Mark Twain and "Life on the Mississippi"

Mark Twain

HORST H. KRUSE

and "Life on the Mississippi"

The University of Massachusetts Press   Amherst

For Ursula, Bettina, and Anna

Acknowledgments

This book could not have been published without the help of many people and institutions. I am grateful to the American Council of Learned Societies and Richard W. Downar, the Director of its American Studies Program, as well as to the Deutsche Forschungs-gemeinschaft for liberal grants that enabled me to pursue my research and to turn my findings into a manuscript. Robert E. Spiller, Henry Nash Smith, and Paul Gerhard Buchloh have taken a particular interest in the development of my project; Professor Smith and the late Frederick Anderson were genial hosts during my stay at the Mark Twain Papers in Berkeley and gave me the benefit of their familiarity with the archives and all phases of the author's life and work. Many libraries and institutions have been helpful in giving me access to their materials and permitting me to publish or to use them, and I owe special thanks to Robert H. Hirst (General Editor, Mark Twain Papers, The Bancroft Library, University of California, Berkeley), Charles A. Ryskamp and Herbert Cahoon (The Pierpont Morgan Library, New York City), William H. Bond and Carolyn

Jakeman as well as Rodney G. Dennis and Helen D. Willard (The Houghton Library, Harvard University), Donald A. Gallup and David R. Watkins (Yale University), Mrs. Connie G. Griffith (Tulane University Library), Mrs. Edith Salsbury (Hartford, Connecticut), Chester Davis (Perry, Missouri), Ralph Gregory (Florida, Missouri), and Carl A. Kallgren (West Redding, Connecticut).

Sections of an early version of the manuscript were read by Evan Alderson and Frederick Anderson, and a German version was accepted as a Habilitationsschrift by the Philosophische Fakultät, Universität Kiel, and published by the Karl Wachholtz Verlag, Neumünster. The English version of this study, however, would not have been published were it not for the continued interest and kindness of Henry Nash Smith and Everett Emerson. Professor Emerson, in particular, insisted that the original version appear in the United States and frequently took time out from his own work in the Mark Twain Papers to help me bring the manuscript up to date, to answer queries, and to take expert care of the many details involved in the production of the book. It is with gratitude that I record his contribution to the present study. My assistants in Münster, especially Rolf Niemann and Gabriele Werner, helped me to check and recheck references, read proof, and update the index. All important decisions in shaping and reshaping the book I have shared with my wife, who also deserves credit for an expert reading of the Morgan manuscript of *Life on the Mississippi*. The staff of the University of Massachusetts Press has been extremely cooperative. Pamela Campbell has been a skillful, patient, and obliging copyeditor, and Mary Mendell has contributed her designer's expertise.

H. H. K.

Contents

Foreword

Some intriguing mysteries of the personality of Mark Twain can
never be fathomed to their depths, even such evident ones as the
author's preoccupation with duality. But an enormous amount of
information is available about America's favorite writer. Hundreds
of his letters and dozens of his notebooks survive, as well as both
manuscripts and notes the author made while at work. Literary
scholarship, aided by such resources, can contribute both knowl-
edge and understanding, and the present state of the art of understanding Mark Twain is at an advanced stage. Horst H. Kruse's
study is a significant contribution, for it advances the understanding of one of Mark Twain's very best works, *Life on the Mississippi*,
both by the organization of information and by the application of
the intellect. Thoroughly and thoughtfully, Kruse examines as has
no one before all the evidence, including the surviving manuscript.
While readily accessible at the Pierpont Morgan Library in New
York City, it has been heretofore largely ignored.

Kruse answers, definitively, many questions, especially ones concerning Mark Twain's intention and his achievement. What kind of book did he have in mind when he returned to the Mississippi River in April 1882? How did what he was to write relate to what he had already written, the papers on "Old Times on the Mississippi" composed in Hartford in the winter of 1874–75? How did the course of composition of what he wrote after his return from the river reflect his original plan? Or did he abandon his intention? What are the origins of the strong vein of social criticism found in some of the chapters? How was Mark Twain's belief in progress reflected in his famous attack on Sir Walter Scott? Why was his growing pessimism so little apparent in *Life on the Mississippi*, written just before he completed *Adventures of Huckleberry Finn*? The answers reveal much about Mark Twain's art and mind.

An earlier version of this book was published, in German, in Kieler Beiträge zur Anglistik und Amerikanistik, volume 8, as *Mark Twains "Life on the Mississippi"*: *Eine entstehungs- und quellengeschichtliche Untersuchung zu Mark Twains "Standard Work"* (1970). Like nearly every other Mark Twain specialist, I was long ignorant of Kruse's study. But while reading Henry Nash Smith's recent *Democracy and the Novel* I came across a reference to it and resolved to read it during an anticipated sojourn at the Mark Twain Papers at the University of California, Berkeley. There I found the book. Soon the last sentence of the foreword caught my eye. Translated, it reads, "An English version of this work may be found in the Mark Twain Papers of the University of California Library, Berkeley." The English version was literally within my reach, and soon I was sharing my gratification and enthusiasm with Professor Smith, who was temporarily back at his old post as editor of the Mark Twain Papers. To cut a rather long story short, with my encouragement and, more important, that of Henry Nash Smith, Horst Kruse returned to the study of *Life on the Mississippi* and now gives us this significantly amplified version, enriched, for example, by the location of an important additional source and by new information about Mark Twain's relationship to Isaiah Sellers, from whom he allegedly stole his pen name.

To grasp the magnitude of Kruse's accomplishment, one should understand that when he began the work, the many pieces of information here fitted together were widely scattered, in Cambridge, New Orleans, New York, and Berkeley, among other places. None of Mark Twain's notebooks had been edited, and an important volume of correspondence that has since appeared was still in preparation. Now in this revision, both published versions and the original manuscripts are cited. The revision itself has been a major undertaking, since many books and articles, published after the publication of the German version, have had to be accommodated. Since my own year of residence at the Mark Twain Papers permitted me to be of some assistance to Professor Kruse as he reviewed and revised his book, I wish to thank the staff of the Mark Twain Papers, and especially Henry Nash Smith, for their aid. I thank too the officials of the Pierpont Morgan Library.

With this publication we are enjoying once again a sense that America's Mark Twain was indeed a citizen of the world.

Everett Emerson

Preface

The complexity of Mark Twain's work, little recognized during his lifetime, has been a challenge for the scholar and the critic ever since the publication of Albert Bigelow Paine's *Mark Twain: A Biography* in 1912 and that of Van Wyck Brooks's *The Ordeal of Mark Twain* in 1920. Much of what has been said about the author in an attempt to explain the totality of his work and his personality has come to be recognized as thesis rather than proven fact. New evidence has been turning up and will continue to turn up for some time to come. To avoid theses and also to prepare more adequate evaluations of the author's achievement, Mark Twain scholarship has begun to concentrate on specific phases and aspects of the author's biography and of his activities, literary and otherwise, as well as on individual works. In studies of the latter sort, attention is being paid increasingly to the genesis of the writings as one way of explaining their complexity and of reducing the margin of error in statements about the author's intentions. The findings arrived at by means of this method have been valuable in several respects: they have corrected a great many assumptions about the writing of most of Mark Twain's major works, they have been the basis of significant re-evaluations, they have corrected details in the author's biography, and they have uncovered important facts for a definitive life of Samuel Langhorne Clemens.

Life on the Mississippi, though it continues to be an important work in the Mark Twain canon, both in its own right and because of its relation to *Adventures of Huckleberry Finn*, has not yet been found deserving of a detailed study. Most frequently it has been approached in the manner in which Bruce Dudley, the protagonist in Sherwood Anderson's novel *Dark Laughter* (1925) approached it, reflecting "that Mark Twain, when he went back to visit the river after the railroads had choked to death the river life, that Mark might have written an epic then. He might have written of song killed, of laughter killed, of men herded into a new age of speed, of factories, of swift, fast-running trains." The reader who approaches the book—particularly the chapters added after the author's Mississippi trip of 1882—in this spirit is likely to conclude, with Anderson's hero, "Instead of which he filled the book mostly with statistics, wrote stale jokes." [1] To be fair to Mark Twain, *Life on the Mississippi* cannot be read with the idea that its author might have written something else instead, for plainly he never intended to write something else. Bruce Dudley's opinion, we may assume, reflects Anderson's reading in Van Wyck Brooks's *The Ordeal of Mark Twain*. [2] Brooks, in trying to prove that Mark Twain, the gifted writer, had yielded to his environment and failed to fulfill the promise of his talents, chose his evidence to fit the preconceived thesis. [3] But whatever selection and manipulation of biographical data he may have found necessary elsewhere, he needed none for *Life on the Mississippi*. Unwittingly, Mark Twain's official biographer, Albert Bigelow Paine, had performed the task for him. By publishing two letters and thus suggesting that they contained a representative description of Mark Twain's work on the book, and by basing his account in the official biography of the author on these letters, he had provided materials that precisely fitted Brooks's thesis.

While the thesis has long since been repudiated, the letters concerning the writing in 1882 of the second part of Mark Twain's book have continued to be quoted and to be seen as containing an adequate characterization of the composition of the work. [4] Seemingly disparaging statements made in these letters, moreover, have frequently furnished an excuse for not taking the work too seriously. Some critics, who have seen meaningful patterns in the chapters of the second part of *Life on the Mississippi*, have found these practically incompatible with the account of the writing of these chapters provided in Mark Twain's letters.[5] Scholars must have been puzzled, too, by still another incompatibility, that which exists between Mark Twain's discrediting statements in the letters and the high opinion he held of the book after its publication.

These unresolved problems demonstrate that, the volume of Mark Twain scholarship notwithstanding, an objective basis for an adequate appreciation of *Life on the Mississippi*—"almost universally considered one of Twain's greatest books, being numbered along with *Tom Sawyer* and *Huckleberry Finn* as one of his three great contributions to American literature"[6]—has not yet been established. The aims of this study therefore are to give an exhaustive account of the genesis of *Life on the Mississippi*, of Mark Twain's intentions in writing the book, of the materials and the sources reflected in it, of the specific use made of such materials, and of the impulses that influenced the writing. The period considered comprises the eighteen years from 1866, when the author first mentioned the plan of writing a book about the Mississippi, to 1883, when *Life on the Mississippi* was finally published, but the main emphasis is on the course of composition during 1882, when the bulk of the manuscript was written.

For a genetic study whose primary emphasis is on fact rather than interpretation, the chronological order of presentation here followed naturally suggests itself. But it has been chosen also because it is a convenient way of demonstrating that the establishment and consideration of an exact chronology is indeed indispensable, not only in solving the immediate problems that arise in connection with this study, but also for an interpretation and an understanding of Mark Twain's work and of his personality.

History is not the kind of "plot-maker" that E. M. Forster expects the novelist to be. Occasional loose ends and dead matter must be accepted by the historian as part of the story. They have been included here for the sake of completing the record and in the hope of offering use for other projects concerning Mark Twain. History also suggests chapters of uneven length and of uneven interest, and it does not always provide meaningful labels for them. Readers who are not prepared to follow its devious ways are referred to both the Appendix and the Index, which are designed to guide them more readily to specific information and to the findings of this study. A systematic presentation, however, cannot be taken to reflect the very complexity of the impulses at work in the actual process of composition. These can best be perceived in following the interpretative procedure practiced by the literary historian.

Such a procedure presupposes a familiarity with the author's writing as a whole as well as with all aspects of his personality. In addition to readily accessible published works and documents this study draws on manuscripts and unpublished materials by and about Mark Twain and on contemporary sources in these archives and libraries: The Mark Twain Papers, The Bancroft Library, University of California, Berkeley; The Pierpont Morgan Library, New York City; Theater Collection, Rogers Memorial Room, Houghton Library, Harvard College, Cambridge, Massachusetts; Berg Collection, New York Public Library, New York City; Yale Collection of American Literature, Morse Collection, Beinecke Library, Yale University, New Haven, Connecticut; Manuscript Division, Tulane University Library, New Orleans; Mark Twain Memorial Library, Redding, Connecticut; Trinity College Library, Hartford, Connecticut; Mark Twain Museum, Hannibal, Missouri; Mark Twain Memorial, Florida, Missouri.

My specific obligations to staff members of these institutions have been acknowledged elsewhere in this study.

Mark Twain and "Life on the Mississippi"

Introduction

The few genetic studies that exist of *Life on the Mississippi* have usually been presented to support an unfavorable critical evaluation of the work. The outlines of the composition presented in such accounts accordingly have tended to stress negative factors, and what little was known of the actual composition seemed to justify this procedure. Thus it has been assumed that when Mark Twain had bound himself by contract with his publisher, James R. Osgood of Boston, to expand the "Old Times on the Mississippi" contributions to the *Atlantic Monthly* (written between October 1874 and June 1875 and published in seven installments in the *Atlantic* in 1875) to the size customary for a book to be published by subscription, he was faced with the problem of providing materials for this project. It has further been assumed that lack of time exacerbated this problem, and that he was thus forced to consult and use materials and sources that would not otherwise have been included in the manuscript.[1] This assumption rests primarily on a letter written by Mark Twain to William Dean Howells and published with the date of October 30, 1882. In it the author complains about "the spur and the burden of the contract" and then proceeds to give an account of the progress made on the manuscript the previous day (by implication, October 29, 1882): "I went to work at nine o'clock yesterday morning, and went to bed an hour after midnight. Result of the day, (mainly stolen from books, tho' credit given,) 9500 words. So I reduced my burden by one third in one day. It was five days work in one. I have nothing more to borrow or steal; the rest must all be writing. It is ten days work, and unless something breaks, it will be finished in five."[2]

In all accounts of the composition and the sources of *Life on the Mississippi* this letter is quoted and interpreted as referring to Mark Twain's extensive use of the "historians of the river" and "accounts by early nineteenth-century travelers." While DeLancey Ferguson adds "an advertising booklet put out by a railroad company"[3] as another source, and Walter Blair lists the "insertion of two unusually irrelevant and inferior passages evidently salvaged from leftovers from *A Tramp Abroad*" and "borrowing or adapting passages from *Huckleberry Finn*" as additional signs of Mark Twain's "difficulty in stretching the manuscript to a satisfactory length,"[4] Dewey Ganzel states that "the books from which Twain 'stole' were memoirs of travelers—for the most part English travelers—who visited the United States between 1815 and 1850."[5] The editors of the *Mark Twain-Howells Letters* annotate the letter in the same manner.[6] There are several facts, however, which reveal that the assumed relationship between the pressure of a deadline and Mark Twain's reliance on travel literature cannot actually have existed, and which therefore show that the rationale behind Mark Twain's use of sources has not yet been adequately explained.

Documents relating to the composition of *Life on the Mississippi* show that the chapters in which substantial quotation from travel books occurs (chapters 27 and 29) had already been written, reproduced in a typescript,[7] and sent to Osgood's firm in Boston before October 30. This and other reasons to be given later suggest a re-examination of the date of Mark Twain's letter. Evidence presented below in chapter 5 firmly establishes that it was actually written on October 3, 1882, but the corrected date still does not permit its account to be interpreted as a reference to the author's use of the travel memoirs: the receipt of the three portions of the typescript had already been acknowledged by September 16, September 29, and September 30 in letters from W. Rowlands of Osgood's firm to Mark Twain in Elmira. The last of these was redirected to Hartford, where the author had returned on September 29, 1882.[8] The three batches acknowledged by Rowlands comprised pages 161 to 233 and Appendix pages 234 to 238. Existing portions of the typescript[9] and Osgood's list of suggestions for revisions and omissions of October 29, 1882,[10] the page references of which are based on the typescript received by him in September, show that Mark Twain had definitely completed the manuscript up to the first half of chapter 44 while still in Elmira. The autograph manuscript in the Pierpont Morgan Library[11] shows a pencil note at the point where the typescript broke off: "Eighth batch will continue that sentence. It will be copied & forwarded presently."[12] This note supports the assumption that the rest of chapter 44 and a substantial part of the eighth batch (consisting of the second half of chapter 44, chapters 45 to 47, and an excised chapter on Southern political slavery)[13] had also been completed in manuscript in what Mark Twain at the time must have considered to be a final form. Since his typist in Elmira apparently was unable to copy everything that Mark Twain had written there, and since he was not willing to leave the untyped portion behind, the eighth batch accompanied him to Hartford where it was to see several revisions and additions at a later time. Either because these revisions occupied him until the rest of the manuscript was completed or because his Hartford typist left it to be copied last, this eighth batch remained in manuscript and had to be forwarded in this form when the typist fell ill with scarlet fever late in December 1882.[14]

Besides the letters from Osgood's firm and the page references to the typescript in Osgood's autograph note of October 29, 1882, the consecutive paging of most of part II of the Morgan manuscript also serves to indicate the time of the composition of Mark Twain's comments on the travel books. Since chapters 27 and 29 are not insertions and since, apart from omissions, the sequence of chapters in the manuscript corresponds to that of the published text, it is safe to conclude that they were written well before the end of September, for by that time the manuscript, as we have seen, had grown at least to chapter 44, possibly even to chapter 47 and the excised chapter which originally followed it. Mark Twain's note in chapter 37 that on "August 8 . . . I was writing one of these foregoing chapters"[15] shows that by that date he had definitely begun the task of composing the second part of his book.

Since the writing of the tourist chapters thus occurred at a relatively early date in the course of the composition of *Life on the Mississippi* and since Mark Twain's reading of the travel accounts preceded even this relatively early date, there is no immediate justification for considering the travel literature as something resorted to under the pressure of time or an unwelcome contract (which, even if not too welcome, did not call for a completion of the manuscript before October 1), and we may speculate as to what determined Mark Twain in his use of these and the various other sources to be investigated. Why should he have continued to incorporate materials in a similar fashion? Why should he have turned to the European Middle Ages, for instance, and to other subjects seemingly extraneous to his proposed book? Questions of this kind can only be answered when placed in a wider context. The context most relevant here is that of Mark Twain's original plans for his Mississippi book and of the intentions which determined the composition of *Life on the Mississippi*.

Planning a Standard Work   II

(1866–1882)

1 Like most of Mark Twain's books, *Life on the Mississippi* had a long and complex genesis. But its history is well documented, and a consideration of it contributes greatly to an understanding of the final work.

The idea of a book about the Mississippi occurred to Mark Twain long before his return to the river and the subsequent composition in 1882, and even before the writing of the "Old Times on the Mississippi" series for the *Atlantic Monthly* in 1874–75. In 1866 and again in 1871 Mark Twain showed an interest in the Mississippi as a subject for a book. In a letter from San Francisco written on January 20, 1866, the author informed his mother that he had begun a book "on an entirely new subject," and that the last hundred pages "will have to be written in St. Louis, because the materials for them can only be got there." As early as this he calls the project a "pet notion of mine," [1] and the abiding interest it held for him also speaks from an interview of March 3, 1866, reported in the Unionville (Nevada) *Humboldt Register* of March 10, 1866. Shortly before his departure for the Sandwich Islands, he told the paper's San Francisco correspondent about his plans for the near future. He stated, so the correspondent writes, that "he would leave, in a few days, for the Sandwich Islands, in the employ of The Sacramento Union. Will be gone about two months. Then will go to Montana for same paper, and next Fall down the Missouri river in a Mackinac boat—he's an old Mississippi pilot—to New Orleans, where he intends writing a book." [2]

There is no evidence that he actually began such a book at any time in the 1860s. But more than five years later, in a letter of November 27, 1871, to his wife, written from Bennington, Vermont, where a lecture circuit had taken him, Mark Twain referred again to the proposed work: "When I come to write the Mississippi book, *then* look out! I will spend 2 months on the river & take notes, & I bet you I will make a standard work." [3] The use of the definite article indicates that the plan must have been of some standing, and it is quite possible that it had never left him since his San Francisco days. Persistent traits in all three statements would seem to indicate this. Despite a whole youth spent by the Mississippi and a term of nearly four years as a cub pilot and a pilot on the river itself, Mark Twain consistently regarded a return to the region that is to be his subject as an essential part of his preparation. The enthusiasm regarding the proposed book that is obvious in his letter of 1871 indicates that he is discussing his next literary venture, and it may well be that the book was not written at that time because a trip to the Mississippi, the apparent conditio sine qua non of a work about the river, could not then be undertaken. The closest Mark Twain got to the region which then interested him most was the Ohio River, "once alive with steamboats and crowded with all manner of traffic; but now a deserted stream, victim of the railroads. Where lie the pilots? They were starchy boys, in my time, and greatly envied by the youth of the West. The same with the Mississippi pilots—though the Mobile & Ohio Railroad had already walked suddenly off with the passenger business in my day, and so it was the beginning of the end." [4] This letter of January 9, 1872, from Steubenville, Ohio, to Olivia Langdon Clemens perhaps intimates why Mark Twain was so eager to collect materials for his Mississippi book: the "widest-awake epoch" of the river was fast becoming history, and Mark Twain considered himself its only privileged and authoritative historian.

Mark Twain's letter of November 27, 1871, indicates more than simple enthusiasm about the project. The use of the term "standard work" certainly implies the author's confidence in his ability to write a successful book. Such confidence is obviously based on the satisfaction he derived from the recently completed manuscript of *Roughing It.* The protracted composition of that book was begun in July 1870, and though Mark Twain could not meet the deadline of January 1, 1871, he did not lose interest in the subject. By May 15, 1871, he had come to consider his work "a bully book" and "a starchy book."[5] His satisfaction with the manuscript continued and obviously eased the habitually wearying lecture tour which he undertook late during the same year, for on December 8 he informed Redpath & Fall, his agents in Boston, that "from this time I shall talk nothing but selections from my forthcoming book 'Roughing It.' "[6] The motive of advance publicity may have influenced this decision as it had the advance publication of chapter 36 of the second volume of *Roughing It* among Mark Twain's "Memoranda" in the *Galaxy* for April 1871.[7] But he also found the selections excellent material for his lecture purposes, for he added, "Tried it last night. Suits me tip-top." Albert Bigelow Paine, his biographer, also mentions that "the *Roughing It* chapters proved a success, and continued in high favor through the rest of the season."[8]

The reference to the Mississippi book in his letter of less than two weeks earlier to Olivia Langdon Clemens clearly implies that he believes such a book will surpass even *Roughing It.* A number of factors suggest that such confidence derives mainly from the successful development of a structural device—the travelogue and the concomitant process of initiation of the narrator-hero[9]—and that in its structure the Mississippi book will be an improvement over the book about the West. It is true that Mark Twain was delighted when his brother Orion, instead of "a foolscap page of items" he had been asked to jot down,[10] furnished a detailed "little memorandum book."[11] The author, who had remembered "next to *nothing* about the matter [of the overland trip],"[12] was now able "to make quite a coherent narrative of the Plains journey instead of slurring it over and jumping 2,000 miles at a stride."[13] It is also true that in *The Innocents Abroad* Mark Twain had relied on the actual progress of the *Quaker City* excursion to provide the narrative basis for his book,[14] and that later he was to use the same structural device again and again, not only in "travel books" like *A Tramp Abroad* and *Following the Equator,* but also in fictional works like *The Prince and the Pauper, Adventures of Huckleberry Finn,* and *A Connecticut Yankee in King Arthur's Court.* There is also reason to assume that the two trips he made to England in 1872–73 to collect material about that country did not result in a book because he lacked "a factual narrative as a basis." [15]

But is it actually safe to conclude that Mark Twain's confidence and enthusiasm about the Mississippi book resulted from the fact that in *Roughing It* he had perfected a narrative technique that only needed to be applied to different materials to make a successful book? And is it safe to conclude that the Mississippi book was not written in 1872 or even in the 1860s because Mark Twain could not undertake a trip to provide him with a factual narrative to serve as a basis for that book? A closer examination of the documents relating to the embryonic stage of the idea that resulted in the 1883 publication of *Life on the Mississippi* seems to me to cast doubt on such assumptions. When on May 15, 1871, Mark Twain told his publisher, Elisha Bliss, that he found *Roughing It* to be "a bully book," he was about "two-thirds done." It was then that he was writing "with a red-hot interest" and an abiding attention, which, if it lasts but long enough, will enable him "to scratch out half of the chapters of the Overland narrative." [16] Since he seems quite eager to perform this act we may conclude that Orion's diary did no more than provide a starting point for the composition and that the chapters devoted to the journey, in Mark Twain's often faulty estimate of his own work, lost their importance as the work grew. On August 10 he plainly stated that he considered it a pity not to be able to "leave off all of the Overland trip." [17] If a successful handling of materials in *Roughing It* at all contributed to the author's confidence in the new project, the techniques of the second volume, not the travel narrative of the first, seem more likely to be responsible for it. Similarly, the interview and the letters of 1866 and 1871 quoted above do not convincingly demonstrate that the conditio sine qua non of a return to the Mississippi is for the purpose of keeping a diary to serve as the basis for the narrative structure of the book. On the contrary, the letter and the interview of 1866 stated that the author wanted to remain in St. Louis or New Orleans to obtain the materials he needs. When in 1871 he wrote that he "will spend 2 months on the river & take notes," it is unlikely that all this time and all these notes will be devoted to establishing a basis for a factual narrative. It can also be argued that the countless trips up and down the river which the author had made as a pilot had left him enough memories and even copious notes from which to reconstruct a factual narrative for his book.[18] But apparently Mark Twain's plan for the book did not emphasize his own experiences. The very fact that—when William Dean Howells asked Mark Twain for a contribution to the *Atlantic Monthly* in 1874—he needed the prodding of Joseph H. Twichell to convince him that there was literary use to be made of predominantly *personal* reminiscences seems to indicate that earlier plans for the Mississippi book had not centered on autobiographical material. It should also be noted that the author had no difficulty in writing the seven installments *without* first having returned to the river. It is only in the course of the writing of the contributions to the *Atlantic Monthly* that the plan of a return to the Mississippi is revived, but Mark Twain's correspondence with Howells clearly documents that this plan has nothing to do with the composition of the magazine contributions themselves. The "Old Times on the Mississippi" series, then, was obviously not the book whose plan dates back to 1866 and 1871.

When Mark Twain told his wife that he was certain that the Mississippi book would be "a standard work," an obvious implication of the term is that the author was confident of its success. In this sense "standard work" is not a generic term. But its use—different from that of the term "classic," which was later defined by Mark Twain as "a book which people praise and don't read"[19]—has certain generic implications, and it is apt to characterize the author's intention, the plan for the book, and the final product. Though Mark Twain does not provide a definition of what he means by "standard work," an essential aspect of its meaning is given by the context in which the term appears in the letter of 1871. It is a work that does not rest on invention and memory so much as on observation and, in modern terms, the "field trip." A standard work is not fiction, like *Adventures of Huckleberry Finn*, nor autobiography, like much of the "Old Times on the Mississippi" series (which he was able to write without having returned to the river). Since Mark Twain's confidence in his ability to write a successful book about the Mississippi derives from *Roughing It*, the use of the term "standard work" suggests a book somewhat like it, particularly in its reportage of the historical and sociological aspects of the Sandwich Islands, which did grow out of a field trip rather than a pleasure excursion, out of observation rather than invention. It is interesting to note, therefore, that there is a kind of link between these two books as early as the 1866 interview. Of the three trips proposed there, the two that were actually undertaken helped to provide basic materials for *Roughing It* and *Life on the Mississippi* and to determine the shape of either work. In the prefatory note to *Roughing It* the author calls attention to this fact. Though he mentions that the book is "merely a personal narrative, and not a pretentious history or a philosophical dissertation," he stresses that it contains "quite a good deal of information," particularly information about "an interesting episode in the history of the Far West, about which no books have been written by persons who were on the ground in person, and saw the happenings of the time with their own eyes. I allude to the rise, growth, and culmination of the silver-mining fever in Nevada."[20] The unmistakable pride Mark Twain takes in being able to convey this authentic information deflates the seriousness of his apology for not being able to "retain [his] facts." It also significantly connects this prominent aspect of *Roughing It* with what he much later felt to have been one of the chief motives for the composition of *Life on the Mississippi*. In 1895, in an interview published in the Winnipeg *Tribune*, he said that he found the subject of the Mississippi to be "a virgin field" for literature: "No one could write that life but a pilot, because no one else but a pilot entered into the spirit of it. But the pilots were the last men in the world to write its history. . . . Here then was my chance, and I used it."[21]

It would seem to be more than a coincidence that there are definite correspondences between these sentences and a letter of about 1890, the famous "Letter to an Unidentified Person," which actually contains Mark Twain's most adequate and most convincing statement of his literary credo. The long catalog of his work and experience in various fields, whose rhetoric by far exceeds the usual style of a personal letter, gives due emphasis to his years as a Mississippi pilot and ends with the following climax: "Now then: as the most valuable capital, or culture, or education usable in the building of novels is personal experience, I ought to be well equipped for that trade. I surely have the equipment, a wide culture and all of it real, none of it artificial, for I don't know anything about books."[22] This avowal of factual reporting and of personal experience as subject and theme of his own works demonstrates that "Old times on the Mississippi" and particularly *Life on the Mississippi* are perfect realizations of his program as a writer.[23]

Roughing It contributes another important aspect to a definition of the term "standard work"; not only are personal experience and the field trip necessary, but a research library is also essential: before Mark Twain began to write about the Sandwich Islands he could pride himself on having read every available book on the subject and, by doing so, assert his authority as a historian and social commentator. The purpose of conveying information and instruction in *Roughing It* was undoubtedly foremost in the author's mind. He implicitly stated this when the experience of giving readings from the book led him to philosophize about the different functions of the spoken and written word. Readings from the book were "to merely entertain, not instruct," [24] the book itself, however, was to do both.

Such documentary and historiographic intentions make the Appendix an integral part of *Roughing It* and the standard work. Mark Twain presumably intended more than humor when he prefaced the supplementary material in *A Tramp Abroad* with a pertinent observation by Herodotus, "Nothing gives such weight and dignity to a book as an Appendix."

Finally, the meaning of "standard work" must be seen in terms of potential popularity and universal appeal. If a subscription book is to be successful, it is as important that it delight as it is that it instruct, and the yarns and humor are as important as the statistics. [25]

In his letter of November 27, 1871, the author implies that whatever traits of this sort *Roughing It* already shows, his standard work on the Mississippi will contain them in a more pronounced and therefore more effective form. It is in terms of this definition that the phrase "standard work" will be used subsequently.

What evidence there is of the embryonic stage of the plan for the Mississippi book indicates that, had the plan been realized at that time, the result would have been essentially like the second part of *Life on the Mississippi*. Though it is futile to speculate about the shape of a book never actually written, it can be assumed that the work would have used a travel narrative of some sort, but indications are that such a structural device would have been subservient, though essential, to the idea of a standard work.

2   The significant feature of the early references to the idea that Mark Twain later developed into *Life on the Mississippi* is that from the very beginning the idea included a strong interest in the historical and documentary aspects of the subject. An interest in such materials for the Mississippi book seems to have persisted through-

out the years that intervened between 1866 and 1882. It characterized not only further references to the proposed book, but also Mark
Twain's specific plans for a return to the river. If this interest did not
show itself in the "Old Times on the Mississippi" series of 1875,
that fact is proof that the magazine contributions were in no way a
realization of the project of the standard work about the river—
though there can be no doubt that Mark Twain soon planned to
incorporate them in that work. Although in the course of writing
that series Mark Twain thought that he had tapped a nearly inex-
haustible source and on January 26, 1875, told William Dean
Howells that he had agreed to utilize it in a book for Bliss,[26] the
discovery of such materials did not ever make him desist from his
plan of a return to the Mississippi. On the contrary, the agreement
with his publisher lent urgency to his attempts to persuade Howells
to accompany him on such a trip. The plan of a joint excursion to be
undertaken early in 1875 is first mentioned in a letter of December
18, 1874, and "was possibly a scheme developed in conversation
with Howells during Clemens's recent visit [of December 15]."[27]
But curiously, it was not Howells but James Redpath, his former
lecture agent, who had been his first choice as traveling companion.
An unpublished letter marked "November 29," almost certainly of
1874, contains a fairly detailed plan which reflects previous ideas
about the making of the book at the same time that it foreshadows
the actuality of 1882:

Nov. 29.

Dear Redpath:

Can't lecture this winter; but I have a notion of going west about May 1,
to make a lagging journey down the Mississippi, dining pilots & pumping
stuff out of them for a book— & paying expenses & making money by
talking "Roughing It" thrice in New York, once in Cleveland, twice in
Chicago, once in Louisville, twice in St. Louis, once in Memphis, & twice
in N.Orleans.

This is my idea, provided I can finish my present book by May 1— & no
doubt I can. Would like you to do the trip both *for* me & *with* me— but
should want you to have a sort of leatherhead to go *before* us all the time, &
attend to minor arrangements & details because I should want you yourself
to stay right *with* me from the first day to the last, & *talk*, & *lie*, & *have* a *good
time*. Think this over & see what notion you arrive at about it.

YoursClemens.[28]

We may assume that despite Redpath's willingness to humor his star lecturer he found that he was unable to accompany Mark Twain, although he probably agreed to make the necessary arrangements for a lecture tour. A discussion of Redpath's negative decision presumably led to a somewhat rash agreement on Howells's part. On second thought he seems to have lost the initial enthusiasm and began to find all sorts of excuses for not being able to go, while Mark Twain became more and more persistent. One of Howells's subterfuges was that he remembered having promised his wife a spring vacation in Bethlehem, Pennsylvania. To this Mark Twain replied on January 12, 1875: "We *mustn't* give up the New Orleans trip. Mrs. Clemens would gladly go if her strength would permit, but can't Mrs. Howells go anyway? I think she would find it very pleasant. I *know* she would. We can *put off* New Orleans until March 1st, & then that would do in place of Bethlehem. You just persuade her." Since Howells had vaguely indicated that the question of time and money had also influenced his negative attitude, Mark Twain added in a postscript, "I know how we can make our expenses going to N.O., but you'd just lose money going to Beth[lehem]." [29] He was probably referring to the lectures he had suggested to Redpath. When despite the intimation that Mark Twain would have defrayed all expenses, Howells definitely refused in a letter of February 16, the former seems to have rejoined with an outright offer to pay him for the trip. But Howells, "touched and flattered that you want my company so much as to be willing to pay vastly more for it than it's worth," [30] had to refuse again. Mark Twain must have feared this all along, for on February 12 he tried to interest James R. Osgood in the steamboat trip from St. Louis to New Orleans and back: "[Howells] is not sure, now, whether he can go or not, but I hope he *will*. But in *any* case, don't you want to take a pleasure trip about that time? I wish you would go. Think of the gaudy times you & Howells & I would have on such a bender!" [31] But neither he nor John Hay could be persuaded. So, finally, Mark Twain himself gave up the trip for the time being. Its plan, however, continued to occupy him; on May 7 he wrote Howells: "If I live a year, I will make one more attempt to go down the river, for I shall have lived in vain if I go silent out of this world and thus lengthen the list of the 'lost arts.' Confidentially, I'm 'laying' for a monument." [32]

It should be noted that the plan for revisiting the river and Mark Twain's almost desperate effort to find a companion occupied him most after he had begun the composition of the "Old Times on the Mississippi" series and when consequently he had already devised a narrative structure perfectly suited to the presentation of its materials. Since this structure could easily have been extended to include further memories and other materials, there is additional reason to assume that the main purpose of the trip was not to provide a factual travel diary as a basis for the narrative structure of the proposed book. The evidence presented above, moreover, indicates that the unpremeditated use of personal reminiscences of the river had revived the "standard work" idea and that the purpose of the trip was the same as that given in 1866 and 1871. One of the letters to Howells affords a further glimpse of the actual program. Forwarding a note from Strother Wiley, a pilot he had known on the Mississippi, the author added that he had been "wondering if [Wiley] were still alive & if we might have the good luck to go to New Orleans with him." Wiley, Mark Twain stated parenthetically, "is brim full of river reminiscences," [33] and naturally would have been a perfect source for some of the information needed for the standard work. Another letter to Howells shows that the method of digression—which has been taken to betray lack of materials, pressure of a deadline, and general irritation during the composition of 1882—was clearly a part of the plan for the book, even in 1875. Referring to an article on "Old-Time Oriental Trade" written for the *Atlantic Monthly* by W. L. Fawcette, a Mississippi pilot, Mark Twain commented, "Good for Fawcett! The idea of a Mississippi pilot writing profound essays upon so imposing a subject as Ancient Oriental Trade! I think I'll ring that into a chapter, for the honor of the craft." [34]

Having written the last installment of "Old Times on the Mississippi" Mark Twain returned to the manuscript of *The Adventures of Tom Sawyer*. It has frequently been noted that the composition of the *Atlantic* series helped to fill the tank of recollection and inspiration for that book, which had run dry on September 2, 1874. [35] But there may also be another and more immediate connection between the postponement of both the Mississippi trip and the composition of the standard work on the one hand and the further exploitation of personal recollections in *Tom Sawyer* and *Huckleberry Finn* on the other. It will be recalled that on January 26, 1875, Mark Twain had informed Howells that he had agreed to write the proposed Mississippi book for his publisher Bliss. When he told Howells on February 20 that he had postponed the trip until June he mentioned that he wanted to "buckle in on another book for Bliss, [and] finish it the end of May." [36] On March 1, he sent the same information to the publisher himself: "I've put off the Miss. River trip till June, & shall write a new book meantime." [37] "Another book" and "a new book" probably mean a "different" book, different from the work he had originally promised Bliss. Though he may not have been bound by a contract, there seems to have been a firm promise, for on June 21, apparently in reply to Howells's suggestion that he publish *Tom Sawyer* serially, Mark Twain wrote: "If I only had the Mississippi book written, I would surely venture this story in the Atlantic." [38] *Tom Sawyer*, of course, would have been completed anyhow, but Mark Twain's early return to the manuscript and its speedy completion can also be explained by the fact that the author needed a substitute for the standard work which originally he had agreed to write for Bliss.

Albert Bigelow Paine states that "the plan for revisiting the river and the conclusion of the book were held in abeyance for nearly seven years." [39] While it is true that the return to the river and the completion of the second part of the book did not take place before 1882, another plan for the trip may have existed in 1877. On April 14, Mark Twain told Mrs. Fairbanks that he could not attend her son's wedding, indicating that he should "either be in the neighborhood of New Orleans, then, or hard at work on a book." [40] The trip was referred to once again in 1881. On July 17, Mark Twain informed George Washington Cable that "Howells is still in the mind to go to New Orleans with me in November for the Mississippi trip, & we shall hope to see you then." [41] The project must have been mentioned before, and it is likely that Mark Twain had told Cable about it during the latter's visit to Hartford the previous month. There is also evidence that during the same year the author rewrote an early version of the story of Karl Ritter's revenge (chapters 31 and 32 of *Life on the Mississippi*) for inclusion in his standard work. Since the incorporation of this story has most consistently been seen as a weak point of *Life on the Mississippi* and as proof that Mark Twain's "main consideration" was "to fill out the book to the contract length," [42] it is worth noting that his first attempt to adapt it for the book occurred well before the period when he supposedly lacked both time and material. The use of yarns like the Ritter story, then, is obviously a consistent part of Mark Twain's plan for the standard work.

3 The plan for the Mississippi trip finally materialized in the spring of 1882.[43] By the end of December 1881 it had definitely been decided that James R. Osgood of Boston, his new publisher, was to be Mark Twain's traveling companion and that the trip was to begin in April.[44] At the same time he asked Osgood about "a short-hand reporter to travel with us in the spring . . . a bright, companionable *gentleman.*"[45] He eventually decided on Roswell Phelps, whom he hired for the duration of the trip and the subsequent transcription of the stenographic notes. All documents relating to this excursion firmly connect it with the plan that had existed since 1866.

The trip was undertaken for the express purpose of collecting material for a book. In suggesting a meeting in New Orleans to Joel Chandler Harris, Mark Twain clearly stressed this purpose. He explained that both he and Osgood would have to use fictitious names to escape the interviewers, and he continued parenthetically, "I am making this letter so dreadfully private and confidential because my movements must be kept secret, else I shan't be able to pick up the kind of book-material I want."[46] In chapter 22 of *Life on the Mississippi* he was to say, "As I proposed to make notes, with a view to printing, I took some thought as to methods of procedure. I reflected that if I were recognized, on the river, I should not be as free to go and come, talk, inquire, and spy around, as I should be if unknown." Even in retrospect he seems to have been concerned about his failure of what he now even called the "main purpose" of his visit, "to hunt up and talk with a hundred steamboatmen."[47] But such failure did not defeat his intentions altogether. In the same letter in which he tells his wife about having been found out he also writes, "We are having a powerful good time & picking up & setting down volumes of literary stuff,"[48] and as late as May 13, 1882, a caption of an interview published in the St. Louis *Globe-Democrat* restates the original motive in calling the venture "A Round Trip on the Mississippi in Search of Book Material."[49] Though Osgood's willingness to accompany him may have induced Mark Twain to go at that particular time, the idea of putting the material to be collected to literary use not only existed, it also was certainly Mark Twain's own, not that of his publisher.[50]

A general plan for the Mississippi book existed, as we have seen, long before the author started on the trip, but its outlines are more clearly perceptible for the first time in his notebook of 1882. Entries like "Get Kellogg's Andersonville experiences through short-hand reporter," "Cases of pilots burning at the wheel," and "Bixby running Island No. 10 during the war,"[51] made as early as February 1882, as well as his plan to include in the book a map of the Mississippi from St. Louis to New Orleans in twenty full-page pieces[52] and to get statistics of width, length, and volume of the river from an encyclopedia[53] indicate a strong interest in the kind of material that was intended to make the book a standard work rather than an extension of the series of predominantly personal reminiscences begun in "Old Times on the Mississippi." But it was also the kind of material that could easily make critics believe it to have been chosen out of desperation rather than out of intention, because he lacked incidents more suitable for a continuation of the *Atlantic* series. There is no reason to assume that Mark Twain was not full of enthusiasm when the long-deferred trip finally got under way,[54] but his notebook indicates that already at this time (at a point in the course of the composition of *Life on the Mississippi* when a possible burden of the contract and a possible lack of time and materials had not yet made themselves felt) he planned the use of material from the historians of the river and of travel accounts by foreign visitors. In his notes he reminds himself of Francis Parkman as a source for something about La Salle's trip and, shortly after his return, of Charles Dickens for "a note on Cairo."[55]

Although various projects in the several agenda for the trip jotted down in his notebook[56] were not successfully completed, he returned with two notebooks (his own and that kept by his stenographer)[57] containing more than 450 items (varying from a single word to nearly 1,300 words in length) relating to the trip and to the projected book. The majority of these notes are documentary rather than personal, and most of these were to develop into sentences, paragraphs, and chapters in the manuscript, though sometimes, as will become evident, they were supplemented and changed by the use of other source materials. Only two of the notes make a connection between the material and the presentation of the "Old Times on the Mississippi" series. One is a reminder to "Tell, now, in full, the events preceding & following the Pennsylvania's explosion: the fight with Brown; the boat steaming down Bend of 103 with nobody at the wheel—the white-aproned servants & passengers on deck applauding the fight—the prophetic talk on the levee between Henry & me that night in N.O. before Pa. sailed on her fatal voyage." The other is in the form of a question: "Begin with a chapter of my experiences as a *pilot*?"[58] While the first of these entries resulted in the writing of chapters 18 to 20, Mark Twain decided against the use of the idea expressed in the second. These entries do not constitute sufficient evidence to assume that he had ever thought of the expansion of the *Atlantic* series in terms of his personal experiences and reminiscences. Even if he had decided to write about his piloting days, such an account would have been no more than a "beginning" (as the author clearly indicates in his notebook entry), after which the idea of a standard work would probably have reasserted itself in the account.[59] The only other evidence in support of a possible intention to expand the original series by an account of his piloting days consists in an interview published in the St. Louis *Post-Dispatch* of May 12, 1882. In it Mark Twain answers a St. Louis reporter's plainly suggestive question whether the new book will treat of the author's early life on the river with "Yes; altogether of that subject."[60] He also adds that it will be finished in about nine months. Knowing that Mark Twain had already bound himself by contract to finish the manuscript by October 1, less than five months after this interview, so that the book could be "in the market for delivery to subscribers on or before April 1 1883,"[61] and considering the many instances of his dislike for reporters, one can probably discount the validity of his statement. One is all the more entitled to do so since Joel Chandler Harris, whom he had met in New Orleans on the same trip and with whom, as their previous correspondence and their common interests indicate,[62] he certainly discussed his literary plans in greater detail than with the reporter, offered a different opinion about the subject of the proposed book. In a review of *The Stolen White Elephant* in the Atlanta *Constitution* Harris wrote that Mark Twain "Only the other day . . . was journeying up and down the Mississippi in search of material for a new volume. Nobody knows whether it is to be a comedy or an emotional drama, but it has been hinted that the reconstructed Missourian will endeavor to repay some of the venerable pilots who puff, and blow, and gas on the Father of the Waters for remembering him so readily."[63]

Further notebook entries of the period preceding the actual writing reveal another kind of material that was to become important in the composition of the book. Reminders such as "Throw in incidents from many lands—Cal., the black negro we saw entering Jerusalem, &c" and "Whenever want to lug in an incident, be *reminded* of it by passing Hat Island or some other locality,"[64] as well as recurrent entries about specific incidents of this nature clearly indicate a return to the episodic method of composition of *The Innocents Abroad, Roughing It,* and *A Tramp Abroad*. The resulting inclusions in the manuscript of "two unusually irrelevant and inferior passages evidently salvaged from leftovers from *A Tramp Abroad*," [65] as well as the "melodramatic blather" of the story of Ritter's vengeance [66] are thus as much a part of Mark Twain's original design as are the accounts of the historians of the river, of the early travelers, and the materials collected in the two notebooks. The author's experiences as a pilot, on the other hand, seem never to have ranked high as potential material for the book. Though a resumption of the method of composition used in the earlier "travel" books is the most obvious characteristic of this design, it is also clear that such a plan is modified in the interest of writing a standard work about the river, a work in which the travel experiences of the narrator are of less importance than in *The Innocents Abroad, Roughing It,* and *A Tramp Abroad*.

The following account of the actual composition of the chapters necessary to expand "Old Times on the Mississippi" to *Life on the Mississippi*, as far as it can be reconstructed, reveals more clearly the author's basic intentions and his design for the standard work. It also reveals to what extent and for what reasons modifications of the original plan became necessary. It thus forms a supplement to the outline of "Mark Twain's habits of work, his characteristic attack on his material, the kind of difficulties he customarily encountered, and his usual ways of dealing with them" as presented in Bernard DeVoto's *Mark Twain at Work* [67] and other accounts that refer to the author's works of fiction. [68]

Devising a Narrative Structure III

(Hartford, May–June 1882)

1   Although as early as February 1882, in declining an invitation, Mark Twain wrote, "I am to begin a long journey early in April, and shall need every moment I can get, meantime, to crowd my work forward to a point where I may leave it at a stand-still for a while without detriment,"[1] there is no evidence that, apart from note-book entries[2] and the writing of early versions of the Ritter story and of yarns not originally intended for the book, the actual composition was begun before his return to Hartford. The contract with Osgood gave him four months to complete the manuscript, and he must have planned to do most of his writing at Quarry Farm, Elmira, New York, as was his usual custom. He did begin his composition in Hartford, however, and there wrote at least ten of the forty-six chapters that were to be added to "Old Times on the Mississippi." His varied attempts to get the composition started reflect the problems that he was faced with in having to incorporate the *Atlantic* series as a block into a much larger context, but the development of a narrative structure emerges as the most important achievement of the first period of his writing.

Although Mark Twain's notebook already contained entries related to the introductory chapters 1–3, he actually began his writing with chapters 18–20. In these, following the reminder in his notebook, he told "in full, the events preceding & following the Pennsylvania's explosion"[3] of 1858 in which his brother Henry suffered fatal injuries. His decision not to recount his experiences as a pilot resulted in a brief chapter 21, "A Section in My Biography," in which he brought the narration up to the present and to his return to the river in 1882.

Before he began the actual account of his recent trip, however, Mark Twain followed another point of his plan as documented in his notebook, namely the preparation of "incidents from many lands"[4] for inclusion in the manuscript.

Walter Blair has already mentioned two such passages, "The Professor's Yarn" (chapter 36) and the drownings of Lem Hackett and the boy Dutchy (in chapter 54), as signs of the author's "difficulty in stretching the manuscript to a satisfactory length" and guessed that they were "salvaged from leftovers from *A Tramp Abroad.*"[5] His conjectures about the origin of these two passages is borne out in one instance by two sheets of manuscript which I have found among other unused material from *A Tramp Abroad.* The two sheets (in DV4, MTP) are marked [page] 138 and [page] 163, and the text precedes the first and continues the last sentence of the Lem Hackett-Dutchy story. This clearly shows that the passage was originally intended as a digression occasioned by Mark Twain's thoughts about a sermon which he heard the Reverend Charles Spurgeon preach in his tabernacle in London on August 17, 1879.[6] The paging conforms to that of the unchanged pagination of this part of the Morgan manuscript of *Life on the Mississippi* (MSVI 139–62).[7] Though no precise date for the writing of "A Professor's Yarn" can be established, handwriting, pen, ink, and paper are markedly different from those of 1882, and it is almost certain that it was written before that year. Since it became chapter 36 and its pages were renumbered accordingly, it was inserted during the Elmira period of composition. The manuscript of "A Professor's Yarn," therefore, must have been selected in Hartford to be taken to Elmira as potential or definite material for the Mississippi book.

The third instance of the use of such materials, the incorporation of the Ritter story, which Mark Twain undertook before writing chapter 22, shows most clearly that such incidents and the yarns built around them are a part of the author's original plan. A consideration of Mark Twain's attempts to adapt it for the book also demonstrates significant aspects of his method of composition and the development of a narrative structure, and it therefore justifies a detailed account.

It has frequently been pointed out that Mark Twain found it rather difficult to develop a narrative technique suited to the presentation of his subject matter.[8] "Old Times on the Mississippi," *Tom Sawyer*, and *Huckleberry Finn* may be seen as important stages in the development of a literary technique which met the needs of their particular matter, but *Life on the Mississippi*, the similarity of its matter notwithstanding, is clearly part of a different development. From the point of view of its structure it is, above all, a travel book, and as such it represents the latest stage in the development of a travelogue technique that had been tried out and constantly improved in the writing of *The Innocents Abroad, Roughing It*, and "Old Times on the Mississippi." If we agree with the large number of critics who have found such improvement and perfection to consist chiefly in the fictionalization of the autobiographical protagonist and narrator, in making him younger and less experienced than the author himself was when the events actually happened,[9] then the literary technique of *Life on the Mississippi* clearly marks a relapse. But such a relapse would seem to be accounted for by the fact that a standard work—which *The Innocents Abroad, Roughing It*, and "Old Times on the Mississippi" were never intended to be— requires a change in narrative technique quite in accordance with its different intention. It would seem logical, therefore, that in Mark Twain's conception of a standard work all facts must be presented as neither subjective nor relative, but must be endorsed by authoritative statements and definite opinions on the part of the author. This kind of procedure naturally precludes the use of a fictionalized narrator as an intervening agent. It is typical, however, that Mark Twain seems to have arrived at this conclusion not before his return from the Mississippi, but—as can be gathered from his attempts to integrate the story of Karl Ritter—only in the process of writing his first chapters. However slow to arrive at such a conclusion, later he was all the more eager to profess and to uphold it, for in the course of his book he again and again makes use of his opinions about the authors of works of a similar nature to justify his own procedure.[10]

Internal evidence shows that the story of Karl Ritter's vengeance (chapters 31–32) was originally begun in 1879, at the time
when Mark Twain was busy writing and preparing *A Tramp Abroad*.
It was probably suggested by an experience of his in Munich,
recorded in Notebook 17: "Jan.4/79—Went to Grossen Kirschof &
saw 15 or 20 dead." [11] Even in its printed version the story retains a
reference to his residence at 1a Karlstrasse, Munich, late in 1878,
and his taking up "working quarters a mile from there in the house
of a widow who supported herself by taking lodgers," [12] and the
relation of the actual incident begins with "Toward the end of last
year . . . ," indicating that it was at least *begun* in 1879. But the
narrative presented by Mark Twain is based on more than the
author's personal visit to a Munich morgue and his observation of
its peculiar devices for ascertaining whether a person was actually
dead. It testifies to the abiding appeal that the theme of premature
burial held for the nineteenth century. Quite in accordance with
Edgar Allan Poe's observation—in the first sentence of "The Premature Burial"—that the theme is "too entirely horrible for the
purposes of legitimate fiction," it occurs primarily in the more
popular type of adventure story. Mark Twain himself seems to have
drawn on an anonymous story entitled "My Own Funeral" in the
January *Harper's New Monthly Magazine* for 1857. [13] The availability
of the magazine in both Hartford and Elmira, and the fact that in his
general dependence on this kind of material he favored this particular journal, make it a very likely source. More important evidence is
the fact that the scene of the story is also Munich and that, although
its action is laid forty years in the past, the more recently instituted
device for the prevention of premature burial exploited by Mark
Twain in his own version is already referred to in passing by its
protagonist:

Of late years they have had recourse to another expedient, which . . . was
unknown in my day. They attach to the fingers of the dead body a ring, to
which is fastened the wire of a bell which hangs in the room of the guardian
of the cemetery. The slightest movement of the limbs suffices to ring this
bell, and the watcher, prepared with cordials and restoratives, rushes to the
place, and rescues the wretched creature from the awful position. [14]

Although the date for the institution of this new kind of corpse-
watch implied in Mark Twain's account—eighteen years before the
meeting with Karl Ritter in 1878 [15]—does not comport with the date
implied in this paragraph from the anonymous "My Own Funeral,"

there are further similarities that point to the magazine story as a probable source. But Mark Twain applied the theme differently. If his story was actually begun or written in 1879, perhaps intended to become part of *A Tramp Abroad*, he must already have perceived its latent possibility as a chapter in a book about the Mississippi and perhaps therefore decided not to use it elsewhere. Other internal evidence, however, proves that the story could not have been completed in 1879. In its process of ratiocination the Ritter story makes use of two devices of identification, that of a missing thumb and that of fingerprints. It was only in 1880 that the practicability of the latter method was publicized;[16] Mark Twain could not have known about it in 1879. This fact suggests that the story went through two stages even before its final adaptation for the book. While the process of ratiocination in the original version had presumably been based solely on identification by means of a missing thumb, his interest in fingerprint material led Mark Twain to duplicate rather than replace the original motif when he came to rewrite it. An addition on the verso of MSII [17] 345 shows that only in the course of rewriting did he endeavor to direct particular attention to the new means of identification by having his narrator surround it with mystery before the method is finally revealed in detail.[17] An emendation in the manuscript of a reference to the time of the action confirms that Mark Twain worked from an earlier manuscript when rewriting the story: having already stated that the events happened "toward the close of the war [the American Civil War],"[18] he apparently copied "this was thirteen or fourteen years ago" from the original manuscript, then (clearly at the same time) changed the numbers to "fifteen or sixteen."[19] The first rewriting therefore occurred in 1881. The journey down the Mississippi was much on his mind at this time, since he was planning to go that November with William Dean Howells.[20] Evidence of a third and a fourth stage in the manuscript further supports this date. The third stage consists in a new beginning for the story which replaces its first eleven pages, breaks off in the middle of the line and of a sentence continued on MSII [12] 340, and leaves nearly half of MSII [11] 339 blank. This stage must still have been composed without much regard for the narrative structure of *Life on the Mississippi* as it was later developed, but it already shows the emendation of a reference to the time of the author's proposed return to the Mississippi: "presently," copied from the original beginning of the second version, is immediately changed to "by and by."[21] This emendation indicates that some time had elapsed since the writing of the earlier versions, although Mark Twain neglected to make corresponding changes in the two remaining and more precise time references, either then or in the final version. Both time references, as they now stand, do not fit into either the biography of the author or the time scheme of the book.

Notwithstanding DeLancey Ferguson's opinion that the "farcical postscript" of the Ritter story was added to incorporate it into the book,[22] the logic of the story itself implies that such a conclusion had been intended from its inception. It is natural, therefore, that the author should have thought of it very early in the process of recording in his notebook items to be included in the Mississippi book. A reference to it appears as early as April 1882, before the beginning of the trip: "The bell rings in the Todt Gallerie & turns the watchman's hair grey."[23] This entry probably precedes the third version, which may have been written even before his trip. The Ritter story, then, must have ranked high as potential book material. This being the case, one may further conclude that the plan of a sufficiently loose narrative structure congenial for an adaptation of the story already existed, or else that the story itself suggested the convenience of such a structure. In any event, Mark Twain's interest in the Ritter story at this stage would seem to challenge the thesis of Ferguson and other critics who have found the incorporation of this very episode to be a sure sign of the author's lack of time and materials.

2   Although these investigations into the history of the text clearly confirm the supposition that Mark Twain had intended a very loose structure for his book, the following analysis of his various attempts to make the story of Karl Ritter a part of his work nevertheless demonstrates that he had to resolve a number of problems before he was able to modify the narrative technique of his earlier travel books so that it could also serve the purposes of his standard work.

Chapter 32, which concludes the Ritter story, was not written before Mark Twain's return from the Mississippi. It makes use of details of his trip on the *Gold Dust* from St. Louis to Vicksburg, the first stage of his journey. In introducing into this chapter members of the steamer's crew who were to function in the story as narrators, spinners of yarns, and listeners to yarns spun and reports given by

Uncle Mumford

others (including Mark Twain himself), the author used their actual
names in incorrect spelling. Mr. Dad Dunham, the second mate, is
called Mr. Dad *Dunn*, Mr. Lem S. Gray, the pilot, is referred to as
Len.[24] Both spellings are later corrected, but they are given correctly
in chapter 25[25] and chapter 24,[26] at the point where both persons
are actually introduced into the narrative. Since chapter 24 is part of
a unit of composition beginning with chapter 22 (which was only
later broken into three separate chapters), the composition of chapter 32 precedes that of chapter 22. The manuscript of chapter 32 and
the fourth stage of the manuscript of chapter 31 as well as vestigial
elements in the final version are therefore significant for the documentation of Mark Twain's attempt to devise a narrative structure
for those chapters in the book which deal with what he later called
the "comparatively tranquil present epoch" in the history of the
Mississippi.[27]

Unlike "The Professor's Yarn" (chapter 36), whose inclusion in
the book demanded such an elaborate justification that when reading proof Mark Twain decided it would be better to give none at
all,[28] the Ritter story, in subject matter, in references to the author's
proposed return to the river, and in its clearly intended conclusion,
was already materially part of the book. Mark Twain's problem,
then, was not to relate it to the rest of his materials, but simply to
write out its sequel and thus make it part of a yet-to-be-devised
narrative structure. For this purpose he uses two sets of characters
not previously introduced. The first of these, Thompson and Rogers,
two traveling companions, argues the wisdom of executing Ritter's
last will and convinces the author that it would be better for the sake
of the heir to appropriate the inheritance themselves and send him
a "chromo" instead. While he and his traveling companions are
now all the more eager to go ashore at Napoleon, the second set of
characters, members of the crew of the *Gold Dust*, provides the
anticlimactic information about the disappearance of that town in a
cut-off caused by the Arkansas river. A canceled beginning in the
manuscript of chapter 32[29] shows that Mark Twain's original intention was to insert the Ritter story in its third stage, like "The
Professor's Yarn," as a narrative complete in itself. His plan to go
ashore at Napoleon was to be made known to his traveling companions only in this sequel, their protest was to cause him to "detail
to them the Ritter history, just as it stands in the preceding chapter."
But he immediately decided against the use of this simplest of all
devices for a narrative structure, and instead, as a fourth stage of the

manuscript of the Ritter story shows, introduced his listeners at the beginning of chapter 31. He thus avoided the otherwise inevitable isolation of the story in the structure of the book.

By his attempt to integrate the Ritter story into the book, Mark Twain reveals significant details of his original plan for a narrative structure. The traveling companions are referred to as "the so-called Thompson & the so-called Rogers." This reference, which was later canceled, presupposes an explanation that was to have been provided in the subsequent composition of the preceding chapters. This indicates that Mark Twain had apparently planned a more extensive use of a device which clearly relates the narrative structure of chapters 22–40 to that of *Roughing It* and *A Tramp Abroad*. The "so-called Thompson" and the "so-called Rogers" were to replace the "Mr. Brown," "Harris," and similar characters of earlier travel accounts. Their first appearance in chapter 32 reveals their functional relation to both Brown and Harris: they are a mouthpiece for the author's less genteel attitudes, a projection of traits of his own personality. Although the arguments for the appropriation of Ritter's legacy are chiefly made by Rogers and Thompson, the author—in this passage clearly a fictional narrator—is only too eager to take them up. In the end, to settle the ensuing argument over the distribution of the money, he even claims spiritual fatherhood: "I retorted that the idea would have occurred to me plenty soon enough, and without anybody's help. I was slow about thinking, maybe, but I was sure." [30]

That Mark Twain intended substantial use of the "traveling companion" device of his earlier travel books is further substantiated by the following entry in the author's notebook: " 'Harris' is along, as usual." The continuation of this entry was clearly written at the same time: "And I use false name because it is mysterious & stylish." [31] Both entries are directly reflected in the canceled beginning of the final version of chapter 32. The decision to rename the traveling companion must have been made during the trip, either because Mark Twain was to meet an actual Harris, his fellow writer, in New Orleans, or, more likely, because the name Harris had been used in *A Tramp Abroad*, with implicit reference to the Reverend Joseph H. Twichell, his friend and traveling companion in the Black Forest and Switzerland. The new traveling companions, Osgood and Roswell Phelps, not only account for a new name, they naturally also explain why the role of Harris was split in two. While in the instance of Brown and Harris of the earlier books the account of their adventures often grew out of extended series of notebook entries,[32] Mark Twain's river notes contain fewer such references. But their number and their nature are sufficient evidence that the plan for this device existed quite independently of Mark Twain's attempt to integrate the Ritter story. Two are to be found in his personal notebook: "Southern Hotel—Johnson drew bowl of water —then asked waiter to bring him some water to wash this water"; "Send W. ashore & get preposterous accounts of Thebes, Grand Tower, Cairo, &c. Sometimes he is drunk—sometimes they give him taffy—sometimes he gives *me* the article." The remaining entries are in the stenographer's notebook. Having boarded the *Gold Dust* in St. Louis he has Phelps record a conversation with an Irish vendor of books and papers; the potentially humorous questions are assigned to "Johnson" and "Sampson." On the following day "the stern aspect of Johnson" and his "eagle glances" cause him to be mistaken for the captain of the boat. In Helena, Arkansas, he has his stenographer record, "Had to step careful or a loose board would fly up and hit Johnson on the nose." Johnson's discovery of "a stylish pretty lady—quite a relief to the dismal monotony of the town," recorded at the same time as the preceding entry, concludes the series.[33] Since there is no record of an actual Johnson, since the name is also used later in chapter 22 as an alias for one of the author's party, and since the notes are of the Brown-Harris type, one can safely assume that this Johnson is Harris's substitute. In successive stages of the manuscript of chapter 32 he was to become the "so-called Thompson," the "publisher" Thompson and, finally, the "poet" Thompson. It is obvious that Thompson and Rogers represent Osgood and Phelps.

The use of assumed names in the canceled beginning of chapter 32 deserves particular notice. It is related to two distinct plans that emerge from the documents and afford a valuable insight into Mark Twain's relation to his materials.

It will be recalled that as early as April 2, 1882, the author told Joel Chandler Harris that he planned to follow his "usual course and use a fictitious name (C. L. Samuel, of New York)." Osgood, he added, would have to do the same. The explicitly stated reason was "to escape the interviewers," and to keep his movements secret so as to "be able to pick up the kind of book-material I want."[34] On April 16 he also asked Howells to address his letters to "S. L. Samuel."[35] On the other hand there is the notebook entry quoted above in which Mark Twain justifies the use of an assumed name as

"mysterious & stylish." The context of this entry, its relation to the plan of introducing "Harris" into the account, confirms that the reason is not to be taken seriously. It is obviously a justification intended to be given in the book itself to permit the author to exploit another device used previously as a structural element in *The Innocents Abroad* and particularly in *Roughing It*: the author or his fictional counterpart, the narrator, poses as an innocent or tenderfoot, whose assumed naïveté is the basis of much of the humor, while at the same time enabling the author to incorporate a great deal of factual information. Since the device had been highly successful in previous works, it was natural that Mark Twain should have thought of using it for the purposes of his standard work. In the writing of previous books, however, the device had suggested itself in the very experiences of the author. The subject matter of the second part of *Life on the Mississippi,* on the other hand, if presented in a first person narration by Mark Twain, the now-famous writer, required the deliberate plotting of a disguise on his part, and the furnishing of a plausible explanation for the reader. In this context the device of an incognito serves the exigencies of a literary account of the trip, whereas Mark Twain's actual intention to travel under an assumed name was to meet the exigencies of the field trip. The two plans have different and totally unrelated motivations behind them, but their realization, which can be traced independently, shows an interesting interaction between the realm of the author's experiences and that of his imagination.

As far as the plan for the actual use of an incognito is concerned, Mark Twain proceeded as he had indicated in his letters to Harris and Howells. But apparently the strategy failed very soon. Though his account in chapter 22 of having been recognized by a clerk at his St. Louis hotel need not be factual, an entry in the stenographer's notebook bears all the marks of truth and plainly tells what really happened:

Friday Eve'g Apl 21st.
Visited the pilot house this morning to get warm, and was betrayed by one of the boys—the pilot on watch. He said, "I have seen somebody sometime or other who resembled you very strongly and a great many years ago I heard a man use your voice. He is sometimes called Mark Twain—or Sam Clemens."

I said, "Then don't give me away" and made no further effort to keep up the shallow swindle. The pilot said he recognized me partly by my voice

"Under an alias"

and face and this was confirmed by my habit of running my hands up thro my hair.[36]

There is nothing to indicate that at any point in the trip Mark Twain returned to the plan. A letter to Olivia Langdon Clemens of April 22[37] and what is known of his actual progress rather confirm the truthfulness of the notebook entry, for Mark Twain was interviewed frequently and became the center of attention, not only during his extended stays in New Orleans and Hannibal,[38] but also as he traveled on board the steamboats. Contrary to his intention, he did not register as Samuel, for on April 23 he was recognized in a Memphis hotel by a man who had noticed the name of Clemens on the list of guests. One notebook entry, however, indicates that the plan for a literary use of the incognito was actually employed. While Mark Twain did not succeed in deceiving the pilots, his strategy of playing an innocent at least duped a fellow passenger during the first or second day on the *Gold Dust*: "He [the passenger from Nebraska] said to Phelps to-day, 'Say, that friend of yours is up in the pilot house. I jest heard him talking & he's an old pilot himself. Now, he's been giving me taffy, representing that he didnt know much about this river. Judging by his conversation I think he knows *all* about it.' "[39]

The idea of making use of the incognito device in the literary account of the journey is first reflected in the author's attempt to find a fictive justification for it. Calling it "mysterious & stylish" naturally suggested itself. Though the actual plan conceived for the journey itself, except in the case of the fellow traveler from Nebraska, had failed altogether, the literary plan devised for the book continued to exist. Mark Twain's personal notebook contains several notations relevant to the structure of the proposed work which were presumably made shortly after the *Gold Dust* had left St. Louis and after Mark Twain had been recognized. Some of these demonstrate how the author plotted various ways in which his incognito might be exposed:

Make my reception by <George> Ed. Gray in pilot house of Gold Dust very rough or sarcastic or something—afterward Len detects voice. Possibly G. recognizes me & "puts up" the rudeness on me. Use the most effective.

The two little boys whom *Len* & I accused of being the late Jesse James & his brother Frank—this talk exposed my voice.[40]

In an entry made a few days later in the stenographer's notebook Mark Twain added another possibility for a use of the incognito device, though he does not indicate how the exposure is to take place: "The pilot thinking I was a greenhorn put up a good deal of remarkable river information on me."[41] These entries show that the literary plan, which had originated independently of the actual plan, now begins to incorporate aspects of the author's experiences, and that in plotting the device Mark Twain wavered between the possibilities of making either himself or the pilot the victim of the deceit. In chapter 24 of *Life on the Mississippi* he decided on a highly complex solution, and it is here that the literary plan and the actual experiences finally merge. Actual experience as well as the exigencies of its literary account determined that the exposure should take place on his first visit to the pilot house. The author's imagination provided his pose as a New England tourist, playing himself "for a stranger and an innocent," while actuality provided the experience of the deceived traveler from Nebraska, whose role is transferred to the pilot to establish a conformity with the literary plan. Reality furthermore supplied the means of discovery, for it was chiefly by his voice that Mark Twain was recognized. The author's intention of "drawing out" the pilot and seeing him "reeling off his tranquil spool of lies"[42] is primarily literary, for the main purpose of the actual plan was to ward off interviewers and admirers, though he also intended to "pump" the pilots for authentic information and stories, and he certainly would not have minded some "authentic lies." As it is, the lies of chapter 24, as will be shown below, are substantially of Mark Twain's own invention. Though the scene incorporates elements of the author's experience, it is fictitious in its basic plot and in its major details.

Seen in relation to the tradition of the pose of the innocent as exploited in previous works the scene marks a vast development in the complexity of the device. It employs neither the simple deceit of the victim used in *The Innocents Abroad,* nor the deceit of the would-be deceiver used in "The Celebrated Jumping Frog of Calaveras County," but a combination of both types. While Mark Twain assumes that he deceives the pilot by his pose, the pilot begins to irritate the unsuspecting author by the enormity of the lies, which has the unforeseen result of making him feel more "like a passenger" than he had expected. To take his revenge the latter greatly annoys the pilot by questioning him about obvious contradictions in his yarns, whereupon the pilot exposes the author's incognito and offers him the wheel and the office of the liar. But Mark Twain rejoins once more, though feebly, by informing the reader: "I had gained a privilege, anyway, for I had been itching to get my hands on the wheel, from the beginning. I seemed to have forgotten the river, but I hadn't forgotten how to steer a steamboat, nor how to enjoy it, either." [43]

The complex denouement of the "fictitious-name business" is of course determined by the exigencies of fiction prevailing over the exigencies of fact. Much later the exigencies of still another plan imposed its structure on the same materials. In a supposedly auto-biographical note which Albert Bigelow Paine included in the biography, Mark Twain states, "I did not write that story in the book quite as it happened." The reader who expects a correction of the story according to the notes quoted above is surprised to find that Mark Twain proceeds to provide an even less probable solution. Though he reduces the number of mutual deceits between him and the pilot, the new and supposedly "truthful" account leaves the author suddenly at the wheel of the steamboat, in "one of the most dangerous places on the river," [44] while the pilot goes to get a cup of coffee. The "explosion" of the author's incognito follows a much more dramatic scene, and the story gains in impact what it loses in complexity. On the basis of the evidence presented above, however, it has to be classified as another of Mark Twain's "literary state-ments"—an attempt to carry the literary principle of deception over into the supposed reality of his autobiography. While the second fictitious account proves how much stronger the literary plan of using the incognito device was than the actual plan of 1882, it was now made to serve the exigencies of the author's popular image. Not only self-dramatization, but also self-idealization is at work in the revised version: the pilot, it should be noted, does not fail to mention that he remembered Mark Twain because the latter had been willing to examine him and endorse his application for a license at a time when others tried to keep the Pilots' Association small.

As far as the composition of Life on the Mississippi is concerned, however, it can be stated that the use of both the device of the "traveling companion" and of the pose of the innocent as docu-mented in the notebooks and preserved in the canceled beginning of chapter 32 clearly shows that the narrative structure originally intended for the standard work is definitely related to that of the author's previous travel books. The appearance of such a formal link between Mark Twain's traditional travel book and the proposed standard work at this early stage of composition suggests that other similarities may equally well be vestigial elements of a traditional plan rather than signs of the author's inability to complete the manuscript without "padding."

3 The development of Mark Twain's plan to use the pose of the innocent and concomitantly use the incognito for himself and his party as traced in the preceding section reveals a break which occurred between the writing of chapter 32, the sequel to the Ritter story, and that of the next unit of composition, chapters 22–24. While the canceled beginning of chapter 32 preserves the use of the incognito, chapter 24, composed subsequently, contains the climactic exposure and the necessary abandonment of the device. Though the canceled beginning indicates that a more extensive use of the traditional device had been intended, its abandonment need have no particular significance in itself. But a similar break in the use of the "travel companion" device suggests that both have a special relevance for a documentation of the development of a narrative structure for the book.

In the chronology of *Life on the Mississippi* chapters 22–24 constitute the beginning of the actual account of Mark Twain's trip of 1882. A marked difference is perceptible, here, between the role of Rogers and Thompson in the sequel to the Ritter story and the rather perfunctory introduction of the two characters. In the manuscript version of chapter 22 the author merely states, "I scraped a couple of friends together, for company."[45] Neither their real names nor their occupations are given, and the use of an incognito is introduced not because it is "mysterious & stylish," as would have comported far better with this pair's function in chapter 32, but for reasons actually quite close to those that determined his own plans in April 1882: "I reflected that if I were recognized, on the river, I should not be as free to go and come, talk, inquire, and spy around, as I should be if unknown. . . . I concluded that, from a business point of view, it would be an advantage to disguise our party with fictitious names." The false names used by the party— Smith, Jones, and Johnson—leave some doubt about the identity of each person. This is further confused when "the young man called Rogers," in a scene slightly reminiscent of earlier Brown-Harris episodes, is found crying over the poor quality of the drinking water. The author remarks, "Rogers was not his name; neither was Jones, Brown, Dexter, Ferguson, Bascom, nor Thompson; but he answered to any of these that a body found handy in an emergency; or to any other name, in fact, if he perceived that you meant him." This is only a half-hearted and barely successful attempt to exploit the traveling companions for comic purposes in the Brown-Harris vein. They are kept along, one suspects, to justify their use in chapter 32, and they are forgotten in the meantime; only the poet reappears once afterwards. Their introduction, moreover, is hardly explicit enough to enable the reader to identify them readily when they reappear in connection with the Ritter story. Mark Twain must have realized this himself when he was reading proof; he managed to modify the defect somewhat by specifying that he enlisted a poet and a stenographer, after he had already made the "publisher" Thompson into the "poet" Thompson throughout the manuscript of chapter 32. While Rogers and Thompson thus cease to function as traveling companions in the Brown-Harris tradition, Mark Twain does not abandon the idea itself. A part of the intended function of the pair is transferred to another person whom he had met on the Mississippi trip—Dad Dunham, second mate of the *Gold Dust*. In *Life on the Mississippi* the author calls him Uncle Mumford and honors this "mate of the blessed old-time kind"[46] by "assigning to him some of his own ideas and favorite curses,"[47] as well as by giving him some of his own experiences and yarns recorded in the notebook.[48] From the point of view of the subject matter this substitution is an altogether more fortunate development of a tested literary device of Mark Twain's, for the poet and the stenographer could hardly be said to "belong" on the Mississippi, and their personae certainly would not have guaranteed the kind of authenticity befitting a standard work.

The difference in the role of the traveling companions between chapter 32 and chapter 22, the actual order of their introduction into the narrative, is indicative of still another difference between the two sections which is even more important for the narrative structure of the book. In the Ritter story sequence the narrator had been perceptibly fictionalized. Such fictionalization, it should be noted, occurred independently of using the pose of the innocent and the incognito, for it is apparent only in his conversation with the traveling companions, where dissimulation on his part is superfluous. In chapter 22 the narrator becomes more nearly the author about to revisit the river. Here the identity between author and narrator is closer, in fact, than in any of the preceding travel books. It is in such capacity that he functions throughout the chapters still to be written. This identity of narrator and author, Mark Twain must have found, was better suited to the intended emphasis on factual reports and material about the Mississippi. The function of the narrator in the very first stage of the composition of chapters 21–60, thus, has been modified in the interest of the documentary aspect of the standard work about the river. Still, Mark Twain must have been pleased with the effective conclusion of the Ritter story reached by means of his fictionalized narrator, because even at the sacrifice of consistent characterization and against his publisher's advice,[49] he insisted on including the story.

The establishment of this close identity between author and narrator was to have far-reaching consequences in the composition of the book. The unity, or its lack, is now provided, and to a certain degree even justified, by the author's discursive mind; it is not the artistic unity derived from the use of a fictional narrator and a consequently restricted point of view. This stance permitted Mark Twain to depend on the river notebooks for a large number of chapters. Chapter 22, in the paragraphs that follow the introduction of the traveling companions, is largely a commentary derived from a series of notebook entries. Some of these are actually quoted in the text. The first three are taken nearly verbatim from the stenographer's notebook,[50] and their source is identified accordingly. The fourth is apparently made up in the same vein. It should be noted that they all refer to the author's overland trip from New York to St. Louis, not to the Mississippi itself. Similarly, the book ends when the Pennsylvania road rushes him "to New York without missing schedule time ten minutes anywhere on the route."[51] Therefore it is clearly Mark Twain's journey that provides the frame for chapters 22–60. Commentaries on St. Louis are similarly based on notebook entries, though these are incorporated into the text. Most of these, as well as those about the river and its steamboats (in chapter 23 and the beginning of chapter 24), concern changes that the author notices; they reflect the normal reaction of one who has been absent a long time. This dependence on notebook facts about the Mississippi, its towns, and the author's experiences was supplemented at a later time by the use of other documentary material. Chapter 22, for example, contains two substantial additions and one footnote which is not part of the manuscript.[52] All of these additions reflect a reading in travel books[53] and were presumably made in Elmira not before late in July, for reasons to be discussed below.

The availability of his notebooks at the time of the composition had another curious effect. Early in 1882 Mark Twain had begun an extended series of entries to be used for an invective against Whitelaw Reid of the New York *Tribune*, avowedly as a revenge for calumnious attacks on him. His extended research on this subject resulted in a huge mass of material gathered before he bothered to verify the rumor of such attacks. When it proved to be utterly without foundation, he abandoned the project and in a letter to William Dean Howells complained about the waste of time.[54] The notes for this project occupied the first pages of his personal river notebook. When he came to write chapter 24, in which Lem Gray[55] was to reel off "his tranquil spool of lies" for the author who was playing himself "for a stranger and an innocent,"[56] these notes furnished excellent copy for the liar's description of another liar. They thus helped to fill the place of the authentic information and yarns that Mark Twain had hoped to gather by using an assumed name. The author had intended to elaborate Reid's phrenology so that the more selfish organs in the sternsheets would weigh down the back of his head and make his nose tilt in the air. He had also planned to comment on the size of his feet as belonging to a body that should be nine feet tall. One of his final notes was that if you took the malice out of Reid "he would be reduced three feet & one inch"; if you took the vanity out of him he "would disappear."[57] All of these went nearly verbatim into Lem Gray's description; the only change was that the intended size of the liar was increased to nineteen feet. This provides an instance of Mark Twain's ability and eagerness to appropriate materials and descriptions, by himself as well as by others, for his own purposes and in a newly devised context. It is a model in miniature of further borrowings in the composition of *Life on the Mississippi*.

A similar procedure is evident in the way in which another notebook entry found a somewhat curious reflection in the same passage. The death of Charles Darwin, which had occurred while Mark Twain was on his Mississippi journey, caused the following notation to be made late in May or during the first half of June: "Mention meeting Darwin at Grasmere. . . . Tell how Norton said Darwin always read himself to sleep with my books—& then (Norton) blushed & apologized. I am glad to have seen that mighty man."[58] As far as the subject of the proposed book is concerned, the entry is nearly as extraneous as that of the elephant intended for Huck Finn's escape in the working notes for *Adventures of Huckleberry Finn*,[59] and the author himself obviously did not see a convenient way of bringing it into the book. But he did find an obscure place for the homage intended for Darwin in the yarn Lem Gray told about his adventures in steamboat explosions: " 'I was flung through the roof of the same cabin in Walnut Bend three times in five years. . . . The third time, the man moved away. . . . He was a nervous, sedentary, student-sort of a man, trying to cipher out the Development business, & Survival of the Fittest, & one thing or another, & he said he would rather move than be always being interrupted & bothered so.' "[60] The passage, however, does not survive in the printed version of the book.

The first two paragraphs of chapter 25 in the final version of *Life on the Mississippi* are all that remain of the last chapter of consecutive composition in Hartford. The writing of these and another seven pages of manuscript for this chapter probably occurred before June 20. This portion continues in the vein of the preceding unit of composition and thus confirms Mark Twain's departure from the initial plan of using a fictionalized narrator. The author himself continues to function as the narrator, and his experiences continue to furnish the materials. Consequently, his dependence on the river notebooks is further noticeable.

Another instance of the use of notebook entries may serve to demonstrate, however, that the break in the development of a narrative structure did not affect the choice of the materials to be included in the book. Though the close identity between author and narrator is apt to stress the actual experiences of his recent trip, the factual material that he collected, and his opinions about both, the original plan of incorporating anecdotes and stories into the standard work persisted. As early as 1881 Mark Twain had listed the renaming of California's Devil's Gorge to Jehovah Gap as an item for the book. The anecdote was to be introduced through association occasioned by the Devil's Bake-Oven and the Devil's Tea Table, which were points the author would pass on the Mississippi. Reminders of the episode appear in his river notebook, once before the beginning of the trip and once when the party actually passed the location.[61] It was finally inserted in chapter 25, and Mark Twain must have been disappointed when he found that the anecdote headed Osgood's list of items to be omitted from the manuscript, but in this case he submitted to his publisher's judgment.

The inclusion of similar materials not directly related to the subject of the Mississippi confirms that the narrative structure devised in the writing of the first four chapters of consecutive composition did not exert a selective or a restrictive influence on the materials that Mark Twain had always intended for the standard work. The method of narration by an author-narrator was found to suit his purposes best. Such a method remained wholly subservient to the plan of the standard work; it did not require much attention, nor did it ever exert a strict artistic control over the subject matter.

(Quarry Farm, Elmira, July–September 1882)

1   After June 20, Mark Twain was busy nursing his family and plainly stated: "In the present circumstances I haven't any literary inspiration." [1] A letter of this time to his mother shows that he had probably stopped his composition altogether; he explains that because of his daughter Jean's illness he has "written no letters, attended to no business, not even matters of the vastest importance." [2] He also mentions that he himself suffers from "lumbago & some other diseases." But a letter from Osgood of July 6, 1882, indicates that Mark Twain has reported to his publisher that he is already in better health. [3] On July 14, 1882, he and his family finally transferred to his summer house at Quarry Farm, Elmira, New York.

It is what happened during the two and a half months of his stay in Elmira that determined the exact shape that the proposed standard work was to assume. When he arrived at his summer residence Mark Twain was probably no less confident in his plan than he had been in 1872, and he was certainly as eager to realize it, but in its subsequent execution he was, as usual, subject to a whole range of influences. We can never hope to learn about all of these, but by observing wherever possible the chronology of the composition and by relating it to the evidence that the surviving documents provide regarding his reading and his ideas at the time, we may hope to arrive at a better understanding of both the author and his work.

The manuscript indicates the extent of Mark Twain's "summer's work." He most likely began with the second half of chapter 25, where the writing resumes in a broader pen.[4] The following chapter definitely belongs to the Elmira period; one of its pages (MSII 176) is written on the verso of a sheet of working notes based on the author's reading in accounts by English travelers. This reading, as we shall see, can not have occurred before the end of July. As indicated above, most of the eighth batch (up to chapter 47 and the following chapter on "Southern political slavery") was also written in Elmira before the end of September. Osgood's references to the numbering of the typescript, finally, show that the intervening chapters also were composed in Elmira.

Many of the chapters written in Elmira and after the author's return to Hartford on September 29, 1882, show a greater dependence than the earlier portion on secondary sources both for quotation and documentation. This fact might plausibly be explained by reference to Jean's and Mark Twain's illnesses and his consequently increased awareness of the pressure of the contract, but I see no evidence that these events affected his original plan for *Life on the Mississippi* to any large extent. A summary of the characteristics of Mark Twain's writing before he went to Elmira points to the continuity of both the plan and the actual composition. The author had decided not to use his personal experiences as a pilot, he had established a close identity between himself and his narrator, and he had decided against an extended humorous use of the traveling companions. His frame for the book definitely was to be his journey of 1882, and it was to be kept loose enough to permit the inclusion of "yarns" and "incidents from many lands," some of which he had already begun to use or to prepare. Each of these decisions may be construed as a commentary on the plan documented prior to the beginning of the composition, chiefly in his notebooks. Only two of these decisions show a rejection of ideas that had been recorded for future use, and these rejections tend to consolidate the concept of the standard work.

Although the portion of the manuscript written in Hartford clearly indicates that Mark Twain had finally decided on a narrative structure for the remaining chapters, and although the rest of the book was to be built solely on this foundation, the author did not immediately continue in his writing. It even seems as if his success in developing an overall plan and in getting his composition started along its lines permitted a more careful, considered preparation and use of sources and documentary material.

Before chapter 25 was completed Mark Twain read or reread Charles Dickens's *American Notes,* as he had intended to do, "for a note on Cairo."[5] The note was duly incorporated in the second half of the chapter. Also at this time he turned to the other literary source referred to in his notebook and began to read Francis Parkman's *La Salle and the Discovery of the Great West.* He had long admired the historian and had already been reading his works when, as early as 1881, he recorded items for his book on the Mississippi.[6] His notebooks contain several references to such reading,[7] and his copy of *The Jesuits in North America,* preserved among other books from his library in the Mark Twain Papers, is full of marginalia in his hand. The suitability of Parkman's account of the discovery and exploration of the Mississippi probably caused him to make a detailed plan for the introductory chapters. This explains why, despite his decision not to make changes in the original "Old Times on the Mississippi" series and the consequent absence of a copy of it in Elmira, he now asked Osgood to send him the numbers of the *Atlantic Monthly* in which the articles had been published. In their final form, chapters 1 and 2, which were composed as one unit, depend largely on *La Salle and the Discovery of the Great West.* For chapter 3 Mark Twain turned to the *Huckleberry Finn* manuscript for the largest of the three borrowings from that source. Much as one would agree with George Washington Cable's wish that the raftsmen chapter be restored to the novel,[8] its presence in *Life on the Mississippi* does not warrant the conclusion that it was transferred for lack of other, more suitable materials. Its documentary and historical value (which is clearly emphasized by the author in the new context of chapter 3), rather than its value as "copy," must have determined its inclusion. In addition to the evidence of the notebook, the very fact that the three sources used in these chapters were available in Elmira at the time of composition indicates that their use had been planned in advance, and that in Hartford Mark Twain had already considered the possibility of borrowing from the *Huckleberry Finn* manuscript.

Before Mark Twain actually wrote the introductory chapters, however, he must have reread Captain Marryat's travel memoirs, which did not occur before July 22, and have written chapter 44.[9] Since they also reflect Mark Twain's attack on Sir Walter Scott and the "absurd chivalry business," [10] which begins in chapter 40 and pervades the eighth batch, it is very likely that their writing concluded the composition of the Elmira period. Osgood's request for "your preface, or such introductory or explanatory matter as you choose to prefix," [11] sent on September 22, indicates that the first three chapters had not been received by him; his request may even have induced Mark Twain to write them at that time.

The two other borrowings from the manuscript of *Huckleberry Finn* mentioned by Walter Blair—the Grangerford-Shepherdson feud material and the description of the Grangerford parlor as "The House Beautiful"—also show signs of advance planning. The use of the latter, which resulted in chapter 38, is likely to have occurred shortly after his arrival in Elmira. A renumbering of the pages of this portion of the manuscript [12] indicates composition in advance of the actual context. References to Charles Dickens, however, show that Mark Twain had first read his *American Notes*. Ink and pen, finally, indicate that the chapter was written in Elmira. "A comparison between this description written by the wry and critical humorist and that of the admiring Huck," Blair says, "throws brilliant light upon the comic value of Huck's angle of narration." The comparison also shows that the parlor was refurnished, divested of details expressive of the Grangerfords' character, in the interest of making the symbolism more universal. This refurnishing was not all Mark Twain's; not only did he borrow, as Blair suggests, "the ironic name" from Clarence Chatham Cook's *The House Beautiful: Essays on Beds and Tables, Stools and Candlesticks* (1877),[13] he also appropriated several items described by this self-appointed but widely acclaimed arbiter of household taste. [14] In its original as well as in its final form the chapter mentions Charles Dickens's lack of enthusiasm for the magnificence and palatial grandeur of the steamboats. The term "borrowing" is hardly appropriate to describe the specific use made of all the sources for the chapter (the *Huckleberry Finn* manuscript, Cook's *The House Beautiful*, and Charles Dickens's comments). Ideas and materials from all three sources are brought together in a context unique to the new chapter and not immediately suggested by any of the three sources. The unifying idea is the importance of training (a favorite idea of Mark Twain's, later used more explicitly in *Pudd'nhead Wilson, What Is Man?*, and other writings), in this instance applied to taste. Magnificence and grandeur, the chapter suggests, are relative notions; the nineteenth-century Babbitt, inhabitant of the standardized "House Beautiful," is struck by what did not excite Dickens. Because of his different background and education, Dickens measured the steamboats by comparing them "with the crown jewels; or with the Taj, or with the Matterhorn; or with some other priceless or wonderful thing which he had seen." [15] A nineteenth-century Babbitt, on the other hand, saw a splendor surpassing that of his own parlor. Mark Twain apparently pursues the idea of the relativity of aesthetic judgments, obviously suggested by his reading of Dickens's *American Notes*, and in doing so does not further the proposed subject of his book. The aside, however, serves to introduce the description of both the home of the affluent citizen and the exterior and interior decoration of the steamboat, though—because of the reliance on Cook's book—the domestic description is not quite as localized a summary of social history, ante-bellum taste and household decoration in the Mississippi Valley as Dixon Wecter assumed. [16]

The concluding paragraphs of the chapter, in the original version more clearly than in the revised text, also reflect an actual experience of the recent trip recorded in the notebook. While traveling on the *Charles Morgan*, which Mark Twain boarded on April 26, 1882, he was shocked at the uncleanliness of the waiters and decided to "give this gilt-&-filth sty *rats.*" [17] While the manuscript clearly identified the boat as the *Charles Morgan*, it became a "Cincinnati boat" in the printed version, and the author apparently failed to make sufficiently clear that the "layer of ancient and obdurate dirt" and his criticism applied only to this particular boat. Speculations about his indignation having symbolic meaning in terms of the splendor of the past opposed to the sordidness of the present in the history of the Mississippi are therefore not wholly justified. [18]

None of the four sources, one may conclude, suggests in any way that Mark Twain borrowed because he lacked materials, nor does his skillful combination of them suggest the pressure of a contract. Dickens's observation, Mark Twain's own experience, and the adaptation of the *Huckleberry Finn* passage are all clearly related to the Mississippi and its history, and borrowings from Cook's *The House Beautiful* merely contribute to the topicality of the description.

2   When after the advance composition of chapter 38 Mark Twain returned to a more chronological order of composition, he began to use considerably more borrowed material. This suggests that those critics are right who have related such borrowings to his illness, to the lack of suitable subject matter, and to the pressure of the deadline. But the general plan for the standard work itself seems to contradict the explanation, and another document indicates that the author would have used secondary sources earlier had they been available. In fact, the advance composition of chapter 38 may well have occurred because Mark Twain was still awaiting the arrival of additional material that he thought necessary for the writing of his book.

In an undated letter to Osgood, probably written in the second half of June or early in July 1882, Mark Twain had asked his publisher: "I wish you would set a cheap expert to work to collect local histories of Mississippi towns & a lot of other books relating to the river for me. Meantime all those people who promised to send such things to us ain't doing it, dern them. . . ."[19] This letter reveals that a further purpose and activity of the Mississippi trip had been to collect or solicit printed matter, probably mainly of the nature of descriptive folders such as the booklet which Mark Twain used in chapters 59 and 60. At least one such attempt to obtain documentary material for the book had been successful. Probably when he was still in New Orleans he subscribed to the *Times-Democrat*, to be sent to him in Hartford. Notebook entries show that he was reading the paper as early as June, and before his intended departure for Elmira on June 22 he reminded himself in another entry to file a change of address so that it would continue to reach him at his summer residence.[20] The five overt quotations from or references to current numbers of that paper in the latter part of *Life on the Mississippi*,[21] then, must be taken as the result of advance planning rather than lack of other material. Similarly, references to and quotations from back numbers of the *Times-Democrat*,[22] as well as the three reports in Appendix A, all about the great flood of March 1882, had already been planned before the trip.[23]

The author's request for "local histories of Mississippi towns & a lot of other books relating to the river" may have been made because further material of this nature failed to arrive. Perhaps in reply to this letter, certainly also in reply to other unrecorded specific requests for the numbers of the *Atlantic Monthly* containing the "Old Times on the Mississippi" series as well as travel books and other material about the river, W. Rowlands of Osgood's firm wrote on July 22:

We send you by American express, a bundle containing the seven "Atlantics" containing the Mississippi articles, and a number of "Emerson's Magazine," with "Up the Miss." by J.A. Dallas in it.

We also enclose a lot of books relating to travels in the U.S. by English people in the first half of this century; twentyfive volumes in all. They include Mrs. Trollope, Basil Hall and Marryat, &c.&c. Their average price is about a Dollar per *volume*. Please, return any you do not wish for.[24]

Without doubt, the "books relating to travels in the U.S. by English people in the first half of this century" constitute the largest group of sources for *Life on the Mississippi*. Quotations from and comments on them form the substance of chapters 27 and 29 of the printed version as well as of three chapters omitted from the final version,[25] but they also occur in other chapters of the second half of the book. The specific use made of these sources has been explored in depth by Dewey Ganzel and Walter Blair. While one must agree with Ganzel that "initially Twain had intended to use the travel books as a point of departure for his own comments about the Mississippi Valley in 1882"[26] and with Blair that "he utilized these borrowings and commentaries . . . in developing ideas and attitudes which were tremendously important to him and to the new chapters,"[27] the role of the travel books in the actual composition of *Life on the Mississippi* has not yet been accurately assessed. Osgood's shipment of books, which must have reached Elmira on or about July 22, contained, as Rowlands's letter indicates, mainly travel books. But also included was an article by an American, as a result, perhaps, of the endeavors of the cheap expert that Mark Twain had asked Osgood to employ "to collect local histories of Mississippi towns & a lot of other books relating to the river." One can assume that the shipment announced by Rowlands was not the only one. He also seems to have supplied Mark Twain with a series of fifteen articles by Ralph Keeler, a journalist who had accompanied the author on several lecture tours in and around Boston a decade earlier. These articles had appeared in 1871 under the titles "New Orleans," "On the Mississippi," and "St. Louis" in *Every Saturday,* an illustrated weekly journal published by James R. Osgood and Company.[28] The numbers were apparently taken from the publisher's archives, for Mark Twain returned them quickly. On September 16, together with the first portion of the typescript of *Life on the Mississippi,* Rowlands acknowledged the receipt of "the package of 'Every Saturday.' "[29] On July 26, perhaps occasioned by finding a reference in the travel books just received, Mark Twain asked Osgood to obtain two more works for him, Henry Bradshaw Fearon's *Sketches of America: Narrative of a Journey of Five Thousand Miles Through the Eastern and Western States of America* (1817) and a now unidentifiable book by a writer named Fawkes.[30] Since he would hardly have had sufficient time to determine that the twenty-five volumes received a few days earlier did not contain sufficient material to be used for the composition of *Life on the Mississippi,* it seems Mark Twain now aimed at completeness rather than usefulness in collecting his source material. Such an attempt is strongly reminiscent of similar preparations for the writing of his letters from the Sandwich Islands and the eighteen chapters devoted to that excursion in *Roughing It,* when Mark Twain availed himself of every source of information he could lay hold of, and even went to the extreme of appropriating Jarves's *History of the Sandwich Islands* from a newspaper office.[31] This parallel, as well as the fact that the author's statements in the October 3 letter to William Dean Howells cannot be related to the use of the travel books, suggests that the acquisition of the latter group of sources does not reflect desperation on Mark Twain's part. Nor need a request for such books be the result of a sudden decision; the value of travel memoirs as source material for the standard work must have been obvious to Mark Twain even prior to 1882 when he had read Harriet Martineau's *Retrospect of Western Travel* and probably some of the other travel memoirs used in *Life on the Mississippi.*[32] His procurement of other materials, which will be discussed below, confirms a procedure preparatory to the composition of a standard work.

In the course of his reading—or rereading—of these books, which must have occurred late in July and in the first half of August, he took notes which, in the actual composition of the chapters based on them, he treated much like the kind of working notes he had previously prepared for other books. Dewey Ganzel discusses in detail the sheet of such notes that has survived as the verso of MSII 176 of the Morgan manuscript.[33] Although I do not agree with his identification of a sheet of the working notes that Walter Blair and Bernard DeVoto attribute to the composition of *Huckleberry Finn*, I do agree that there must have been more such notes. All of these, however, were used almost immediately for the composition of the chapters devoted to comments on the travel accounts.

Of these chapters, the two omitted ones which were to have followed chapter 40 were composed first, and only much later were they fitted into the sequence of the narrative. The manuscript shows a renumbering of the pages throughout this portion (MSII 562–612 were originally numbered 3–53) and also establishes that the list of authors consulted was prefixed to this portion when it was incorporated in the manuscript; at the same time, the original beginning, which possibly consisted of an incomplete list of authors, was discarded and replaced by MSII 561. But the list as presented on this page [34] is still not complete. Dewey Ganzel noted the absence of Ernst von Hesse-Wartegg's *Mississippi-Fahrten: Reisebilder aus dem amerikanischen Süden (1879–1880)* and Francis Parkman's *The Discovery of the Great West* in what he considers to be the author's "list of sources." [35] It is obvious, however, that Mark Twain had not intended to be exhaustive in listing the foreign travel writers. In concluding the paragraph he explicitly stated, "There are others, but their books cannot be purchased now." [36] There are specific reasons, furthermore, why the names of Hesse-Wartegg and Parkman should not have been included. Not only were their writings not used in the two chapters that in the manuscript followed the list, but also Hesse-Wartegg had, unlike the tourists whose names were given, only very recently visited the United States. In identifying his *Mississippi-Fahrten* as the source of a quotation about a yellow-fever epidemic in Memphis in chapter 29, Mark Twain mentions that it was "just published in Leipzig." [37] He had a good reason to stress this fact, for the book was not yet available when he wrote the chapter; the quotation and the author's commentary do not appear in the manuscript and were inserted only when he read the proofs. This suggests that there were indeed more shipments of books from Osgood's firm, and that either the "cheap expert" or Mark Twain himself, and probably both, continued the search for documentary materials. [38] The insertion of this additional quotation from the travel memoirs when Mark Twain already knew he had "enough book" further demonstrates that the author's interest in such materials extends beyond the Elmira period of composition and the actual writing of those chapters which critics originally found to reflect a careless padding. The absence of Parkman from Mark Twain's list is, of course, explained by the fact that he was not a foreign tourist and that his book was not, as Ganzel's use of its early title seems to imply, a travel memoir.

References in correspondence between Mark Twain and Robert Underwood Johnson of the *Century Magazine* confirm that the two omitted chapters based on the author's reading in the travel memoirs were written early in August and thus antedate the composition of preceding chapters. In a letter of August 9, 1882, Johnson attempted to solicit a series of three articles on "Permanent Sources of Corruption in Our Government," suggesting among other items the railroad pass system, to be published in the September issue of the magazine (an issue already scheduled to contain Howells's article on Mark Twain). The next letter from Johnson, dated August 16, suggests that Mark Twain "make a monograph of the remarks on R. R. passes," and, together with his last letter of August 29, clearly indicates that the author, in declining the invitation, had explained that he was already using such remarks in his new book.[39] Mark Twain's comments on the railroad pass system were part of the second of these two chapters, and they were therefore written early in August. The incorporation of one of the working notes for these two chapters in the manuscript of chapter 26 confirms that they were written in advance. It also shows that the author did not resume the chronological order of his composition before the middle of August, when he wrote chapter 26. Thus it was before he made an equally extensive use of material derived from the travel books in chapters 27, 29, and the omitted chapter that was to have followed chapter 29, that he made a discovery that was to have far-reaching consequences, both for the actual process of composition and the final version of *Life on the Mississippi*. He had been forced to make the following admission: "I drudged through all those old books, mainly to find out what the procession of foreign tourists thought of the river towns of the Mississippi. But as a general thing, they forgot to say."[40] As early as the middle of August, therefore, an important project for the preparation of the additional chapters of *Life on the Mississippi*—the collecting and reading of the travel literature—had proved essentially futile. While the tourists did comment on steamboats and scenery, their information as a rule did not extend to the towns along the banks of the river, or else it was not detailed enough for Mark Twain's purposes. The author's wording deserves particular attention; it indicates that he was not interested in the individual adventures of the foreign traveler, of which their accounts contained a full measure. What he had hoped to find and use were opinions on life and institutions in the Mississippi Valley, presumably to provide a perspective on the present. This direction of his research confirms an important point of his plan for the standard work. His reaction to the failure to find the information demonstrates how strongly this plan continued to govern the selection of his materials. Rather than preserve the relation to the Mississippi and include individual adventures he chose to present opinions and observations of historical and documentary value, though these were chiefly related to the cities of the East. Besides observing the outlines of his plan for the standard work, his reaction was also typical of his procedure in another respect. Not only did he decide to compose the chapters later deleted, fully aware that in doing so he was leaving the proper subject of his book, he also continued to make what use he could of his reading in the composition of further chapters. This method parallels the use he made of the attack on Whitelaw Reid, with the difference that now the burden of the contract may have begun to make itself felt.

3   Another aspect of the two deleted chapters composed immediately after Mark Twain's reading of the travel memoirs deserves particular notice: the strong vein of social criticism in these is an even more prominent characteristic than their apparent irrelevancy to the rest of the book. This characteristic sets these two chapters apart from those written previously. Contrary to the impression given by the final order of the chapters in the holograph manuscript, which indicates a concentration of social criticism in chapters 40–48 (including the above-mentioned omitted chapters and a chapter on "Southern Political Slavery" following chapter 47), the order of composition demonstrates that a strong critical impulse was at work even before Mark Twain had written chapter 26. While in the first of the two deleted chapters he directs his criticism against the America of the past and merely leaves the reader to draw his own conclusions about its applicability to the present, in the second chapter he introduces his criticism of the present by observing that "the noticeable features of that departed America are not all gone from us." [41]

    Seen from the point of view of narrative technique, in these chapters Mark Twain appears neither as the recent traveler recounting his experiences (as he does most of the time) nor as a fictionalized narrator (as he does in chapters 42 and 43), but rather as the author himself who records his reactions to specific passages in a number of books he is reading. He becomes more of a social commentator than simply the author of a book about the Mississippi. In a concluding sentence, he admits his deviation from the ostensible subject matter and even attempts to justify the insertion.

Since the omission of these two chapters was prompted by comments made by his publisher [42] and therefore was not made on his own motion, we are justified in interpreting his commentaries as part of the context of ideas presented in *Life on the Mississippi*.[43] It is possible, therefore, to determine more precisely than before the author's position as a social commentator. It has frequently been observed that Mark Twain's attitude in his comments upon the changes that he observed during his trip in the spring of 1882 is ambivalent. Walter Blair summarizes such views when he writes, "Toward both the past as he recalled it and the present which he now pondered he had mixed feelings." [44] The view that Mark Twain was a romantic at heart [45] and committed to progress in theory does not entirely explain the ambivalence. The comparison, in the omitted chapters, between the America of the past as interpreted by the foreign tourist and that of the present as interpreted by the author himself reveals Mark Twain's position as a seemingly impartial observer who identifies himself with neither of the two alternatives. Though he does, in a later chapter, call the nineteenth century "the plainest and sturdiest and infinitely greatest and worthiest of all the centuries the world has seen," [46] he still perceives that not all the flaws and social evils of the past, even those of an immediate national past, have vanished from the contemporary scene. But contrary to the attitude which dominated his later life, he still firmly believes in the possibility of social betterment and moral progress, and that belief is the very foundation upon which his criticism of even the "infinitely greatest and worthiest of all the centuries" still rests. Such an overt commitment to a belief in moral and social perfectibility and the consequent condemnation of sentimentality make apparent the incongruity of an occasional ubi sunt and his nostalgia toward the "flush times" of steamboating on the Mississippi, which even the author's innate "sentimentality" can not entirely explain.

The holograph manuscript of *Life on the Mississippi*, however, contains two curious cancellations that may well help solve this problem. In chapter 45 ("Southern Sports"), after describing the "abundant fascination" that the "sport" of cock-fighting holds for a group of spectators in New Orleans, he originally continued: "All 'civilizations' are legitimate matter for (private, but not public) jeering & laughter, because they are so conspicuously made up of about three tenths of reality & sincerity, & seven tenths of wind & humbug; but it seems to me that the civilization which is always preaching pity & humanity, & then for a change—".[47] The sentence was crossed out before it had been completed, and the manuscript resumes with another matter. It is not difficult to see what caused the cancellation. Mark Twain must have noticed, first of all, that while publicly asserting that all "civilizations" are but matter for private ridicule, he was actually contradicting the statement he was making. While the humorous effect to be derived from such a method might have persuaded him to proceed, he must also have realized that the sentence would weaken his carefully worked-out argument against Southern culture and Southern society, the theme of a sequence of chapters begun with chapter 40, and culminating in his attack on Sir Walter Scott.[48] Given these reasons for a cancellation, there is no need to assume that Mark Twain should not have, at least momentarily, believed in the truth of his statement. His later views of the "damned human race" make such a belief appear thoroughly plausible, and another cancellation of a similar nature in *Life on the Mississippi* itself helps to confirm this. Commenting, in chapter 48, on the credulity of the clients of a spiritualistic medium, the author writes: "Of course every man in this world is in one way or another a fool, & is well aware of it; but why should he be *this* kind of a fool?"[49] Again the author canceled the sentence, realizing that by making this statement he was undercutting the effect of his "progressivistic" argument, made, in this case, by a conscious attack on superstition and credulity as medieval rather than modern characteristics.

What makes these canceled passages so interesting is, of course, their direct contradiction of Mark Twain's overt advocacy of the belief in the moral and social perfectibility of mankind, one of the most pervasive themes of *Life on the Mississippi*. Mark Twain's own decision[50] to cross out the statements seems to have been a deliberate check of impulses beyond rational control. His incipient pessimism is beginning to cast doubt on the overtly maintained belief in human perfectibility. Such ideas latent in his thinking must have led him to question tacitly the premises of his position as a social commentator and a moralist. If there were social values to be found at all, his pessimism would imply, they could be found to reside in the past as well as in the present, in the "flush times" of steamboating as well as in the days of the River Commission and the powerful tug.

The canceled chapters document the existence of a critical attitude toward the present as well as the past. Since this attitude became apparent following the completion of that part of the book devoted primarily to his reminiscences but before the bulk of the writing in accordance with his plan for a standard work, it probably contributed to the emergence of the ambivalence of the author's attitude in *Life on the Mississippi*. His doubts of his progressivistic assumptions, however, were covert and subconscious, and when they crowded to the surface, Mark Twain was careful to cross out the statements that embodied them as soon as a more rational thinking regained control over his creative process.

There were several important external influences on the types of rational control that Mark Twain imposed on his creative impulses. Rational control is constantly enforced by society and authority. For Mark Twain as a writer it was most clearly exercised by William Dean Howells, who functioned, as their correspondence and other records of their exchanges show, as his literary conscience, in the nonpsychological sense in which F. Scott Fitzgerald used the term for Edmund Wilson. But in a larger sense, society itself—Mark Twain's readers and those who made known their demands, the publishers—also exercised such a control. Hamlin Hill has clearly shown one aspect of this process in his investigation of the demands that the method of subscription publication made on Mark Twain and how the author consciously strove to meet such demands.[51]

Mark Twain's attack on the railrod pass system and on "noticeable features" of a "departed America" in the two omitted chapters discussed above already indicates the presence in the latter half of *Life on the Mississippi* of the impulse toward social and moral criticism. Robert Underwood Johnson's request for some articles on "Permanent Sources of Corruption in Our Government" could only confirm both the author's inclination and his belief in his capabilities to function as a critic. Johnson's request for Mark Twain's views on this particular matter, however, was admittedly prompted by reading the manuscript of William Dean Howells's critical appraisal of Mark Twain as a writer, to be published in the *Century Magazine* for September 1882:

Something in Mr. Howells's very interesting paper on you and your writings . . . induces us to think that the proposition we are about to make will not be unwelcome to you—at least not distastefull.—We propose that you should write for the Century say three papers on the Permanent Sources of Corruption in our Government—not primarily the passing scandals. . . . We mean a serious exposition of the ways that are dark of the professional politician. . . . Does the idea strike you favorably? We think it would make a hit, and help on the Millenium a notch or two. Besides it is the next thing to do.[52]

Mark Twain's contributions, obviously, were to have supplemented—and implicitly to have supported—Howells's contention that the author possessed "an indignant sense of right and wrong, a scorn of all affectations and pretense, an ardent hate of meanness and injustice."[53] But as early as June 1882, Mark Twain himself had already seen Howells's manuscript. Commenting upon it in a letter to its author he wrote: "Of *course* it pleases *me*—that goes without saying—& I hope the public will be willing to see me with your eyes. I shouldn't ask anything better than that. Well, I am mighty glad you had time & the disposition to write it."[54] One can hardly overestimate the effect on Mark Twain of Howells's evaluation and praise. It has been pointed out repeatedly that the article constitutes the first full-length appreciation, transcending "the obscurities of . . . book notices."[55] Nothing is more plausible, in view of Mark Twain's continued and widely documented dependence on Howells's critical judgments,[56] than that thus praised he should have seen his "indignant sense of right and wrong," his "scorn of all affectations and pretense," and his "ardent hate of meanness and injustice" vindicated, and that he should have felt called upon to exercise these faculties more fully even than before. Howells's ideas almost certainly, then, gave added impetus to Mark Twain's critical inclinations. But they also led Mark Twain to impose rational control on such criticism according to the principles that Howells felt had governed it from the very beginning of Mark Twain's career.

At the same time, Mark Twain's reading of Howells's manuscript may well constitute a final factor that contributed to his modification of the original plan for the standard work about the Mississippi. It is, however, difficult to determine precisely the extent to which Howells's remarks influenced the book, for Mark Twain's previous works such as *The Gilded Age* had of course also contained their measure of social criticism. But since even his standard work, a book actually intended to serve completely different purposes, now became a vehicle for severe social criticism, it would seem safe to conclude that the author is availing himself of the very manuscript he is producing to supply the kind of proof that Johnson had asked him to furnish—albeit in different form—to vindicate Howells's assertion. If later he was to comply with the wishes of his publisher and excise the chapters devoted exclusively to social criticism, one may assume that the original idea of the standard work, which asked for a higher degree of objectivity, was reasserting itself, but one may also assume that the impulse resulting from Howells's appreciation and Johnson's request had abated and that now the question of selling the book in the very region that he was attacking was beginning to exert a different kind of rational control.[57]

4   While the use made of travel books in the two omitted chapters discussed above can be interpreted as a sign of the author's difficulty in stretching the manuscript to a satisfactory length, the conjecture that his use of travel accounts had long been planned is supported in two ways. As soon as he received these books he interrupted the consecutive composition of the chapters devoted to the beginning of his trip in order to ascertain the usefulness of the material and to compose two chapters for an eventual insertion in the manuscript. He now also made several additions in the completed manuscript of chapter 22 which increased its documentary value. MSII 89A–E contain observations on St. Louis by Charles Augustus Murray, contrasted with those made by the author "some forty-five or fifty years" later, an instance, certainly, of the use Mark Twain had hoped to derive from a larger number of travel accounts. On the following page he added as a footnote remarks about the city made by Captain Marryat.[58] MSII 93A–D constitute another addition, summarizing the history of river traffic and ending with a significant *ubi sunt*: "Where now is the once wood-yard man?" A similar use of the formula occurs in the last of the two omitted chapters: "And where now is the whittler? Does he still vex the foreign tourist with his universality and his never-tranquil jack-knife, or is he gone down into the shades forever, with the vanished woodyard-

man of the Mississippi? He does seem to have passed utterly away and left no heir." [59] The relation established here between the two paragraphs indicates that the former was added about the time that the latter was written. Presumably both reflect Mark Twain's reading in the travel books. This suggests that the travel books contributed not only to the composition of those chapters that contain direct references to them, but also to the development of attitudes reflected in other chapters. [60]

After Mark Twain had received the travel memoirs, read them and taken notes, composed two chapters commenting on them and made several additions in previously written chapters, he returned to writing chapters consecutively. During the preceding period of composition he had developed a narrative structure suitable to his overall plan. Now, in writing chapters 26–47 in the order in which they finally stood, he continued to follow his plan and the modified structure. Notebook entries, additional documentary material already collected and still to be procured in the course of the composition, and passages already prepared for interpolation in the narrative constitute the materials. The distribution of such matter shows a careful alternation of the three groups of sources, despite the fact that the places for the insertion of three of the prewritten chapters (31, 32, and 38) and some of the paragraphs taken from the memoirs of the English travelers were determined by the narrative basis of the author's actual journey of 1882.

The manuscript of chapter 29 demonstrates that Mark Twain's research in the travel books was not confined to the period immediately following their arrival in Elmira. Having drawn on Captain Marryat's memoir already in the writing of chapter 28 and having completed at least the following chapter, he returned to the second volume of the *Diary* to tear out a four-page account of Murel and his gang, "a colossal combination of robbers, horse-thieves, negro-stealers, and counterfeiters, engaged in business along the river some fifty or sixty years ago." These pages were inserted in the completed chapter [61] after having been slightly edited and prefixed with the author's commentary, a comparison of Murel with the recently assassinated Jesse James.

Other additions in chapters 28 and 29 also reflect the arrival or discovery of source materials subsequent to the composition of these chapters. Chapter 28 was extended to accommodate a clipping from the Cincinnati *Commercial* and the author's comment on its statistical information [62] as well as a reference to Edward Atkinson's remarks on Mississippi River Improvement[63] which Mark Twain put into Appendix [C] B. Edward Atkinson, whose opinion, according to Mark Twain, "comes as near ranking as authority as can the opinion of any individual in the Union,"[64] had stated his views in an article written April 14, 1882, and published in the *New York Herald*. The article was reprinted in the New Orleans *Times-Democrat* (April 28, 1882), where Mark Twain presumably found it when screening its numbers for items to be incorporated in the book. Chapter 29 contains an addition about industrial and commercial developments in Memphis[65] and later also was to include three paragraphs about the city's immediate past that were taken from Ernst von Hesse-Wartegg's *Mississippi-Fahrten*.

Mark Twain's research in the old travel books may seem to suggest that in his return to consecutive composition he was likely to appropriate still other and more extraneous sources in order to make up for time lost in his reading and for failure to find suitable materials in sufficient quantity. His use of materials about Southern feuds in chapter 26, the first chapter written after he had stated his conclusion about the lack of usefulness of the travel books, particularly encourages this conjecture. But despite Walter Blair's interpretation of the "retelling of the Grangerford-Shepherdson-Watson-Darnell feud story augmented with new information"[66] as a sign of Mark Twain's difficulty in stretching the manuscript, I see no evidence that the use of the story indicates lack of other materials. The procurement of additional information about feuds which the author remembered from his time on the river had actually been part of his agenda for the Mississippi trip: "Going down, use the little packets all the way, & stop somewhere every day. . . . New Madrid (1 hour). & ask about the old feuds. . . . Compromise? . . . Natchez. (Duels)." Though the plan was not realized in the manner anticipated in these entries, he did obtain the information he sought from a pilot. The beginning of the stenographer's record reads, "Darnell & Watson were the names of two men whose families had kept up a long quarrel," and in stressing the names it indicates that the subject itself is familiar. In the course of the pilot's report Mark Twain himself took over and in two paragraphs related his own memories of the case. Though direct correspondences of words indicate that the *Huckleberry Finn* manuscript was consulted for the composition of chapter 26, the use of the feud material and its inclusion at this point was determined by a preconceived plan, by the chronological sequence of the trip and that of the resultant notebook entries. In the stenographer's notebook the pilot's and Mark Twain's accounts of the feuds are preceded by a lengthy account of the pilot's war experiences;[67] in chapter 26 the same order is preserved.

5   A close study of the sources of the remaining chapters of this period of composition, however, reveals that the failure of the travel accounts to yield suitable material in sufficient quantity did have an effect on the composition. While a large dependence on the travel books themselves seems to be totally in accord with the plan for the standard work, and while the Ritter story and its sequel and "The House Beautiful" were conceived and rewritten to become an integral part of the fabric of that work, the relation of "The Professor's Yarn," "Hygiene and Sentiment," and "The Art of Inhumation" to the subject matter of the rest of the chapters appears tenuous at best. Although Mark Twain had kept the narrative structure deliberately loose in order to include yarns and narratives, the manuscript shows that he had some difficulty in accommodating "The Professor's Yarn." The story had been written several years earlier, and its pages were now bodily incorporated in the new manuscript.[68] Since it dealt with the outwitting of three professional gamblers on their way to California, the historical fact of the ousting of gamblers from Vicksburg was made to provide the far-fetched occasion for telling it. In a cancellation in the introduction of the story at the end of the preceding chapter he called it "worth preserving," then thought better of it and merely stated that it was "called out by gossip concerning the once-famous lynching & banishing of gamblers by the enraged citizens of Vicksburg, near fifty years ago. . . . "[69] When he came to read proof he owned up and then wrote: "I insert it in this place merely because it is a good story, not because it belongs here—for it doesn't."[70] This statement, however, may belie his actual opinion, and it may well reflect that the difficulty of accommodating "The Professor's Yarn" was primarily one of technique. The inclusion of the story, therefore, need not necessarily signify lack of more appropriate materials. For, as has been mentioned above, the manuscript of the yarn must have been selected in Hartford to go to Elmira, and at that time, anyway, Mark Twain must have considered it to be suitable material for the standard work.

    No such reasons, however, can be found for the inclusion in the manuscript of "Hygiene and Sentiment" and "The Art of Inhumation." When in late August or early September Mark Twain received and read the September number of the *North American Review* he found in it an apparently most welcome inspiration for a further chapter as well as some factual information and material for verbatim quotations according to the procedure already followed in his use of the travel memoirs. The article in question is "Earth Burial and Cremation" by Augustus G. Cobb.[71] It concerns a subject that, unlike most of the sources used previously for inspiration and quotation, has no immediate or apparent relation to the Mississippi. The specific use that Mark Twain made of this article affords an insight into his method of composition when dealing with material not directly related to his subject, and since the method marks an obvious deviation from previous compositional procedures, it is worth closer examination.

The immediate result of his reading of Cobb's article was an entry in his notebook: "Funerals in our stupid & expensive way—cremation preferrable. Poor Moore had to pay $26 for *cheapest* coffin. You can cremate a body for one [dollar]. Plague has been produced by bodies 200 years buried."[72] The author thus linked one aspect of Cobb's advocacy of cremation—the high cost of funerals—with an experience that an acquaintance of his had had, and "poor Moore" becomes in chapter 42 of *Life on the Mississippi* "a colored acquaintance" who had to pay twenty-six dollars for the cheapest coffin when he had lost a child, an outlay that he and his family will feel "a good many months."[73] It is easy to see why Mark Twain should take an interest in the social aspect of funerals; what is not so easy to perceive is why he should have thought this material suitable for inclusion in his book about the Mississippi. It is true that when he stayed in New Orleans he made the customary visits to its famous cemeteries, which, like Brooklyn's Greenwood, Philadelphia's Laurel Hill, and Cambridge's Mount Auburn, were favorite tourist sights, but his notebook entries at the time do not show any concern about adverse effects of earth-burial and the superiority of cremation. Nor are the entries explicit descriptions. Even an earlier statement on the subject of cremation, made in Paris in 1879,[74] does not appear to be serious and thus does not explain the ultimate account in *Life on the Mississippi*. In his possible concern about lack of materials in late August and early September, however, Mark Twain must have seen a possibility for the inclusion of such views when he read Cobb's statement that "during the epidemic in New

Orleans in 1853, Dr. E. H. Burton reported that in the Fourth District the mortality was four hundred and fifty-two per thousand, more than double that of any other. In this district were three large cemeteries, in which during the previous year more than three thousand bodies had been buried. In other districts the proximity of cemeteries seemed to aggravate the disease."[75] This link between the subject matter of the book he was writing and the ideas that Cobb's article gave him or reactivated—tenuous as it is— probably determined Mark Twain to consider the material suitable and to use the article for paraphrase and quotation.

In the actual composition of chapters 42 and 43, however, his procedure is different. In its opening, chapter 42 closely resembles an account given in a letter to Annie Elizabeth Taylor of Keokuk, Iowa, written in New Orleans on June 1, 1857, after a visit to one of the famous cemeteries:

Today I visited one of the cemeteries—a veritable little city, for they *bury* everybody *above* ground here. All round the sides of the inclosure, which is in the heart of the city, there extends a large vault about twelve feet high, containing three or four tiers of holes or tombs (they put the coffins into these holes endways, and then close up the opening with brick), one above another, and looking like a long 3- or 4-story house. The graveyard is laid off in regular, straight streets, strewed with white shells, and the fine, tall marble tombs (numbers of them containing but one corpse) fronting them and looking like so many miniature dwelling houses. You can find wreaths of flowers and crosses, cups of water, mottoes, small statuettes, etc., hanging in front of nearly every tomb. I noticed one beautiful white marble tomb, with a white lace curtain in front of it, under which, on a little shelf, were vases of fresh flowers, several little statuettes, and cups of water, while on the ground under the shelf were little orange and magnolia trees. It looked so pretty. The inscription was in French—said the occupant was a girl of 17, and finished by a wish from the mother that the stranger would drop a tear there, and thus aid her whose sorrow was more than one could bear. They say that the flowers upon many of these tombs are replaced every day by fresh ones. These were fresh, and the poor girl had been dead *five years*. There's depth of affection! On another was the inscription, "To My Dear Mother," with fresh flowers. The lady was 62 years old when she died, and she had been dead *seven years*. I spent half an hour watching the chameleons—strange animals, to change their clothes so often! I found a dingy looking one, drove him on a black rag, and he turned black as ink—drove him under a fresh leaf and he turned the brightest green color you ever saw.[76]

Apart from furnishing an excellent basis for a study of the development of his art, this letter shows that although in *Life on the Mississippi* Mark Twain had decided to shift the focus of the narrative to the present, he did not entirely rely on the observations and experiences of his recent trip and the sources consulted for his writing. As late as 1882, he was apparently able to visualize and reproduce what he had seen twenty-five years earlier and to present it in nearly the same terms. When his notebooks and other sources failed him, his memory supplied the details. But the elements of the description are structured differently in the letter and in the book. The intended effect of chapter 42 of *Life on the Mississippi* occasions a selection of detail and a reinterpretation of the scene. Like the Mississippi River, which appears all-beautiful to the inexperienced passenger but is frequently dangerous to the experienced pilot, the cemetery also is open to reinterpretation. For the young Sam Clemens it is merely an isolated idyl, but for the grown-up author it has begun to be a symbol of corruption and impending destruction—even though in this particular instance an incipient pessimism is still alleviated by a mild kind of humor. After brief mention of the peculiarities of the New Orleans cemeteries and their "graceful and shapely" architecture, Mark Twain now proceeds to social commentary (in comparing the "city of the dead" favorably to that of the living) and moral commentary. He compares the sorrow expressed by fresh flowers to "a milder form of sorrow" which "finds its inexpensive and lasting remembrancer in the coarse and ugly but indestructible 'immortelle.' " The little chameleons creeping along the marble fronts of the vaults are now no longer up to their reputation; "They change color [only] when a person comes along and hangs up an immortelle; but that is nothing: any right-feeling reptile would do that." The lightness of tone seems incongruous with the subject, but it serves a definite purpose. When the author presently remarks that he has been trying in vain "to get down to the sentimental part" of the subject of graveyards and then concludes that "there is no genuinely sentimental part to it," he has the reader prepared for his lecture on cremation. His arguments are twofold. First, he stresses the lack of hygiene and the danger to health connected with the custom of earth-burial and in support of his arguments includes a long quotation from Cobb's article (with an acknowledgment). Secondly, he compares the high expense of earth-burial to the low cost of cremation; in support of this he quotes from an address given before the Chicago Medical Society by Dr. Charles W. Purdy (source identified in the text). The example of the "colored acquaintance" ("poor Moore" of the notebook) concludes the chapter. In a reference to a possible end of "threadbare burial witticisms" and a resurrection of "mildewed old cremation jokes that have had a rest for two thousand years" Mark Twain maintains the lightness of tone in this section, but the main function of the conclusion is to prepare the reader for the next chapter. Here—in accordance with his dictum and belief that nothing survives ridicule—he presents the "Undertaker's Yarn" with its macabre exposé of the business aspects of burial. This chapter ends with the author's statement, "As for me, I hope to be cremated,"[77] and leaves the reader with the impression that, however tenuous the relation of his advocacy of cremation is to the ostensible subject matter of *Life on the Mississippi*, he has presented a sincere and well-argued case for cremation.

A comparison of the final text with both the manuscript and Cobb's article reveals Mark Twain's manipulation of sources. The manuscript shows that the four paragraphs of quotation from the article[78] consist of four independent items from four different pages of the *North American Review*. Only the first of these is copied in the author's hand; the rest are clippings, slightly edited and pasted into the manuscript. Besides the four paragraphs retained in the final version, the manuscript contains three additional clippings inserted between the second and the third paragraph, and two more clippings following the last of the retained paragraphs. Cobb's article shows that what in the manuscript and in the final version stands as Mark Twain's own transition from the first quotation to the second is also copied verbatim from the article.[79] While in his presentation the author gives the impression that in order to substantiate his argument he has done particular research and consulted still another source, his second quotation in fact also derives from Cobb's article. In appropriating it, he extended the quotation marks on the clipping,[80] thereby making Cobb's next sentence, in a slightly edited form, appear a part of Purdy's address. Following the second quotation, in a paragraph deleted from the final version,[81] Mark Twain continues in the vein of "macabre wit"[82] and satire developed earlier in the chapter where he stated that "a dead saint enters upon a century-long career of assassination the moment the earth closes over his corpse."[83] In language which foreshadows the Connecticut Yankee's application of business terminology to sacred and sacral subjects he states that even though "the relics of St. Anne, up yonder by Quebec, have now, after nineteen hundred years, gone to curing the sick by the score, . . . a Saint never *quite* squares up, . . . for his buried dead body *kills* people, whereas his relics heal, only; they never restore the dead to life."[84] Mark Twain originally wrote that usually, when a saint "has squared up—like St. Swithin, or St. Thomas à Becket—<he takes in his sign,> he goes out of business. Therefore, as regards St. Anne, let us collect while we can."[85] It is surprising to find that this apparently thoroughly Twainian lack of reverence is clearly prefigured in Cobb's article. Tracing the origin of the custom of earth-burial, Cobb mentions that "inanimate 'temples of the Holy Ghost' by the score were encased in the niches and corners of churches, and many a moldering monk unintentionally counterbalanced the good deeds of his life by the disease that he generated after his death." He calls "the innumerable prodigies which were performed by the relics of St. Stephen, . . . above seventy miracles, of which three were resurrections from the dead in the space of two years," "incidents of unquestioning and childlike faith, . . . [illustrative of] the intellectual capacity of the age," which helped "to explain the preference of early Christians for burial."[86]

Part of Mark Twain's irreverence and similarly an indelible trait of his writings is his antisentimentalism: "I will gradually drop this subject of graveyards. I have been trying all I could to get down to the sentimental part of it, but I cannot accomplish it. I think there is no genuinely sentimental part to it. It is all grotesque, ghastly, horrible."[87] The manuscript, however, shows "sentimental" in both instances to be an emendation of "serious"[88] and reveals Mark Twain's introduction of the subject to be a direct reflection of Cobb's statement that "on investigating the condition of graveyards, all sentiment clustering around the tomb is quickly dispelled, and a state of things horrible in its nature and dangerous in its effects arrests our attention."[89] In this instance of borrowing, then, Mark Twain not only appropriated specific material, he also adopted the structure of argument and the tone from his source.

This tone may well have been reinforced by a second source directly reflected in this chapter. The topical references to "The relics of St. Anne, up yonder by Quebec," which "have now, after nineteen hundred years, gone to curing the sick by the score," are based on his reading of W. George Beers's "The Canadian Mecca," a report of a trip to the shrine of Ste. Anne de Beaupré, published in the *Century Magazine* for May 1882.[90] Beers explicitly states that he has "no more faith in La Bonne Ste. Anne than in the dozens of other shrines [he] has seen in Europe,"[91] an attitude that leads him to a mild tone of mockery when he comes to discuss the alleged miracles wrought by the relics of St. Anne.

Mark Twain's argument for cremation itself, however, is not quite so extraneous to the ostensible subject of the book as the materials alone might lead one to assume. On a not insignificant level, *Life on the Mississippi*, at least as much as other books written by the author, is also a record of the progress of mankind, shown in a specific sphere of activity. Other cases in which Mark Twain appropriated seemingly extraneous ideas, such as his praise of the benefits of the French Revolution and his condemnation of Sir Walter Scott's contributions to a revival of the "absurd chivalry business," along with a large number of commendations of mechanical and architectural improvements in the Mississippi Valley, confirm the existence and the importance of this level. Though it does not justify a departure from the subject matter of the book, it is understandable that if such a departure were at all necessary, it should have taken this direction. Cobb's introductory paragraph alone must have been sufficient to attract Mark Twain's attention, because it reflects what he himself believed:

Time and experience test the works of man, and the highway of progress is covered with the fragments of countless inventions. The creeds, the dogmas, the social regulations of one age, become the by-words or the antique curiosities of the next. Men do what they can, and coming generations pardon their errors, but judge their works as they ought. —What is good, lives; what is bad dies—this is the general rule.[92]

Another paragraph in Cobb's article points not only to the moral and social criticism of chapter 42 itself, but also to the criticism of Sir Walter Scott and the values he is made to represent in chapters 40, 45, and 47: "Realizing what burial is, it would seem easy for a confirmed inhumationist to change his belief and agree with Dr. Anelli that *burial recalls the Middle Ages, and even the times of barbarism, while cremation represents progress and civilization.*"[93] The consecutive pagination of the manuscript shows that the chapters devoted to the attack on Sir Walter Scott were composed in their final order, both before and after the writing of chapters 42 and 43. Mark Twain's attack on the custom of earth-burial and his advocacy of cremation are therefore part of the larger context of the author's critical attitude, and it is obvious that the immediate source of his notebook entry concerning the preferability of cremation had an influence that extends beyond the composition of chapter 42 and contributed to the context of his criticism of the reactionary aspects of Southern culture and society. While in Cobb's article two different funeral customs are made to represent two different worlds— the Middle Ages on the one hand and progress and civilization on the other—in Mark Twain's own juxtaposition the same two worlds are represented by the literary works of Sir Walter Scott and Don Miguel de Cervantes Saavedra.[94]

While it was obviously Cobb's article that inspired chapter 42, the reference to burial witticisms toward the end appears as an interpolation in the manuscript and may well indicate that Mark Twain conceived of incorporating chapter 43 with the "Undertaker's Yarn" only in the course of composing the previous chapter. For reasons already indicated, chapter 43 constitutes a genuine complement of the argument of chapter 42 by virtue of its satire of the custom already under attack. As suitable material for a standard work about the Mississippi, however, it is even less relevant than the earlier chapter. Mark Twain could easily have changed this had he paid more attention to references to place and time. As they stand, they imply Hartford or Elmira as the scene and the composition of "one of the preceding chapters"[95] as the time. Neither of these establishes any relation with the matter of the river.

In the light of a comment made by Henry Adams on the role and function of the *North American Review*, Mark Twain's use of Cobb's article assumes the proportions of a cultural phenomenon. In *The Education of Henry Adams*, reflecting on the *Review* when he joined its permanent staff in 1868, he writes:

Few writers had ideas which warranted thirty pages of development. . . . An article was a small volume which required at least three months' work. . . . Not many men in England or France could write a good thirty-page article, and practically no one in America read them; but a few score of people, mostly in search of items to steal, ran over the pages to extract an idea or a fact, which was a sort of wild game—a blue-fish or a teal—worth anywhere from fifty cents to five dollars. Newspaper writers had their eye on quarterly pickings. The circulation of the *Review* had never exceeded three or four hundred copies, and the *Review* had never paid its reasonable expenses. Yet it stood at the head of American literary periodicals; it was a source of suggestion to cheaper workers; it reached far into societies that never knew its existence; it was an organ worth playing on. . . .[96]

Although the account, for obvious reasons, is somewhat subjective, and although by 1882 the *North American Review* had begun to appeal to a wider audience, had increased its circulation and become a monthly, whatever conditions prevailed in 1868 to justify Adams's assessment of its role still seem to have pertained in 1882. Not only Mark Twain, whom even Henry Adams would not have wanted to label as a "cheaper worker," but also the journalists referred to seem to have appropriated Cobb's article. In October 1882, the *Century Magazine* devoted its "Topics of the Time" column to "Murder by Burial," and concluded,

Indeed, the whole matter of our burial customs is one which urgently needs revision. It is astonishing that, in connection with risks so many and various as are involved in our modes of burying our dead, there should have been, in modern times, so little care and forethought. The dwellers in proximity to grave-yards who have been poisoned by their drainage, include a vast multitude whose number has never been reckoned.[97]

If Mark Twain read the concluding sentence[98]—"Anybody who shall institute a wholesome reform in this matter will make himself a benefactor of his generation"—he must have seen ample justification for his deviations from the given subject of his book. It was sufficient, certainly, to reject, as he did, Osgood's suggestion to "Rewrite the Graveyard chapter . . . omitting the Extracts and the cremation business, but keeping the Undertakers story."[99] Instead, he decided merely that he would have "some of the statistics knocked out."[100]

The *Century* column's last sentence, in fact, can be read as a commentary on the serious purpose behind Mark Twain's writing, and as his critics were beginning to show a greater awareness of this purpose the author himself was apparently devoting even more attention to it than in his previous works.[101] Later in the book, in anticipation of Howells's comparison of his work with that of Cervantes,[102] Mark Twain invoked a model for his procedure when he wrote:

A curious exemplification of the power of a single book for good or harm is shown in the effects wrought by *Don Quixote* and those wrought by *Ivanhoe*. The first swept the world's admiration for the medieval chivalry silliness out of existence; and the other restored it. As far as our South is concerned, the good work done by Cervantes is pretty nearly a dead letter, so effectually has Scott's pernicious work undermined it.[103]

6   The model of Cervantes was to serve Mark Twain again and again. Hank Morgan's challenge of the chivalry of England, indeed,

of "the massed chivalry of the whole earth," and his boast of having broken "the back of knight-errantry" [104] have been interpreted as an indication that the author was "beginning to conceive of himself as duplicating the feat" of Cervantes's destruction of Spain's chivalry by means of a book. [105] Besides other elements which reappear in *A Connecticut Yankee*, Mark Twain's chapters of *Life on the Mississippi* written after August 1882 foreshadow his role as a nineteenth-century Cervantes attacking, in the name of common sense and progress, not only "grotesque 'chivalry' doings and romantic juvenilities," but also other "dreams and phantoms; . . . decayed and swinish forms of religion; . . . decayed and degraded systems of government; the sillinesses and emptinesses, sham grandeurs, sham gauds . . . of a brainless and worthless long-vanished society." [106]

The juxtaposition of Scott and Cervantes at the end of chapter 46 merely epitomizes critical endeavors most readily discernible in chapters 40, 41, 42, 43, 45, 46, and in three omitted chapters which in the manuscript follow chapters 40 and 42. Nevertheless, it has elicited much comment, presumably because of its apparent originality. The discovery of germinal notebook entries, immediate sources, and larger contexts of ideas for a great many chapters and passages in *Life on the Mississippi*, however, suggests that similar "origins" and contexts may be found for the extended criticism of Scott and the values he is made to represent.

The attack on Sir Walter Scott and the "wild proposition" in chapter 46 "that he is in a great measure responsible for the war," [107] however, is without an immediately recognizable source. Neither the river notebooks nor other documents contain direct references to it. When Mark Twain actually visited Baton Rouge and the state capitol building (the report of whose restoration in *Life on the Mississippi* triggers the attack), he merely noted: "Apl. 27. Landed for half an hour at Baton Rouge. In the Capitol (now being repaired.) Much damaged during the war." It was only after his return, probably early in June, that he made the following entry: "Baton Rouge cost $125000—sound boats cost toward a million.—one is sham & the other real." [108] But the reference here is obviously to the steamboat "City of Baton Rouge," which was piloted by Horace Bixby and on which Mark Twain traveled from New Orleans to St. Louis. It had been built the previous year at a cost of $150,000. [109] Another entry, apparently also made before June 21, reads: "Make no end of Chas. Lamb, & people who have been educated to think him readable, & really *do* think him so. The same prejudice of education in favor of some other passè [sic] authors." Though the entry is not overtly related to the Mississippi book, the items immediately preceding or following it are clearly intended as notes for it:

"So sorry you warn't here at the Mardi-Gras" (silly, but they admire mystery, romance, &c. For instance, nobody knows who is Rex.
Remus & Cable.
. . .

The romance of boating is gone, now. In Hannibal the steamboatman is no longer god. The youth don't talk river slang any more. Their pride is apparently railways—which they take a peculiar vanity in reducing to initials ("C B & Q")—an affectation which prevails all over the west. They roll these initials as a sweet morsel under the tongue.
South still in the sophomoric (gush) period. All speech there is flowery & gushy—pulpit, law, literature, it is all so.[110]

A comparison between this sequence of entries and chapter 46 of *Life on the Mississippi* shows an almost total congruity of subject matter; the entry concerning Charles Lamb and some other passé authors is the only one not reflected in the book. Instead, Sir Walter Scott figures prominently in the chapter. In contrasting him with George Washington Cable and Joel Chandler Harris, Mark Twain leaves no doubt that he considers him to be passé, and there is some justification for the conjecture that Scott was substituted for Lamb. Entries concerning New Orleans in the stenographic notebook make the substitution seem logical: "It is still in the romantic dark ages here. They fight duels for the merest trifles, but the French fashion of small swords probably prevails; also the French immunity from danger. . . . They have not got rid of flowery and fulsome speech in the newspapers and are consequently high-colored in expression high-wrought rhetoric & eloquence. Too much puffery & mention of personal names."[111] It must also be remembered in this connection that despite the somewhat surprising use that Mark Twain made of *Ivanhoe*, *Kenilworth*, and *Quentin Durward* in his preparation of *The Prince and the Pauper*,[112] he had conceived a disdain for "Walter Scott's artificialities" as early as 1874,[113] a disdain he expressed as late as 1903 in two letters to Brander Matthews.[114] And it should be noted that in September 1882, during his stay in Elmira, he presented his daughter Clara, then twelve years old, with a copy of *The Poetical Works of Sir Walter Scott*.[115] It is quite possible that Mark Twain, whose reading was not confined to potential sources for *Life on the Mississippi*, also read this book at the time. Earlier in the composition of the book itself, however, Scott had already been mentioned. In the prewritten chapter later to be entitled "The House Beautiful," which as chapter 38 had now just found its place in the manuscript, Scott's *Ivanhoe* had appeared as one of the books adorning the mahogany center table of the Southern parlor. But, quite contrary to the spirit of the subsequent charge of the effect of Scott's writing on the character and the politics of the South—which would definitely require the conspicuous presence of his works among those "piled and disposed, with cast-iron exactness, according to an inherited and unchangeable plan"—Mark Twain merely says that "maybe *Ivanhoe*" can be found there, too. [116] At this point in the composition of *Life on the Mississippi*, that is, early in his stay in Elmira, he uses Scott's book, therefore, as merely one example of artificiality and the love of romanticism. Though there can be no doubt that Sir Walter Scott was an available substitute for Charles Lamb to characterize an outdated literary style, the larger applicability of a criticism of Scott—which made the substitution worthwhile also from the point of view of Mark Twain's subject matter and his theme of progress—must have emerged at a later time, perhaps from other sources, and for reasons other than mere availability. In addition to the general influence of William Dean Howells's praise of Mark Twain as having "a scorn of all affectations and pretense" and "an ardent hate of meanness and injustice" and the specific influence of Augustus G. Cobb's article on "Earth Burial and Cremation" I should like to suggest a number of possible sources that individually or jointly helped to develop Mark Twain's attack on Scott and the resulting eulogy of progress in the context of chapters 40, 45, and 47.

If Mark Twain, as his use of Cobb's article suggests, was a subscriber to the *North American Review*, he perhaps noticed the following paragraphs in an essay on "False Taste in Art" by Francis Marion Crawford in the July number for 1882:

> The fictitious idea that what is patched and old, if reproduced in fac-simile, will be pleasing, is one of our most wide-spread errors. People forget that whatever beauty there is in the architecture of the irregular English country house, where the "Elizabethan," the "Queen Anne," the "Tudor," and the "Norman" elbow each other for the mastery, is due chiefly to romantic association, recalling, as many of those dwelling-places of ancient families do, the brilliant and stirring traditions of the hereditary lords of a great race. Those homes of warriors and courtiers tell a real

story. . . . But a fac-simile of the original, on a pigmy scale, with every turret and tourelle, rampart, "jutting frieze, buttrice, and coigne of vantage" reproduced in inferior material and planted on the Newport cliff, suggests neither warrior nor courtier. Such houses have no right of existence—no *raison d'être*—in these days.

We cannot create a past embracing many centuries of feudal oppression and robbery, internecine strife, plunder and cavalierdom, nor can we acquire the romantic spirit of fetich worship which clings around the tombs of beheaded kings and murdered princes; nor should we desire to dwell in houses and surround ourselves with objects more appropriate to such a past than to the future we have a right to expect. There are many who know this well enough, and who feel that, the sooner we abandon an elaborate and expensive mediaevalism, the sooner we shall arrive at what we most desire for ourselves and our children. [117]

The view expressed here is not entirely original. The development of a national architecture was as much a matter of concern and debate in the nineteenth century as the development of a national literature, and writings about one of the two subjects frequently referred to the other for purposes of illustration. Crawford's essay merely represents the kind of article which, before and even after the publication in 1891 of the *Architectural Record* and later professional journals, from time to time appeared in the better-known magazines and periodicals of the time. But it is as good an example as any of the kind of argument that Mark Twain may well have encountered in his reading, and one that, given his interest in architecture, he may actually have read.

Mark Twain's abiding interest in architecture and interior decoration frequently finds expression in his works; his notebooks are filled with pertinent observations. Both his own and Olivia's library contained popular and expensive works on the subject. The development of Mark Twain's rendition of interiors which culminated in the description of the Grangerford parlor in *Huckleberry Finn* shows increasing mastery. [118] The Grangerford parlor clearly exhibits an almost Ruskinean equation of architecture and furnishings with the character of its owners. The building and the decorating of his Hartford mansion had occupied Mark Twain for a considerable time and in all probability strengthened his interest. Although the house was ready for occupancy in 1874, "the new home was not entirely done for a long time." [119] In 1881 a kitchen wing was added to the house, and the first floor was redecorated. [120]

As late as 1882 the author excuses Oliva's failure to write to his protégé Karl Gerhardt because of "a long siege of house building and decorating." [121] Mark Twain is certainly drawing on his own experiences when in chapter 51 of *Life on the Mississippi* he compares changes in the river with those necessary in a newly built house: "if you hurry a world or a house, you are nearly sure to find out by and by that you have left out a towhead, or a broom-closet, or some other little convenience, here and there, which has got to be supplied, no matter how much expense or vexation it may cost." [122]

In July or August 1882, as already noted, he consulted Clarence Chatham Cook's *The House Beautiful* for what became chapter 38 of *Life on the Mississippi*. It is therefore highly probable that when he read Cobb's article in the September number of the *North American Review* he also glanced at an article by the author of *The House Beautiful*, entitled "Architecture in America." [123] In it Cook continues the argument begun in *Scribner's Magazine* and his book; he attacks artificiality and uniformity, which are aspects of architecture and interior decoration stressed by Mark Twain in his chapter about "The House Beautiful," and he praises "the cottages and smaller houses of the colonial times, and of the times immediately succeeding the Revolution" as models for imitation and suggestion. The main virtue of their architecture consists in functional design: "A fastidious elegance has never taught the cottager to conceal the facts that cooking, baking, washing, and ironing, go on beneath his roof. No architect has sophisticated away his chimneys behind make-believe battlements, nor tempted his honest gutter to hide itself behind a senseless cornice." The decline of American architecture, according to Cook, is due to the fact that design is no longer the task of the builder, but of the architect:

The Museum of Fine Arts and the Memorial Hall at Cambridge, for instance, are examples of what comes of building getting into the hands of literary, critical men, art-students, with their heads crammed full of remembered bits of Old World architecture, and their portfolios stuffed with photographs of more and more bits. . . . in architecture, as in all our fine arts, notably in the art of painting, the field has fallen into the possession of a set of clever, accomplished, but overcultivated young men who have come back from French and English studios, offices, and pedestrian trips, with a plenty of "material" in their sketch-books, much of it good in its own time and place, but, when worked up into houses for the average American, as alien to his mode of life, to his needs, and to his character, as can be conceived.

American Colonial and Revolutionary architecture was "for a long time despised or simply neglected, while we, in our callow youth, were going through our 'classic' mumps and 'Gothic' measles, and near to perishing with the dreadful visitation of the 'Mansard' malaria." [124] The latter attack may well have induced Mark Twain to make an addition in chapter 43; by way of demonstrating the profit to be derived from his business, he has the undertaker say, "Five years ago, lodged in an attic; live in a swell house now, with a mansard roof, and all the modern inconveniences." [125] It also stands to reason that Cook's advocacy of the simplicity of traditional New England architecture concurred with Mark Twain's own views [126] and contributed to the fact that in the 1880s he could pass negative judgment on scenes amid which he had spent his boyhood and youth. In chapter 42 he praises Quincy, Illinois, as having "the aspect and ways of a model New England town" [127] and thus demonstrates his new aesthetic standard. Its acquisition, as Henry Nash Smith has shown, of course has moral implications as well. It goes hand in hand with the adoption of "the view that democracy is one of the fruits of Progress, that it comes at the end of the historical process begun by industrialization." [128] Cook, who confines his observations to New York City and the New England states, concludes that "Now, we laugh at the architect who, a few years since, was persuading us all to accept his designs for civil edifices and for private houses in the Norman style, the Perpendicular style, and the style of the Pantheon." [129] The restoration of Baton Rouge's state capitol building, however, offered Mark Twain an opportunity to demonstrate that the impulse to admire and preserve "architectural falsehoods" and an Old World architectural style alien to the spirit of progress had not yet disappeared from the American South. But in attacking Southern medievalism, he shows that he fully shared Cook's views.

In one of the omitted chapters written early in August and later inserted after chapter 29, Mark Twain already had reported Thomas Hamilton's observation on an architectural absurdity of Springfield, Massachusetts—"little frame houses with porticos of huge *wooden* Corinthian and Ionic columns"—which, Mark Twain adds, was not confined to that locality. "It was a fashion which swiftly extended itself from one limit of the country to the other; so that to-day there is no town sixty years old in America, which has not one or more specimens of that ridiculous mania lingering in it." [130] In chapter 38 he had already documented this assertion by describing "The House Beautiful"—"the residence of the principal citizen, all the way from the suburbs of New Orleans to the edge of St. Louis"—as a "big, square, two-story 'frame' house, painted white and porticoed like a Grecian temple—with this difference, that the imposing fluted columns and Corinthian capitals were a pathetic sham, being made of white pine, and painted." [131]

Another inspiration, finally, may have come from his reading of William Dean Howells's *Their Wedding Journey*. He had read the novel shortly after its publication in 1871, [132] and he may have reread it in the early 1880s, for Howells's name is among those on a list put together for the proposed *Library of Humor*, and the book eventually contained four selections from the novel. [133] *Their Wedding Journey* is similar to *Life on the Mississippi* in that its narrative structure is also based on a journey undertaken by the protagonists, the Marches, and like Mark Twain's book it makes use of a contrast, that between Canada and New England, to point up the particular traits of each region. Here, too, the indigenous architecture, the kind of building that is in accord with its surroundings, is set up as an ideal and serves as a model in Basil and Isabel March's criticism of foreign architectural styles: "They clung most tenderly to traces of the peasant life they were leaving. . . . They saw the quaintness vanish from the farm-houses; first the dormer-windows, then the curve of the steep roof, then the steep roof itself. By and by they came to a store with a Grecian portico and four square pine pillars. They shuddered and looked no more." [134] An argument that *Their Wedding Journey* directly influenced *Life on the Mississippi* may be made on the basis of this passage as well as on Mark Twain's general dependence upon Howells's opinions and on the basic structural parallel between the two works. Mark Twain's book also contains an ironic reference to Marshall Spring Pike's sentimental song "Home again, home again, from a foreign shore!", [135] which seems to have been suggested by a similar use of that text in Howells's novel almost immediately after the last quotation. [136]

Articles and passages such as the ones discussed above establish a context out of which Mark Twain could easily develop his attack on Sir Walter Scott. But they may also have stimulated opinions that he had held as early as 1853. In a letter from Philadelphia of October 26 of that year, published in the Muscatine *Journal*, he wrote, "I despise bogus brick columns, plastered over with mortar." But the immense distribution branch of the Philadelphia Water Works described in the same letter—"built in a kind of dirty yellow stone, and in the style of an ancient feudal castle" [137]—did not yet prompt the kind of comment he was to give the Louisiana state capitol. Similarly he had attacked a revival of medieval manners and institutions as early as 1870 in "The 'Tournament' in A.D. 1870," which formed one of his contributions to the *Galaxy*. [138] But he did not then relate such tendencies to the vogue of Sir Walter Scott.

In chapter 40 of *Life on the Mississippi* Mark Twain confines himself to an interpretation of the "sham castle" of the capitol building as an expression of the romantic spirit fostered and sustained by Scott's medieval romances. But the attack gains momentum in chapter 45 when he blames the "flowery and fulsome speech" that he had noticed in New Orleans on Scott's influence as well. [139] To document his charges Mark Twain inserted in the manuscript two clippings from the New Orleans *Times-Democrat*, [140] but in a verso addition hastens to exempt the editor, Page M. Baker, whose hospitality he had enjoyed during his visit and whose assistance he had called upon in the course of the composition of his book. [141]

For the context of chapter 46 with its final accusation of Scott, however, Mark Twain used still other ideas and, possibly, additional sources. The paragraphs that contain the new indictment and form the substance of the chapter, constitute an addition. Pages 374–78 of *Life on the Mississippi* were inserted as MSII 733 A–733 O. This pagination indicates that their writing followed that of chapter 47 and possibly also that of the following omitted chapter on Southern political slavery.

Reading directly reflected in chapter 46 concerns the French Revolution, probably chiefly Carlyle's *History of the French Revolution*. According to his own testimony Mark Twain had first read the book in 1871. [142] His biographer states that it was "among the volumes he read oftenest." [143] In 1887, when writing *A Connecticut Yankee*, he told Howells that his most recent reading of the volume had made him see himself as "a Sansculotte! . . . a Marat." [144] Explaining the circumstances that led to this realization, Mark Twain indicates that he has read the book several times since 1871. His correspondence with Osgood and his firm proves that Carlyle was definitely on his mind during his stay in Elmira in 1882. Rowlands's letter of July 22, which announced the shipment of travel books, shows that Mark Twain had also ordered sets of Carlyle's *History of Friedrich II. of Prussia Called Frederick the Great*, *Oliver Cromwell's Letters and Speeches*, and *Life of John Sterling*.

Having answered Rowlands's question concerning "the style of edition" preferred he received the works in ample time to read the *History of Frederick the Great* before leaving Elmira. His notebook contains references to and quotations from the thirty-volume *Library Edition of Carlyle's Works* published by Chapman and Hall.[145] Regardless of what explanation may be found for the fact that Mark Twain, when supposedly desperately concerned about meeting the obligations of the contract for *Life on the Mississippi*, took time to read extensively in the works of one of his favorite authors, the reading constitutes evidence that Carlyle's image of history was among the ideas that influenced his thinking at the time. It has already been observed that, in addition to the sources consulted expressly for the purpose of documenting *Life on the Mississippi*, his readings not directly related to the Mississippi were beginning to find their way into the book; a newly stimulated interest in the English historian, therefore, may well have contributed to the context of ideas presented in chapter 46.

As already indicated, another favorite book of his, *Don Quixote*, which he read as early as 1860, similarly served as inspiration from time to time during his career.[146] Like Carlyle's *History of the French Revolution*, it provided an impetus for the writing of *Huckleberry Finn* and especially for that of *A Connecticut Yankee*, but its use in the two novels finds its parallel in chapter 46 of *Life on the Mississippi*. The specific use made of it in the climactic closing paragraph of the chapter, its citation as "a curious exemplification of the power of a single book for good . . . ,"[147] is latent already in a notebook entry of 1881. In the style of allegory that reached its perfection in *A Connecticut Yankee* he enters the following idea for a plot: "Don Quixotte [a spelling still used in the *Life on the Mississippi* manuscript] is defended against Arabian Nights Supernaturals by Telephone Telegraph &c & successfully."[148] His opinion of the suitability of Cervantes's book to symbolize a victory over the medieval chivalry business and his allegiance with the party of progress, then, are clearly evident before these ideas first appeared in print in chapter 46 of *Life on the Mississippi*. If, however, he was not familiar with Byron's critical dictum concerning the effect of Cervantes's book on the chivalry of Spain, and if he had not planned to include a comment on it in *Life on the Mississippi*—and there is no reason to believe this—then Walter Blair is correct in assuming that Frances Trollope's repetition of the statement that "Cervantes laughed Spain's chivalry away"[149] contributed substantially to the

development of the final attack on Sir Walter Scott. The fact that
Mrs. Trollope's work is drawn on most frequently in Mark Twain's
use of travel books and that he quotes from her account in the very
chapter in which he launches his attack on Scott, supports this
assumption.

The contrast established between Cervantes and Scott as representatives of two worlds is also reminiscent of a contrast between
two figures in another of Mark Twain's immediate sources. In *La
Salle and the Discovery of the Great West,* Francis Parkman had
juxtaposed "the humble Marquette" and "the masculine form of
Cavalier de la Salle" as representatives of the same two worlds, "the
one, with clasped hands and upturned eyes, seems a figure evoked
from some dim legend of mediaeval saintship; the other, with feet
firm planted on the hard earth, breathes the self-relying energies of
modern practical enterprise." [150]

In setting up his basis for a criticism of the negative effect of
Scott's writings in the South, Mark Twain refers to the crimes of the
French Revolution and of Bonaparte as counterbalanced by "two
compensating benefactions," the breaking of "the chains of the
ancien régime and of the Church," and "the setting of merit above
birth"—"great and permanent services to liberty, humanity, and
progress." [151] In making this reference he is drawing on ideas
already presented in *A Tramp Abroad* and in notebook entries made
in preparation for it. In chapter 26 of that book he had called the
French Revolution "hideous but beneficient," and stated that "the
world owes a great deal to [it]." [152] The notebook entries concerning
the French Revolution were made in connection with elaborate
notes on the French people and nation. They occur in Notebook 18
(formerly 14) and are discussed at length by Walter Blair. [153] The use
of other material from this notebook indicates that it was available
when Mark Twain worked on *Life on the Mississippi,* and the wealth
of reading on the subject of the French Revolution reflected in those
entries establishes a broad basis for his ideas. Though he seems to
have gone beyond Carlyle's interpretation when he stressed the
"compensating benefactions," other sources had anticipated his
evaluation. [154] By the time he wrote chapter 46 of *Life on the Mississippi,* he could also just have read H. M. Hyndman's statement that,
although in England "to this day . . . the French Revolution and the
Reign of Terror are quoted in almost every middle-class household
as standing warnings against any attempt of the people to organize
themselves in earnest," nonetheless,

at the present moment efforts are being made to correct the ideas which have been current with regard to the leaders of the French Revolution among the working-class. Lectures are constantly delivered and pamphlets distributed in the growing radical and democratic clubs, which run quite counter to the middle-class idea of that great upheaval. Robespierre, Danton, St. Just, Couthon, and even Marat are rehabilitated completely, and held up to admiration as men who sacrificed themselves to the good of the human race.[155]

The effect of the context of these definite and potential sources, either as direct material influences or as reminders of materials and ideas available to him, was enormous. Though initially related to the subject matter of the book he was writing, Mark Twain's comments on romantic and reactionary tendencies he had observed in the South unloosed with almost uncontrolled fervor ideas that had been slowly accumulating. These thoughts had lain dormant from the time he decided to make *A Tramp Abroad* a milder sort of book than his preparatory notebook entries would have led one to predict. In the resultant polemics in *Life on the Mississippi* he of course transcends the limits of considered judgment that had distinguished the style of the standard work up to that point. The manuscript shows that in actually writing the additions in chapter 46 he first carried the argument as far as stating that "but for the Sir Walter disease . . . the South would be fully a generation further advanced than it is."[156] He then resumes to blame the creation and the persistence of rank and caste on Scott, and after another pause unleashes the final indictment by holding Sir Walter "in a great measure responsible for the war."[157] Each pause has him return to the manuscript with renewed vigor and increased charges. Walter Blair notices that "Mark Twain is unusually tentative as he makes this qualified suggestion, and of course it is easy to attack him."[158] The manuscript, however, shows that some of the qualifications are additions; *perhaps, rather,* and *wild* [proposition] are not part of the initial outburst. By making these additions Mark Twain indicated an awareness of the shakiness of his thesis. Still, in its initial and its qualified form the indictment of Sir Walter Scott directly parallels and anticipates similar outbursts in chapters 13 and 20 of *A Connecticut Yankee*, where in one instance the same materials and the same ideas, as Howard G. Baetzhold has shown, make it appear "as if Twain were bearing down hard on the pen."[159] Besides materials and ideas themselves, then, the very method of composition connects *Life on the Mississippi* with *A Connecticut Yankee* and thus stresses the importance of the former book as a rehearsal, not only (as is commonly held) for *Huckleberry Finn*, as far as it remained to be written, but also for the later novel, the relevant parts of which he wrote as much as five years later.

The preceding account of the development of Mark Twain's attack on Sir Walter Scott and the values he represents seemingly contradicts the argument that *Life on the Mississippi* is the result of the author's plan for a standard work rather than of his inability to meet the deadline of a contract with Osgood that he had signed without much thought and against better judgment.[160] But the account also shows that for various reasons the author consciously modified the plan as documented in letters and notebooks prior to the composition without ever actually abandoning it. All of these modifications, including that which gave rise to the elaborate strain of social and moral criticism that culminates in the attack on Sir Walter Scott, occurred at the very beginning of the Elmira period of composition. There is no evidence that at this time the conditions that have been blamed for the alleged inferiority of the second part of *Life on the Mississippi* actually prevailed. We may therefore conclude that the attack on Scott and Southern backwardness constitutes a deliberate effort on Mark Twain's part to establish a clear link between the idea of the standard work, which he had had since 1866, and the idea of progress, whose conscious and outspoken champion he had since become. As the author's notebook entries about Southern unprogressiveness indicate, it was during the Mississippi trip of 1882 at the latest that he thought of the possibility of combining both ideas.

The very nature of such modifications of the plan for the book, furthermore, shows a return to working habits, devices, and techniques employed in the composition of earlier works rather than a recourse to methods of composition occasioned by encumbering circumstances. In the most prominent instance of Mark Twain's function as a social and moral critic—the attack on Sir Walter Scott and his influence on Southern culture—one finds that its sources, contrary to those obtained for the standard work as originally conceived, are not the result of deliberate collection and advance planning. Throughout the chapters devoted to such criticism the author demonstrates his ability to assimilate materials taken from sources not consulted primarily for the purpose of documenting aspects of the specified subject of his book.[161]

This ability to assimilate materials, to make them part of his own argument, and thus to give them the stamp of his own personality and style is one of the chief characteristics of Mark Twain's procedure as a literary artist. Walter Blair in "The French Revolution and 'Huckleberry Finn' " and in *Mark Twain & Huck Finn* conclusively demonstrated that "Twain's manipulations of his materials are more revealing than his borrowings," and that a "thorough integration of seemingly remote materials suggests artistry of a high order." [162] It would obviously be wrong to interpret evidences of the same "artistry" in *Life on the Mississippi* as less ingenious and less successful.

7   Although the elaborate attack on Sir Walter Scott and his influence in the American South reflects a wide use of materials that Mark Twain had found accidentally in the course of his reading, he continued to pursue the basic idea of the standard work. This is evident in the very same chapters. The incorporation of such materials again presupposes the well-planned and extensive procedure of procurement which emerges as the characteristic trait of Mark Twain's effort.

Thus, on August 21, 1882, he wrote to John Henton Carter ("Commodore Rollingpin") of the St. Louis *Post-Dispatch*, a friend of his who had interviewed him and with whom he had kept in touch during the trip. [163] In his answer of August 23 Carter informed him, "In regard to the matter in the Republican I would say you can still have it if you wish to go to the expense of having the matter set in large type and printed on clear paper. . . . I think $20. would cover the expense of resetting the Republican matter—Perhaps less. There would be no charge except the printers bill." [164] The matter referred to certainly is the extract from the diary of Captain Isaiah Sellers originally published on September 6, 1860, in the St. Louis *Missouri Republican*'s "Special River Correspondence" column under the heading "A Veteran Navigator—Early Steamboats—Fast Time Thirty Years Ago—Signals &c." It did not reach Mark Twain until much later, when it was inserted in the completed chapter 50 ("The 'Original Jacobs' "), which in itself constitutes an insert in the manuscript. [165] To all appearances, the biographical sketch of Sellers had been written fairly early during the Elmira period, probably in July or early August, and was waiting to be inserted at the appropriate place in the narrative. This is shown by the fact that no mention is made of Sellers in the manuscript of chapter 49, which is wholly devoted to "Episodes in Pilot Life." It was, presumably, only in the course of writing the third paragraph of what is now chapter 51—and, significantly, at a place where he caught himself making the kind of comparison between present-day steamboat travel and that of the past [166] for which he had once lampooned Captain Sellers—that Mark Twain realized he had passed the place where the prewritten pages about the captain might best fit in. So he went back in his manuscript to the end of the sequence of episodes about pilots in chapter 49 to insert it there as a new chapter by adding the appropriate pagination and renumbering the subsequent manuscript pages to the point where he had stopped. Only after the chapter had actually found its place in the manuscript did the author add (as MSIII 63 B) the material that had since arrived from Carter. But on MSIII 63 A he erroneously introduced it as having been written at the time of Captain Sellers's death, whereas internal evidence based on the published portion and the four unpublished paragraphs canceled by Mark Twain and preserved in the Morgan manuscript conclusively proves that it was indeed written in 1860,[167] while Sellers did not die until March 6, 1864.[168] This error further confuses the account of the origin of the author's use of his nom de plume and at first glance would seem to corroborate Mark Twain's assertion that Sellers had died before he himself began to use what he claimed to have originally been the captain's pseudonym. But the explanation in this instance is a different one. The matter from the *Missouri Republican* as reset for the author bears no date, and since it actually constitutes a kind of summary of Sellers's career based on his diary it must have led Mark Twain and perhaps John H. Carter as well to assume it to have indeed been written at the time of the captain's death. Mark Twain, in any case, probably because the material arrived only after the chapter had been completed, did not read the text with sufficient care to discover that it had been published in 1860 and, what is more obvious in the text, that Sellers was still alive at the time of its writing.[169]

In his letter Carter further promises, "The other matter I will look into at once. . . . Will write you again soon concerning statistics etc.," and he also included a picture of Dad Dunham, second mate of the ill-fated *Gold Dust*, the original of the fictionalized Uncle Mumford of *Life on the Mississippi*. This picture was used for an illustration on page 305 in the first edition of the book. About a month earlier, Mark Twain had asked Osgood to write Carter for another illustration, a photograph of the monument that Captain Sellers had ordered to be erected on his grave in Bellefontaine Cemetery. In his letter to Osgood he added, "I stole my nom de plume from him, & shall have considerable to say about him, for out there he was 'illustrious.'" In a postscript to this letter he mentioned still another document to be included in the chapter devoted to Sellers. He asked Osgood to get in touch with Captain John A. Stevenson of New Orleans: "He has the article—my first—which made Capt. Sellers so angry. Said he would give it to me, but at the time I didn't think I needed it.—But I do." [170] The reference obviously is to some material by Mark Twain which was printed in the New Orleans *Daily Crescent* of May 17, 1859, and is generally if somewhat inadequately referred to as his Sergeant Fathom letter. It is a burlesque of Captain Sellers's river news or "memoranda" of May 4, 1859, which was published with the captain's own signature ("Isaiah Sellers") in the New Orleans *True Delta* on May 7, 1859, as well as of similar information based on Sellers's journal (which Sellers seems to have readily made available to newspapermen) that was published in the same paper on March 22, 1859. According to the pattern observed in actual river reports, this was preceded and introduced by a character sketch, in this instance a burlesque of the captain as "Sergeant Fathom," based on the biographical information contained in either number of the *True Delta* and also, one may presume, on information well known among the Mississippi pilots of that day. As published in the *Daily Crescent*, these two burlesque sections themselves were preceded by still another text, a slightly longer version (signed "I. Sellers") of Captain Sellers's letter of May 4, 1859. [171]

This material in its entirety constitutes the "article," and apparently it was this which Mark Twain had been offered when he saw "his old-time friend" Stevenson in New Orleans. [172] An entry in his stenographer's notebook made in that city between May 1 and May 4 shows that the author indeed discussed Captain Sellers's biography as potential material for his book during his stay there: "The great Isaiah Sellers died in Memphis about 1863. Buried in Bellefontaine Cemetery St. Louis. There is a monument over him which he had constructed during life. It represents him standing at the pilot wheel. He was detested by all the other pilots because he could antedate them so far in river reminiscences." Another notation made about the same time in his own notebook also seems to refer to Sellers: "And there is the Oldest Pilot, full of strange lies & wordy brag, who is proud to remember how he started <as s> at the bottom round." [173] His personal relations with the captain, however, are not touched upon, and a detailed and documented account of the origin of his nom de plume in particular does not seem to have ranked very high as a potential subject for the book, so that at the time he obviously felt he did not need the matter from the *Daily Crescent*. When he had decided to exploit the natural relation between his own biography and that of Sellers and to use the opportunity afforded by his book about the Mississippi to give the story of his pseudonym, he immediately tried to obtain the article that Stevenson had offered him. For some reason, however, he chose a fairly complicated way of procurement. Rather than write Stevenson himself, he asked his publisher to get Horace Bixby to ask Stevenson for it and then send it to Osgood, who in turn was to pass it on to Mark Twain: "Won't you ask Bixby to get it for *you*? Say you want to see it, and will return it if required." [174] This is probably why the material, as in the case of the matter from the *Missouri Republican*, was not available at the time of the writing of chapter 50 and why the portion that Mark Twain eventually used had to be inserted in the completed manuscript and introduced in a footnote on a verso. [175]

The account of Captain Sellers and Mark Twain's relation to him and the story of his nom de plume, therefore, were written from memory, without the documentary support of any of the data contained in or possibly sent along with the article from Stevenson. But these things were written by Mark Twain on the supposition that they would be verified, substantiated, and documented by the very article that he expected to arrive and that he had obviously planned to use for substantial quotations. As he can hardly be expected to have remembered which facts the article actually contained, the supposition practically extends to all the factual material in chapter 50. This, together with the notebook entry in which the author antedates Sellers's death by one year, establishes beyond all doubt that at the time of the writing of this chapter Mark Twain actually believed he had taken his pseudonym from Captain Isaiah Sellers upon the latter's death in 1863. This also establishes that Mark Twain believed the other erroneous information contained in the chapter to be true, namely that Sellers's "brief paragraphs of plain, practical information about the river" [176] had appeared in the New Orleans *Picayune* (not in the New Orleans *True Delta*, where two such items have since been found) and that his own burlesque of Sellers's river news had appeared in the *True Delta* (not in the

New Orleans *Daily Crescent*, where it was published on May 27, 1859). By implication, finally, this also establishes that he actually believed these very assertions to be true as early as May 29, 1877, when he first made them in a letter to the San Francisco *Daily Alta California*, which was published in that paper on June 9, 1877. Since this letter was apparently written as a rejoinder to recent accounts in the Eureka, Nevada, *Sentinel* and the *Alta* about the "barroom" origin of the sobriquet "Mark Twain," [177] here is proof that the author himself, his "creative memory" [178] notwithstanding, did not invent what Guy A. Cardwell calls the "orthodox" version in order to cover up or to suppress what he must have considered to be a less creditable story. It is possible, however (though not very likely in light of the facts here assembled), that accounts of the "nautical 'Mark Twain' " as "sung out to and by bartenders" in Nevada [179] at a much earlier date provided the original impetus for the author's "creative memory" to produce the more creditable, "orthodox" version. But then that very same process must also have operated to make him forget that particular impetus.

The article that Stevenson had offered him arrived in due course as a clipping. But Mark Twain, as Cardwell remarks, got "more than he asked for." [180] He also received a holograph in pencil of the original Sellers letter of May 4, 1859, a transcription of which stood at the head of the burlesque matter in the *Daily Crescent* of May 17, 1859. There is no record when these two items actually came, other than that Mark Twain had by then completed his chapter on Sellers. Nor is there an accompanying letter from Stevenson, possibly because Bixby acted as mediator. Therefore Mark Twain seems not to have learned where his burlesque had actually appeared. [181] Nor did the material give him any reason to correct his manuscript concerning the information about the paper in which Sellers's items had been printed. An important discrepancy, however, lies in the fact that both the holograph manuscript of Sellers's letter and its printed version at the top of the article are signed "I. Sellers" rather than "Mark Twain." Unlike the matter from the *Missouri Republican*, this document is too brief for him to have overlooked this, and the discrepancy is too obvious for him to have ignored it. He simply does not seem to have done anything about it. For while the burlesque itself, lengthy as it is, probably did not strike him as useful material now that the chapter had actually been completed and its emphasis, quite in accordance with the original plan for the standard work, had remained on Captain Sellers rather than on the author himself, he decided that the letter should be included in the manuscript. It was inserted on the verso of MSIII 72 as a footnote containing the Sellers item which "became the text for my first newspaper article," and the author's introduction reads: "The original MS. of it, in the captain's own hand, has been sent to me from New Orleans." [182]

The reliability of this information has long been doubted by scholars. The "original manuscript" has been held to be a burlesque version made by Mark Twain at the time he wrote the Sergeant Fathom letter, and the handwriting, therefore, could not be that of Sellers, either. [183] But the manuscript itself has not been adequately examined by those who have concerned themselves with the problem. As preserved as an attachment to the holograph of *Life on the Mississippi* it is indeed in a hand which is clearly not Mark Twain's, and the fact that it is torn and partly illegible would seem to bespeak its age. Moreover, it is full of the grossest misspellings and stylistic lapses:

Dear Sir

My opinion f[torn] Benifit of the citysans of [torn] orleans the water is higher this fare up then it has Bin Since 1815. My op[torn] is that the water will [torn] 4 feet deap in canal [torn] next June Mrs [torn] agree with me.

Yours with out enny hasitatue

I. Sellers

P.S. Mrs Turners plantation at the head of Big Black Island is all under water and it has not bin Since 1815.

I.S. [184]

These are the very oddities that also characterize the few surviving passages from Sellers's logbook, [185] and there can be no doubt that Mark Twain is correct in asserting that the letter is indeed in the captain's own hand. The text of the letter printed in *Life on the Mississippi*, therefore, is by no means an exact transcription of it. With the exception of two minor points, however, the text is identical with that printed in the *Daily Crescent*. [186] In fact, it is obvious that it was actually transcribed from the clipping provided by Stevenson. This is corroborated by the instruction Mark Twain gave to his copyist in the manuscript itself: "Preserve the pencil letter, but do not copy it."

These facts indicate that Captain Sellers's letter as rendered in the *Daily Crescent* of May 17, 1859, and in *Life on the Mississippi* is not, as has been believed since the publication of Ernest E. Leisy's

"Mark Twain and Isaiah Sellers" in 1942, a burlesque of an "authentic" version as printed in the *True Delta* of May 7, 1859, and that it is not, as has more recently been maintained by Cardwell, "partly spurious, revised so as to open Sellers to satire or burlesque." [187] Both versions are based on the original of May 4, 1859, and the version given by Mark Twain, ironically, is much closer to it than that of the river editor of the *True Delta*. Ivan Benson, when examining the log of Captain Sellers, found entries in it "so badly written as immediately to raise doubt that Sellers ever wrote anything himself for the newspapers." [188] But Sellers did write for the newspapers, and the newspapermen, in addition to correcting his mistakes, felt free to edit his notes and turn them into more readable accounts, as was done by the *True Delta*. Mark Twain, however, was also interested in the very oddities of the captain's pompous style, and it was the original of Sellers's letter—obtained, no doubt, from the office of the *True Delta* [189]— rather than the version printed in that paper to which he referred in his extended burlesque in the *Daily Crescent*. The transcription of the Sellers letter of May 4, 1859, at the head of it, therefore, is probably his own, and this may also explain why in 1882 he was able to identify the captain's hand. The assumption, moreover, that Mark Twain should knowingly have credited Sellers with a letter not actually written by the captain does not at all comport with his procedure outlined above. The very fact that he did not bother to explain the signature "I. Sellers"—as Albert Bigelow Paine later did by saying that "Captain Sellers, as in this case, sometimes signed his own name to his communications" [190]—and did not attempt to change it to "Mark Twain" in order to substantiate what he had said in the text of his chapter 50, would seem to prove that there was no need for the kind of circumstantiation required for the promulgation of a deliberately false account.

If Mark Twain realized—as he may perhaps have begun to do when he found that Sellers did not sign himself as "Mark Twain"—that there was a discrepancy between the account written from memory and the facts recorded in what constitutes historical documentation, this realization did not cause him to revise, either on paper or in his mind, the account he had first given. His creative memory takes precedence and overrides whatever doubt is cast upon it by historical evidence. Despite the wealth of biographical documents he left at his death, his own biography—not as a fictitious construct deliberately fashioned to fit the pattern of Eastern respectability but as shaped by his imagination and *actually believed in*—is more important to Mark Twain than all historical fact. The material offered him by Captain John A. Stevenson and thought by Mark Twain actually to constitute his *very first article* does not mean anything to him personally and does not interest him as long as he does not need it for his book. A holograph letter that he assumed was written by the venerable Isaiah Sellers himself is simply marked and inserted as a page in his manuscript and thus relinquished to possible perdition. His is the mind of a writer, therefore, not of the historian. "If this is not life," he might well have told a critic of his own version of his biography, echoing a famous contemporary, "then so much the worse for life."

For other materials to be used in the composition of the remaining chapters he wrote to the editor of the New Orleans *Times-Democrat*. This letter was written on September 22, presumably when he had finished the last manuscript portion to be typed in Elmira and thence to be forwarded to his publisher, and when he was projecting or already writing the next portion of the book. In reply to his request Page M. Baker sent "the articles you asked for." [191] These articles presumably concerned materials published in the *Times-Democrat* prior to Mark Twain's own subscription to the newspaper, such as the three articles about the Mississippi flood of 1882 used in Appendix A and the excerpts from journalistic reports used in chapter 45. In procuring the articles about the flood he again followed a notebook memorandum made before the Mississippi trip. While at that point he had planned to include "Yarns about the great overflow of March '82," [192] he now stressed the historical and documentary value of those accounts. But at the same time he also used them to demonstrate peculiar characteristics of Southern style and the influence of the works of Sir Walter Scott.

The above survey of Mark Twain's efforts to procure materials for his book during his stay in Elmira is certainly incomplete, though all records I have been able to find are listed. On the basis of these, however, Mark Twain's procedure can be characterized as an attempt to document or to expand ideas for his book which, as his notebooks prove in all instances, he had had even before he began the actual composition. In addition to the entry indicating the projected use of matter concerning the flood, the intention to write about Isaiah Sellers is documented both in Notebook 20 and in Notebook 21, [193] the entries of which more clearly than those of the personal notebook constitute memoranda to be used in the course of the composition. The author's account of his nom de plume, despite the attention it has been given here and elsewhere, actually remains wholly subservient to the initial plan of presenting Sellers's biography. Also sizable verbatim quotations not previously mentioned, which exist largely in the form of clippings in the Elmira portion of the manuscript [194] and therefore seem to suggest lack either of time or of creative energies during this period, are foreshadowed in a lengthy notebook entry about the experiences of "A War Pilot" [195] in which Elliot (corrected to Ellet in *Life on the Mississippi*), Farragut, and the gun boat *Essex* are referred to. One need not belabor the point, therefore, that the extensive procurement of source materials as well as the extensive use actually made of such sources in the text of *Life on the Mississippi* was not occasioned by what his biographer called the maddening "menace of his publisher's contract" and the fact that the book "refused to come to an end." [196] Rather, they prove the truth of Mark Twain's early contention that he would have to return to the Mississippi to be able to gather the materials that he needed for his standard work.

8   The record of Mark Twain's summer's work is not complete, however, without a consideration of the possible effect of his repeated illnesses during this time. Late in June and early in July, while Jean suffered from scarlet fever, the author claims that he himself "was stretched on the bed with three diseases at once, and all of them fatal." [197] In a letter to his mother he explains that he suffers chiefly from lumbago [198] which, together with the duty of nursing, leaves him without "any literary inspiration." [199] A communication to his publisher, however, seems to have indicated that he is "likely to get off . . . easy." [200] But after the family had moved to Elmira on July 14, Mark Twain apparently saw a doctor a week later. [201] In a letter of August 13 to Samuel E. Moffett, his wife describes him as being "hard at work on a new book," but she adds, "I have never seen him when he worked with so much difficulty—that is his head so sore & tired that he cannot bear to have the simplest question asked him, or be compelled to talk at all, so our evenings are mostly spent in playing Cribbage. . . . " The account may be somewhat exaggerated, for Mrs. Clemens continues, "Therefore you will have to say to the lady that it will be impossible for him to grant her request," and she concludes by saying that except for Jean, "We are all now pretty well." [202] On

September 18, however, he wrote his publisher, "I have been half dead with malaria ever since you left [Osgood had sailed for Europe on August 8]; & these last few days am two-thirds dead. I work all the time, but accomplish very little—sometimes as little as 200 words in 5 hours." While here his illness may have served as explanation for his failure to bring the manuscript nearer completion—"I shall peg along, day by day, but shan't be through when we leave for home two weeks hence"[203]—it also served as an excuse for not having written to Joseph H. Twichell. On September 19 he apologized, "I was simply compelled to deny myself all such satisfaction, & religiously save up *every* little wayward & vagrant suggestions of intellectual activity & hurry to apply it to *work* before it weakened & died. Never was a book written under such heavy circumstances. I am full of malaria, my brain is stuffy & cloudy nearly all the time. Some days I have been five hours writing two note-paper pages."[204] As late as October 9, he tells his mother, "Every body here is well but myself, and in my case some doctors think it is malaria, and some think it is laziness. I am taking medicine for both."[205] There can be no doubt that Mark Twain's illness delayed the completion of the manuscript so that it could not be submitted by October 1. While on September 22 Osgood still hoped that the project could be carried out as planned,[206] by October 14 he had learned better. He now attempted to persuade his author to undertake a lecture tour in February, "so as to help the canvassers on their last two months work."[207] Though its publication was delayed, the manuscript of *Life on the Mississippi* itself does not show any effects of Mark Twain's illness. In mentioning that he "had been sick" in his letter of October 3 to Howells he merely states that he "got delayed,"[208] and even in enlarging on his difficulties with the book in his letter of November 4, he makes no mention of his illness.[209] Obvious signs of "unconcealed haste and inattention" pointed out by Bernard DeVoto[210] can refer only to the printed text and are the result of revisions undertaken later.

"Trying to Build the Last Quarter of the Book" V
(Hartford, October 1882–January 1883)

1 When at the end of his stay in Elmira Mark Twain "expressed" the completed portions of the typescript to Osgood, he stated that the "eighth batch" would be forwarded presently. If he himself believed the assertion, he was mistaken. It is true that some of this section had been written, and that materials he had requested because he planned to use them in further chapters of this portion arrived at the time of his return to Hartford, but nonetheless he needed another three months to complete the manuscript.

The length of time Mark Twain devoted to writing the last quarter of the book suggests that he had indeed considerable difficulties in concluding his project. Repeated complaints in a number of letters written during this period and indications in one of these that he "borrowed" or "stole" in order to be able to finish his work confirm this. The establishment of a chronology of the genesis of the manuscript as begun above, however, has revealed that the use of "borrowed" materials was not confined to the last three months of the composition, to the period during which Mark Twain complained about his inability to bring his book to an end. From the very beginning of his composition he had relied heavily on a great variety of sources. The use of such sources, moreover, has been shown to have been a part of his plan for the book ever since Mark Twain first conceived his standard work about the Mississippi. Conversely, then, it might be argued that the lagging progress of Mark Twain's composition was occasioned by the fact that he had now exhausted the materials and sources he had collected for use in his standard work. But in view of the large number of notebook entries still unused and the great amount of borrowed materials actually incorporated into the last quarter of the book, so general a hypothesis must appear equally untenable. If an explanation is to be found for the fact that upon his return to Hartford Mark Twain encountered more than the usual amount of difficulties, it is again necessary to establish as complete a record as possible of the progress of the composition and the impulses that attended it.

The first assumption to be made is that life in the city, as opposed to that on Quarry Farm, offered inevitable distractions. Mark Twain himself was clearly responsible for some of these. Stopping over in New York on his return from Elmira, he wrote a note to George Washington Cable, informing him that "A week hence, we shall be all straightened up, there; & then we shall be glad & willing & anxious to see you on any date thereafter—you to name it & give us notice & we will go to your train & fetch you. Be *sure* you come." [1] In Hartford itself he found Charles Dudley Warner and Joe Twichell returned from long trips to Europe, but he still managed to work on the unfinished chapters of the eighth batch. On October 16, in one of the three letters urging Cable not to delay his visit, he optimistically announced, "And besides, I shall finish my book this week, I think, for I have already just finished writing all I don't know about New Orleans." [2] This, together with the use of the articles from the *Times-Democrat*, indicates that chapters 45, 46 and perhaps 47 were written or completed at this time. Since the burden of the contract was momentarily removed because of the postponement of the publication date, the spirit of optimism is understandable. On October 20, Osgood paid him a visit, and Cable finally arrived also, and as a result work was interrupted once more. But apparently Cable was helpful in discussing the book and providing further source materials. A letter went out to Mrs. Cable in New Orleans with a list of books in Cable's library to be loaned to Mark Twain, expressly for use in the composition of the remainder of *Life on the Mississippi*. After Cable had returned home, he informed his recent host, "I sent the books to you a day or two ago, (on the 4th). Mrs. Cable had failed to find them all and even now they do not conform exactly to the list you kept." [3] When acknowledging the receipt of the shipment on November 11, Mark Twain added the following postscript: "Please send me a New Orleans directory of this or last year. I do not know the price but inclose five dollars at random." [4] This indicates that since Cable's departure the concluding chapter of the eighth batch, which was the deleted chapter following chapter 42 in the manuscript, had been written. Following MSII 772, as the text and a note for the printer [5] show, the author had planned to use four pages of the directory to demonstrate the incongruity between variegated national origin and uniform voting behavior of the people of New Orleans. On December 2, Mark Twain acknowledged receipt of the directory, which had apparently been sent to him by Cable's niece, Miss Helen M. Cox, whom he had also met during his trip. [6]

Since the majority of the chapters about New Orleans were already written when Cable's books arrived, and since further remarks about the city and its surroundings, as well as additions in the completed chapters, do not reflect newly acquired sources, it is not possible to determine which titles the shipment contained or if Mark Twain used the materials at all. It may be inferred, however, that Mark Twain took advantage of Cable's useful collection of sources for his historical writings about the South. The original intent to use such sources for *Life on the Mississippi* becomes obvious when on January 15, 1883, Mark Twain writes Cable, "I have just finished my book at last, & was about to return the volumes you so kindly lent me." [7]

An extensive use of sources is further documented in Mark Twain's letter to William Dean Howells, which has been published with the date of October 30, 1882. This letter, the document most frequently quoted in connection with the composition of *Life on the Mississippi*, cited erroneously as characteristic of the author's mood and interpreted mistakenly as relating to the use of travel memoirs, remains a puzzling and misleading piece of evidence, and therefore deserves particular notice.

Having complimented Howells on the success of the last installment of *A Modern Instance*, which had appeared in the October number of the *Century Magazine*, Mark Twain continues:

We have only just arrived at home, and I have not seen Clark on our matters. I cannot see him or any one else, until I get my book finished. The weather turned cold, and we had to rush home, while I still lacked thirty thousand words. I had been sick and got delayed. I am going to write all day and two thirds of the night, until the thing is done, or break down at it. The spur and the burden of the contract are intolerable to me. I can endure the irritation of it no longer. I went to work at nine o'clock yesterday morning, and went to bed an hour after midnight. Result of the day, (mainly stolen from books, tho' credit given,) 9500 words, so I reduced my burden by one third in one day. It was five days work in one. I have nothing more to borrow or steal; the rest must all be writing. It is ten days work, and unless something breaks, it will be finished in five. We all send love to you and Mrs. Howells, and all the family.[8]

Certain dates and facts referred to in Mark Twain's account are obviously incompatible with the accepted date of the letter itself. The author's correspondence as well as readdressed envelopes preserved in the Mark Twain Papers confirm Arlin Turner's conjectured October 16, 1882, date for Mark Twain's note to Cable. They establish that he and his family had left Elmira on September 28 and, after spending the night in New York, proceeded to Hartford in the afternoon of September 29. Obviously, then, the family had not "only just arrived at home" on October 30. There would also have been time, in the course of a month, to see or contact Charles Hopkins Clark, managing editor of the Hartford *Courant* and co-editor of the *Library of Humor*, about "our matters." The matter in question certainly is the *Library of Humor*, and Mark Twain's statement may well be apropos of Howells's letter from London of September 1, in which he had written, "I suppose Clark has the consumption again: I don't get any material from him for the Library of H."[9] Mark Twain himself had initially been involved in the project; in the spring of 1882 he had brushed aside Howells's question about his ability to do his "share of the reading at Elmira while . . . writing at the Mississippi book"[10] by answering, "I think there is no reasonable doubt that I can read all summer without any inconvenience. I can read all Saturdays and Sundays and also an hour each evening perhaps. This added up makes about a month of pretty steady reading and ought to accomplish the business."[11] But DeLancey Ferguson is wrong in stating that "the

Library of American Humor, which continued to be a millstone about his neck, interfered further with the book" [12] during the stay in Elmira. A new agreement reached on April 1 between Howells and Clark and submitted to Mark Twain by Osgood, the intended publisher, indicates that Mark Twain was now relieved of the possible burden, at least during the initial stages, by the reorganized procedure. Clark was to do the first reading and submit his selections to Howells, who in turn was to forward them to Mark Twain. [13] One of the items in a notebook list of matters to be done before the Mississippi journey consequently reads, "Put away the Library of Humor books." [14] Its cancellation indicates that he attended to it, and I see no evidence that he returned to the project at any time during the remainder of the year. It may be assumed that Mark Twain was not able to show as much concern about this matter as Howells, who had been promised the sum of $5,000 for his share in the work and who was perhaps eager to "earn" the money. But in view of the fact that in the course of October Mark Twain permitted many other matters to take him away from his writing it is likely that he also should have attempted to stir up Clark, particularly since, as co-editor, he was also in the author's pay.

Mark Twain's complaints about "the spur and the burden of the contract" and the number of words still to be written are equally incompatible with the date of October 30. As has been shown, the immediacy of the burden of the contract had disappeared by October 14. The number of words still lacking was twice mentioned as 30,000, as early as September 5 to Joel Chandler Harris [15] and again in a revised estimate to his publisher on September 18. On October 16, however, as has been noted, he told Cable that he would probably complete the book that week and that he had just finished writing "all I don't know about New Orleans." It can be inferred, therefore, that by the end of October the number of words still needed must have been reduced somewhat, if not considerably.

The reference to the closing installments of *A Modern Instance* in the October issue of the *Century Magazine* also points to the beginning rather than the end of October. Despite the urgency of the contract Mark Twain had followed the novel with great interest and was likely to read its conclusion as soon as it was available. He did in fact read it while he was making a desperate effort to finish his book.

The evidence thus seems to indicate that the letter was dictated early in October. An examination of the original typescript reveals that its date actually is October 3. The misdating resulted from a combination of idiosyncrasies: those of Mark Twain's typist and the use of a typewriter with sans-serif capital types only. Throughout 1882 and 1883 the typist consistently abbreviated "2nd" and "3rd" as "2D." and "3D."[16] The date of Mark Twain's letter to Howells thus reads "OCT.3D.1882." It is further confirmed by the sequence of the additional correspondence of this period between Mark Twain and Howells as given in the *Mark Twain-Howells Letters*.[17]

The new date, however, still does not establish a relation between the account of the author's process of composition and the extensive use of travel memoirs. But the description is sufficiently realistic to reflect Mark Twain's actual procedure and to warrant an attempt to relate it to his work on the book. However neither the printed version of *Life on the Mississippi* nor the Morgan manuscript contains sections that fully fit the description. The only part of the last portion of the manuscript that contains sections "mainly stolen from books, tho' credit given" and that vaguely approaches the description are chapter 59 and its corresponding part in the appendix (Appendix D of the printed version) and the final chapter 60. But although the latter portion of the manuscript permits the conclusion that it need not have been written consecutively,[18] Mark Twain's later complaints about the "broken continuity"[19] caused by Osgood's suggested revisions make it unlikely that he began the composition of the remainder of the book with its final chapters. It seems equally unlikely that he should have led Howells to believe that these chapters reflected more sources than the two books he actually used,[20] or that he was merely attempting to characterize the method of composition and the use of sources followed throughout the summer. The only plausible explanation seems to be that on October 2 Mark Twain actually wrote a portion of some 9,500 words in which, as claimed, he used and acknowledged materials drawn from books, and that what he composed in this desperate and overly long spurt of composition made in a final effort to meet the deadline of the contract did not stand the test of his considered judgment at a later date. This explanation is supported by an unpublished letter not previously related to the history of the composition of *Life on the Mississippi*. On December 2, 1882, while contrary to the predictions made in his letter of October 3 he was still trying to bring the book to a conclusion, he sent a typewritten letter to Edward H. House, which said in part:

I have been waiting, for months, to write you with my own hand, like a Christian. But the book is not done yet, for the powers of heaven and Earth and hell are leagued against it, and it may never be finished at all. I have been on the home stretch, with three quarters of the course behind me, for two full months, and I have been laboriously jogging along all those two months; but what I write on one day I tear up the next, so I make but little permanent advance toward the goal. In the work I have suffered two months of literary gout; all pain and no getting on.[21]

The period of composition here specified includes the date of Mark Twain's letter to Howells. Although the desperate method envisaged for a forced conclusion of the manuscript had been abandoned, the next letter to Howells of November 4 indicates that the difficulties persisted and had even increased:

I never had such a fight over a book in my life before. And the foolishest part of the whole business is, that I started Osgood to editing it before I had finished writing it. As a consequence, large areas of it are condemned here and there and yonder, and I have the burden of these unfilled gaps harassing me and the thought of the broken continuity of the work, while I am at the same time trying to build . . . the last quarter of the book. However, at last I have said with sufficient positiveness that I will finish the book at no particular date; that I will not hurry it; that I will not hurry myself; that I will take things easy and comfortably, write when I choose to write, leave it alone when I so prefer. The printers must wait, the artists, canvassers, and all the rest. I have got everything at a dead stand-still, and that is where it ought to be, and that is where it must remain; to follow any other policy would be to make the book worse than it already is. I ought to have finished it before showing it to anybody, and then sent it across the ocean to you to be edited, as usual. . . .[22]

The general outline of the composition provided in these two letters replaces that of the account given upon his return to Hartford in his letter of October 3. A consideration of the composition of the final portion of the manuscript, therefore, cannot be undertaken with the supposition that it reflects extended borrowings for the purpose of completing the book and meeting the deadline of the contract. Obviously the author actually took as much time as he said he would, for even in late December the book had not yet come to an end, and obviously he maintained a high critical standard in his selection of materials throughout the writing, for he apparently repeatedly excised sections he had composed and he rearranged and edited those he retained. Chapters 48 to 60 thus constitute a conscious literary endeavor, and most of the materials used may be assumed to reflect Mark Twain's considered judgment as to their suitability.

Nevertheless, both letters indicate that Mark Twain found it exceedingly difficult to "build the last quarter of the book." Not lack of materials, but the "broken continuity of the work" seems to have been the main problem. Having mentioned this in his letter of November 4 to Howells he repeated the same complaint in a letter to his brother Orion of November 18: "In order to get a chance to finish my book, I am reading and answering letters only once a week; . . . I am only tolerably well, and full of devilish irritation besides, on account of my inability to work steadily and to my satisfaction on my book."[23] Such complaints are occasioned by Osgood's suggested revisions as well as by frequent interruptions due to Mark Twain's social and business activities in Hartford. While it is unlikely that the broken continuity and the author's inability to work steadily affected the choice of materials for the standard work to any large extent, these handicaps do explain a certain lack of integration of materials into the manuscript: on occasion Mark Twain plainly fails to show why they found their way into the book at all.

2   When after his indictment of Southern political slavery Mark Twain began the composition of the last portion of the manuscript, the attack on Sir Walter Scott appears to have continued its influence. Chapter 48 only seemingly returns to recounting experiences of the recent trip; the sequence really serves as a thread for the presentation of experiences, observations, and commentaries in such a way as to embody ideas Mark Twain developed most clearly in the attack on Sir Walter Scott and in his condemnation of the values of the past. The title of the chapter, "Sugar and Postage," points to the twofold aspect of his endeavors: the presentation of factual information about an important part of the economy of the Mississippi Valley, according to the plan of the standard work; and the launching of an attack on the superstitious belief in spiritualism, according to the ideas of the recently expounded vein of social criticism.

The resulting laudatio of the present apparently prevented the meeting with Horace Bixby (the man who had "learned" Mark Twain the river) from giving rise to a flood of personal reminiscences, which would inevitably have stressed some values of the "flush times" of steamboating. Instead, the bloodshed occasioned by Jackson's victory in the Battle of New Orleans in 1815 is blamed on the absence of "the cable telegraph in those days." This implicit praise of the age of invention becomes explicit in the description of the steam plows on the Warmoth plantation which facilitate the cultivation of sugar cane "after a modern and intricate scientific fashion." [24] Consequently he checked an impulse, documented in his notebook, to give a burlesque account of the sugar-making process in the style of "How I Edited an Agricultural Newspaper," [25] and replaced it by a serious description of the procedure, which the author finds "exceedingly interesting." [26] The particulars of this description are based on notes that his stenographer made during the visit to the plantation. [27]

Much like Ernest Hemingway, Mark Twain had an eye for certain rather mundane situations that can be exploited as symbols in literature. When he and his party, which included several ladies, took a trip to the Warmoth plantation on the tugboat *W.M.Wood* the author made the following note about an actual incident that occurred on May 4: "Parrot on board keeping up constant stream of remarks, some irrelevant, some not. Parrot's swearing *very* inappropriate. (Elaborate this: Parrot makes extremely naughty remarks and the ladies gradually withdraw.)" [28] Mark Twain's notation indicates that he originally intended a humorous exploitation of the situation. In the context of this chapter and following the attack on Sir Walter Scott, however, the same situation is given a more significant symbolic meaning. "Romance and sentiment" are destroyed by the "always this-worldly, and often profane" comments; the "tug's pet parrot" with his "super-abundance of the discordant, ear-splitting, metallic laugh . . . a machine-made laugh, a Frankenstein laugh, with the soul left out of it," is, through the very imagery of Mark Twain's description, clearly identified with the tugboat itself, before whose advance "romance and sentiment cannot long survive." [29] While "sentimental and romantic" are ostensibly introduced as satisfying and desirable qualities, the essence of such qualities is expressed in "pathetic" songs like the inappropriate "Home again, home again, From a Foreign Shore," [30] similar to the titles of books, music, and paintings in "The House Beautiful" and reminiscent of the incongruity between such titles and the real emotions of the Grangerfords in chapter 17 of *Huckleberry Finn*. The true nature of the sentimentality is thus revealed to be false, and identical with the negative Southern romanticism and sentimentality derived from Sir Walter Scott. Consequently, Mark Twain's statement concerning the ostensible desirability of such sentimentality becomes ironic. But while he rationally sides with the parrot, the very imagery that identifies the traditionally antiromantic bird with the antiromantic tugboat also suggests that the author subconsciously has his reservations about the latter, an invention which in this context is made to stand as a symbol for progress: a discordant, ear-splitting, metallic, machine-made, soulless Frankenstein laugh perceptibly weakens the irony concerning the desirability of sentiment and romance. As in the two instances of the cancellations discussed above (of which the second one occurs in this very chapter),[31] the return of a rational control over his materials may now have induced the author to attempt stressing the irony by an emendation: "very sentimental and romantic" thus becomes "satisfyingly sentimental and romantic."[32] But it is only natural that Mark Twain should still betray misgivings; for when he wrote chapter 15 of *Life on the Mississippi* for the *Atlantic* series he had spoken of the "vulgar little tug-boat" which helped to make "the noble science of piloting [a thing] of the dead and pathetic past."[33] Imagery, then, like the two cancellations stresses a dichotomy between overt statement and covert judgment and contributes to the emergence of an ambiguity in the author's feelings concerning his subject.

Conscious as Mark Twain is of his role as a social and moral critic—and doubly so since the praise recently accorded him by William Dean Howells and Joel Chandler Harris and the subsequent inception of his attack on Sir Walter Scott—it is also highly probable that, corresponding to the juxtaposition of *Don Quixote* and *Ivanhoe*, the actual incident of the parrot's interference on the *W.M. Wood* on May 4, 1882, now caused the author to see himself not only in the role of Cervantes, but also in that of the irreverent parrot discouraging the sham romance and the sham sentimentality of the South. The next instance of his antiromanticism follows in the concluding episode of the chapter. Since the report of Mark Twain's experiences during a séance with "a New York spiritualistic medium named Manchester"[34] is only circumstantially related to the subject matter of the book, its incorporation in chapter 48 would seem to illustrate the author's lack of materials. However, an account of the composition of this episode and the following chapters reveals a complexity of procedure and motives which, like much of his work, defies simplification.

As far as Mark Twain's technique is concerned, gossip aboard the tugboat on its forty-seven-mile trip from the Warmoth plantation to New Orleans is now made to provide a loose frame for the incorporation of a full sixty-eight manuscript pages (comprising the conclusion of chapter 48, and chapters 49 and 50) devoted to the narration of episodes. The frame is established when, following the remarks of the parrot, "the male members of the party moved to the forecastle, to smoke and gossip." [35] The existence of the frame is implied at the beginning and in the course of the following chapter 49 and at the beginning of chapter 50,[36] and it is closed at the end of that chapter when the party approaches New Orleans, "the Crescent City lit up with the white glare of five miles of electric lights." [37] The looseness of this frame and its congeniality to Mark Twain's process of "building" this portion of the book is convincingly demonstrated by the insertion into the finished sequence of the manuscript of the twenty-one pages devoted to Isaiah Sellers (the substance of chapter 50). Chapter 49, as its title announces, contains "Episodes in Pilot Life," all of which can be traced to notebook entries or otherwise shown to have a base in fact. The distribution in the two river notebooks of the entries used in the chapter proves that at this point Mark Twain carefully leafed through both documents to extract individual items of an episodic character.[38] In one case, that of an entry concerning "Dad Dunham & the pet bear," [39] the incident is transferred to another person,[40] since in the context of the book Dad Dunham (Uncle Mumford of *Life on the Mississippi*) and the author had already parted company before it could be introduced. This rearrangement of details, the fact that the episodes are based on notebook entries made at different times, and the addition of the chapter about Isaiah Sellers, all establish that the account of the tugboat gossip given in *Life on the Mississippi* is not the record of conversations actually held, but a technical device designed to permit the incorporation of relevant materials which otherwise might not have fitted into the narrative.

Mark Twain's incorporation of the episode of his spiritualistic experiences, therefore, is deliberate. This is all the more obvious since the episode is introduced by association and since the initial piece of gossip about the "pilot . . . become a spiritualist," [41] with which it is associatively linked, cannot, unlike all other items in the sequence, be traced to a corresponding notebook entry or another documentation. It is probable, therefore, that the initial item constitutes an invention for the purpose of introducing the episode involving the author himself. While he refers to his séance with the medium Manchester as having happened ten years ago, its essence as related in *Life on the Mississippi* is reflected in an entry made in Notebook 18 in May 1879, during his stay in Paris:

> Talk with the departed.
> To Henry, (through medium Mansfield)—Pray <move to > try the the [*sic*] other place; <it is better to be less comfortable> you don't seem to have much intellect left, but even that is worth saving, & a change might help."[42]

The entry is marked "A" (meaning perhaps "Anecdote"), a designation Mark Twain used for many items in Notebook 18 which, as the repetition of such items in the working notes for *A Tramp Abroad* indicates, he intended to incorporate in that book. The similarity of both materials and tone in the notebook entry and the manuscript of *Life on the Mississippi*, particularly in the first stage of the episode in which the author supposedly converses with the spirit of his brother Henry,[43] is so obvious that it is safe to conclude that the incorporation of the episode in the Mississippi book constitutes another use of materials originally intended for *A Tramp Abroad*. The same notebook also contains an entry about a dinner in Paris at which "D. D. Home (pronounced *Hume*,) the spiritualist miracle-worker, was present."[44] Although he found the internationally famous medium to be "a very fine fellow," he may have thought differently about his profession as Home described it in his autobiography, *Incidents in My Life*, which was in Mark Twain's library.[45] The author's interest in spiritualism thus suggests that his ridicule of it was more than an attempt to fill out pages of subscription books that refused to come to an end. In planning to use the material in *A Tramp Abroad* and in incorporating it in *Life on the Mississippi* the author merely resumed earlier attacks[46] on a superstition which "had convulsed the Hannibal of his later boyhood,"[47] where "nearly every family [had] two or three mediums in it."[48] It is highly probable, furthermore, that a superstitious belief in spiritualism represented merely another peculiarly Southern sham and that this justified both the invention of a piece of gossip about a "pilot . . . become a spiritualist" and the incorporation of his own experiences with the medium Manchester. As in previous instances of the use of materials written or intended for *A Tramp Abroad*, the charge of padding is not entirely justified. When viewed as an integral part of the chapter whose conclusion it forms, what seems to be an extraneous incident in the gossip sequence actually constitutes a conscious and effective exemplification of the author's identification with the antisentimental parrot, making his "always this-worldly, and often profane" comments to discourage sham romance and sham sentimentality. Cancellations in the Morgan manuscript show that in his antisentimental ardor and in his eagerness to ridicule superstition the author ran to such this-worldly and profane phrases as "the happy cabbage patch" (emended to "spirit land") and "my sainted idiot brother," [49] which subsequently occasioned two extensive revisions of the episode.

3   The briefness of the account of the return trip from New Orleans to St. Louis given in chapter 51 points to the fact that Mark Twain's primary object still was a report on conditions on and along the Mississippi. This portion of the river, however, had already been commented on, and to avoid a gap in the basic narrative structure of the journey the author instead offered a series of reminiscences purportedly occcasioned by his trip. The actual journey on board "the great steamer *City of Baton Rouge*, the latest and swiftest addition to the Anchor Line," "was accomplished speedily," [50] and the author explicitly stated his regret. Notwithstanding this statement, when reading Harriet Martineau's account of a journey over the same distance that took several days, he had made the following marginal notations: "Think of this weary slow travel!—Two days out, to Natchez—we went there in 22½ hours." [51] In finishing the chapter the author reverted to the use of statistics and included figures from the St. Louis *Globe-Democrat* about church attendance in that city, providing a circumstantial justification for these by concluding "that St. Louis was in a higher state of grace than she could have claimed to be in my time." [52]

At the end of the gossip sequence and following the "grotesque romance" of a steamboat clerk, Mark Twain had remarked, "Such are the actual facts; and not all novels have for a base so telling a situation." [53] For a long time he had wanted to disclose similarly grotesque facts, and their actual relation to St. Louis now provided an opportunity for him to do so. After his return to Hartford he reminded himself in a notebook entry of "that convict's wonderful letter." [54] The reference is to a letter purporting to have been sent by an ex-convict from St. Louis to a convict in the Massachusetts state prison at Charlestown. In 1872–73 it had caused a great deal of interest, particularly in Hartford, until, due to suspicions voiced by

Charles Dudley Warner, it was finally exposed as having been penned by the convict himself in an attempt to improve his lot. Mark Twain now obtained a copy of the letter, which had been widely circulated among the clergy, as well as two letters concerning its authenticity, from the Reverend Joseph H. Twichell. With the latter's hesitant consent he reported the incident as chapter 52 of his book, and, having crossed out the names of places and persons, bodily incorporated the original correspondence in the manuscript.[55] In view of the misgivings that Twichell had about permitting his friend the use of the letters[56] and in view of the tenuous connection between the subject matter of the book and the story, one must conclude that Mark Twain finally resorted to the use of extraneous material to fill out the remaining chapters. The manuscript version of his introduction of the account is clearly reminiscent of the difficulties he had had in making "The Professor's Yarn" a part of the book: "Upon that text I am going to depart from the direct line of my subject, now, & make a little excursion. But no apologies are necessary, & I offer none. I intend to reveal a secret which I have carried with me nine years, & which I have often wanted to disclose."[57]

Although Mark Twain's procedure in these two chapters seems to parallel earlier deviations from the direct course of the narrative and the subject matter under discussion, the argument needs to be made that chapters 51 and 52 mark a clear departure from previous habits and methods of composition. Quite apart from the external circumstances to be adduced from documents considered above, both the materials used and the techniques employed in incorporating them point to such a break. In the gossip sequence immediately preceding the two chapters the author had apparently exhausted his supply of items and episodes either directly related to the lower Mississippi or sufficiently representative of river life to be transferred to that locality, while the vital information concerning this region of the Mississippi Valley had, of course, been presented in earlier chapters built around the author's progress downstream. The resulting substitution of remnants of vaguely relevant information, supplemented with personal reminiscences of no relation to the ostensible subject matter, betray no perceptible selection and order. Technically, an organizing principle, like those that in previous instances had provided for the integration of materials from various sources into larger units, is totally absent in chapter 51. And although "The Professor's Yarn" as well as "A Burning Brand"

demonstrates lack of materials, of creative impulse, and of successful incorporation in the manuscript, a comparison of the author's
technique used in both instances clearly shows that of the earlier
chapter to be more acceptable.

While chapters 51 and 52 thus indicate the existence of a break
in the composition of the book as well as the general direction of the
departure from the use of materials and techniques followed up to
that point, the composition of the next four chapters (53–56) confirms such observations. Both the original plan for the standard
work and the modifications arrived at in the course of the composition had allowed, and even called for, the use of humorous yarns
and "incidents from many lands." Now, however, the author had
begun to turn to a different kind of material, that of personal
reminiscences, apparently finding a justification for their introduction in the localities visited in 1882. While the first part of the book
had of course been entirely devoted to reminiscences, there is an
obvious difference between those scenes and the memories exploited now. The former had been mainly concerned with Mark
Twain's piloting days, and when they reached beyond that into his
boyhood, they had been directly connected with the Mississippi;
they had also been of a general rather than a personal nature. The
reminiscences of chapters 53 to 56, on the other hand, are all concerned with his boyhood in Hannibal and are highly personal.
Though the presence of the Mississippi is felt throughout, the
author obviously does not exploit the connection. Nor does he
proceed to a consistent exploitation of the contrast between the past
and the present as the major integrating principle of the book. In
the beginning of chapter 53, before the actual sequence of these
reminiscences sets in, the author mentions "the large and flourishing town of Alton, Illinois," and Louisiana, Missouri, "a sleepy
village in my day, but a brisk railway-center now." But only twice
in the course of the sequence does he return to the theme of material
progress, once in a comparison of the "shabby little brick church
called the 'Old Ship of Zion' " of his day with the "trig and rather
hilarious edifice" now in its place, and again in the concluding
paragraphs of chapter 55, which constitute an explicit and extended
comment on the flourishing state of Hannibal in 1882:

It is no longer a village; it is a city, with a Mayor, and a council, and
water-works, and probably a debt. It has fifteen thousand people, it is a
thriving and energetic place. . . . The customary half-dozen railways center
in Hannibal now, and there is a new depot which cost a hundred thousand

dollars. In my time the town had no specialty, and no commercial grandeur; the daily packet usually landed a passenger and bought a catfish, and took away another passenger and a hatful of freight; but now a huge commerce in lumber has grown up, and a large miscellaneous commerce is one of the results. A deal of money changes hands there now.

But when the author mentions that Bear Creek, though "a famous breeder of chills and fever in its day," "is hidden out of sight now, under islands and continents of piled lumber, and nobody but an expert can find it," [58] a note of regret over the lost playground creeps in and confuses the reader as to the author's intended effect. The manuscript, furthermore, reveals these paragraphs to be a later addition; MSVII 25 was torn in two parts, its upper half now being followed by a twenty-five-page insert which begins with the overt praise of the present condition of Hannibal. The lower half of MSVII 25 appears later in the manuscript and indicates that the chapter originally was to have ended with the coachman episode, now the conclusion of chapter 56. Since the first instance of these comments on progress and material advancement does not belong to the actual sequence, while the second is obviously ironic, and the third constitutes an addition, all three demonstrate the ambiguity of the author's attitude. But they are neither sufficiently frequent nor sufficiently integrated to prove a definite relationship with the pattern dominating the preceding chapters of the second part of the book.

Similarly, further evidence of an antiromantic and antisentimental attitude in the remembered episode of the carpenter—"a romantic, sentimental, melodramatic fraud . . . who had had his poor romantic head turned" by reading Robert Montgomery Bird's *Nick of the Woods* and whose plagiaristic inventions the author had believed—does not become part of the earlier critical program. Its significance is that of an individual experience, one of many which Mark Twain had had as a boy. The episode merely marks a return to a theme explored a year earlier in "A Curious Experience," the story of a boy who posed as a Southern spy because he was "a ravenous devourer of dime novels and sensation-story papers." [59] The implicit criticism of dime novels and sensation-story papers in "A Curious Experience" is as general as that of Bird's book in the episode in *Life on the Mississippi*. There are other reasons why the latter cannot be construed as a specific attack on contemporary Southern literature. *Nick of the Woods* was published in 1837 and its action is laid in the Kentucky of 1782, illustrating a frontier society rather than the post-war one that Mark Twain was criticizing, and the melodramatic lies of the carpenter were exposed already by Sam Clemens of Hannibal, not by Mark Twain of Hartford.

The valuable biographical information contained in these four chapters, their foreshadowing of materials used in *Huckleberry Finn*, and their intrinsic "appeal of finely-sensed psychological analysis, of drama, and of truth," [60] have generally blinded critics who assess their role in *Life on the Mississippi*. While in these values they may surpass the rest of the materials in the second part of the book, and while Kenneth Andrews may be right in saying that Mark Twain's "account of Hannibal springs to life in the midst of the dead chapters because of the reminders he sees there of the past and his sense of subsequent alteration," [61] these chapters nevertheless constitute a deviation from the plan for the standard work and at the same time clearly violate the structure of the book. Up to this sequence the Mississippi journey of 1882 had merely provided a basic narrative structure devised for presenting materials according to the author's idea of the standard work, but it now ceases to function solely as a structural device and gives rise to an overly long sequence of individual experiences of no actual relevance to the subject matter. The insertion of the twenty-four manuscript-page account of the drownings of Lem Hackett and the boy "Dutchy," taken as they were from unused portions of *A Tramp Abroad*, merely signifies that Mark Twain had almost exhausted his materials and was now using a sequence of experiences not originally intended for *Life on the Mississippi*. His awareness of departing from the idea of the standard work and the absence of a principle designed to integrate these materials may have been the reason for adding the paragraphs devoted to evidences of material progress which distinguished the Hannibal of 1882. The very attempt, however, occasioned still another deviation, that of the burning of Jimmy Finn, the town drunkard, which concludes the addition.

4   As Mark Twain's narration moved into new regions, new materials from the notebooks and other sources procured for the composition could be used. This progress also permitted a return to aspects of the plan for the standard work and to integrating principles previously employed. The most obvious of these is the theme of material progress, for which the keynote is set in the opening paragraph of chapter 57:

From St. Louis northward there are all the enlivening signs of the presence of active, energetic, intelligent, prosperous, practical nineteenth-century populations. The people don't dream; they work. The happy result is manifest all around in the substantial aspect of things, and the suggestions of wholesome life and comfort that everywhere appear. Quincy is a notable example—a brisk, handsome, well-ordered city; and now, as formerly, interested in art, letters, and other high things.

Particular attention is given in the final chapters to the symbols also of moral progress—to libraries, reading rooms, colleges and universities, costly churches, grand courthouses, newspapers, and the stately architecture of "honest brick and stone." The author credits Burlington with having "the progressive modern city's full equipment of devices for right and intelligent government, including a paid fire department. . . . "[62] Mention of the latter would seem incongruous in this connection if it were not for a notebook entry in which Mark Twain observed, "N.O. [New Orleans] is still in the dark ages of independent fire Co's. Nothing paid but a Babcock Co. The town *belongs* politically to the independent organizations."[63] An antidemocratic and hence reactionary organization is thus immediately and, as the context of his work would suggest, more than merely metaphorically, linked with medievalism. The absence of such evidences along the Upper River, on the other hand, consequently becomes a sign of democracy and progress. The South, it seems, had in many ways become identified with France, which may well explain why Mark Twain repeatedly returned to Notebook 18 for entries he had made in that country. The Upper River region, on the other hand, was seen as but an extension of New England; Quincy, Illinois, is described as having "the aspect and ways of a model New England town."[64] The thematic use of a contrast between the past and present is thus developed into a contrast between two regions, a development that already foreshadows the idea of a contrast of two civilizations, on which the basic theme and plot structure of *A Connecticut Yankee* was to rest.[65] But whereas the hypothesis that material progress is an essential prerequisite for moral progress is eventually questioned in the novel, it is clearly implicit in the concluding chapters of *Life on the Mississippi*.

However useful the theme of material and moral progress was for a return to aspects of the standard work, its possibilities were definitely limited. Not being used in a fictional context, it did not lend itself to a ready expansion or a variegated presentation. The description of cities along the Upper River, the enumeration of evidences of their material and moral growth, and a sprinkling of statistical information are therefore almost interchangeable. This is not surprising because in most places the author had not even been able to go ashore. Since his notebooks contain none of the details given here, his account is probably based on newspaper clippings like the one which has survived in Notebook 20 and also largely on an informative travel booklet from whose pages he clipped two items for incorporation in the manuscript of chapters 59 and 60,[66] as well as John Disturnell's *Sailing on the Great Lakes and Rivers of America*,[67] a traveler's guide that he either used on his trip or subsequently acquired for the composition of the book. Since episodes were necessary to embellish the rather informative chapter 57, the author drew on his memory for an account of Henry Clay Dean's first public speech given in Keokuk, as told to him by William H. Clagget in Nevada in 1862, and for an experience of his own in Muscatine. The description of the scenery in the chapter entitled "On the Upper River" (chapter 58) is strongly reminiscent of that given by Francis Parkman in chapter 18 of *La Salle and the Discovery of the Great West*, particularly on pages bearing the caption "The Upper Mississippi." But it also reflects a notebook entry made during the trip. Parkman speaks of "a wilderness, clothed with velvet grass; forest-shadowed valleys; lofty heights, whose smooth slopes seemed levelled with the scythe; domes and pinnacles, ramparts and ruined towers, the work of no human hand."[68] Mark Twain's notebook entry reads: "The bluffs all along up above St Paul are exquisitely beautiful. <Some> Where the rough broken, turreted rocks stand up against the sky above the steep verdant slopes, they are inexpressibly rich & beautiful / mellow in color— soft dark browns mingled with dull greens—the very tints to make an artist worship. Remind one of the old houses in Spanish New Orleans."[69] Transferred to the region described by Parkman, the description in *Life on the Mississippi* reads:"The majestic bluffs that overlook the river, along through this region, charm one with the grace and variety of their forms, and the soft beauty of their adornment. The steep, verdant slope, whose base is at the water's edge, is topped by a lofty rampart of broken turreted rocks, which are exquisitely rich and mellow in color—mainly dark browns and dull greens, but splashed with other tints."[70] Similarities to the passage in Parkman's account are quite obvious, and one may well assume that the author used the literary source to supplement his notebook entry.

Following the overt praise of progress and the enumeration of its evidences along the Upper River, a sudden disruption of the tranquil scene caused by "the unholy train . . . with its devil's war-whoop and the roar and thunder of its rushing wheels"[71] introduces a disturbing element into the system of values recently developed. A very material reason may be offered for the non sequitur. There can be no doubt that when Mark Twain was writing these chapters he was eager to finish the book and—as subsequent instances of the use of sources in the two concluding chapters of the book show—eager to utilize materials suited for incorporation. What was needed now was a transition from the notebook entry just incorporated to the next one which promised to be of use for the book:

> 8 yrs ago boats like the Minneapolis used to go into St Paul with 150 people. Man used to say "Got 28 cars of wheat, Captain."
> "I'll take 2 of 'em."
> Now the *Captain* inquires "What you got for us?" "Nuth'n."
> The RR has done it.
> Used to carry loads of harvesters—now they've invented a self-binder & don't *have* harvesters any more.[72]

It is obvious that in order to include and extend the entry the author now must make the railroad the villain rather than the hero of modern historical development. While it would be a simplification to conclude, as Gladys C. Bellamy does, that Mark Twain "was apparently out of sympathy with the 'progress' along the upper Mississippi,"[73] even a momentary reversal of the earlier overt system of values can only be explained by the existence of a subconscious uneasiness about the forces transforming life on and along the Mississippi. Previous reading of Parkman's *La Salle and the Discovery of the Great West* and a possible return to the book for descriptions of the scenery of the Upper Mississippi, combined with a fruitless search for items of historical interest may have confirmed Mark Twain in his departure from the panegyric of progress. It was in connection with the Upper River and the erosion of the Falls of St. Anthony that Parkman had written:

Other changes, equally disastrous, in an artistic point of view, are going on even more quickly. Beside the falls stands a city, which, by an ingenious combination of the Greek and Sioux languages, has received the name of Minneapolis, or City of the Waters, and which in 1867 contained ten thousand inhabitants, two national banks, and an opera-house; while its rival city of St. Anthony, immediately opposite, boasted a gigantic water-cure and a State university. In short, the great natural beauty of the place is utterly spoiled.[74]

Mark Twain used an understatement when in 1882 he wrote that the falls had been chained to produce water-power, "somewhat to the damage of the Falls as a spectacle, or as a background against which to get your photograph taken."[75]

The notebook entry about the adverse effect of the growth of the railroad and the invention of the self-binder on steamboating upon the Mississippi is the last relevant entry made during his trip. His notebooks now contained no more materials to be used in the composition, and the foreign tourist, as a rule, had never ventured farther north than St. Louis. As to the new cities, he "has never heard of these; there is no note of them in his books."[76]

But either during his trip or in his subsequent search for materials Mark Twain had procured the booklet which in *Life on the Mississippi* he inadequately acknowledged as "a Tourist's Guide which the St. Louis and St. Paul Packet Company are going to issue this summer for the benefit of travelers who go by that line."[77] Its description of the scenery along the Mississippi from La Crosse to St. Paul became the basis for a lengthy commentary put into the mouth of a fellow passenger, "an old gentleman who had come to this Northwestern region with the early settlers, and was familiar with every part of it. Pardonably proud of it, too." Burlesque exaggeration of the travelogue points to Mark Twain's stylistic criticism, and the speaker is at last exposed as having "traveled with a panorama."[78]

5   The booklet and Parkman's *La Salle and the Discovery of the Great West*, as well as Disturnell's *Sailing on the Great Lakes and Rivers of America* and an article entitled "Sketches on the Upper Mississippi,"[79] may have directed Mark Twain's attention to Indian legends as a convenient way of filling out the last chapters of the book without actually violating the plan for the standard work. Although no references to Indian legends had appeared in the notebooks, with the exception of Parkman all the sources listed contained the full text of the Sioux legend of Winona. Mark Twain clipped it from the booklet and inserted it on MSVIII 101, introducing it as having been told by the "old gentleman." Parkman, in relating Father Hennepin's journey down the Upper Mississippi, had also referred

to "The 'Lover's Leap,' or 'Maiden's Rock,' from which a Sioux girl, Winona, or the 'Eldest Born,' is said to have thrown herself, in the despair of disappointed affection. The story, which seems founded in truth, will be found, not without embellishments, in Mrs. Eastman's *Legends of the Sioux*." [80] Parkman's qualification of the authenticity of Mary H. Eastman's version of the legend may be responsible for Mark Twain's burlesque version. In inserting the clipping he omitted the ending, for which he substituted a conclusion of his own, having Winona, instead of committing suicide, dash herself on her parents—"a distinct improvement upon the threadbare form of Indian legend." The author's ending and the subsequent inflated comments of the "old gentleman" as to the fate of the girl clearly reflect the antiromantic attitude shown earlier in the book:

'tis said she sought and married her true love, and wandered with him to some distant clime, where she lived happy ever after, her gentle spirit mellowed and chastened by the romantic incident which had so early deprived her of the sweet guidance of a mother's love and a father's protecting arm, and thrown her, all unfriended, upon the cold charity of a censorious world. [81]

Circumstantially "Mr. Schoolcraft's book, published near fifty years ago, and now doubtless out of print," [82] is introduced as containing legends "current among the Indians along this part of the Mississippi," and "written . . . down with strict exactness and without embellishments. . . . " Consequently "The Undying Head" and "Peboan and Seegwun, an Allegory of the Seasons" are incorporated into the manuscript. [83] Mark Twain confined himself to making a few minor stylistic changes in both legends (the substitution of lower case letters for upper case in the source resulted from his having the text retyped on a typewriter with upper case letters only). [84] One of the stylistic changes is of particular interest. In "The Undying Head" Mark Twain substituted "women" for "females." [85] The reason for this can be found in an earlier chapter in the manuscript. On MSII [9] 568, which occurs in the first of the deleted chapters following chapter 40, the author had explained parenthetically that when an Englishman uses the word "female" he "does not necessarily mean a cow or a cat . . . he often means a woman." Later, having "happened to glance into 'Society in America,' " he adds a footnote with the following observation by Harriet Martineau: "This noble word [woman], spirit-stirring as it passes over English ears, is in America banished, & 'ladies' & 'females' substituted; the one to English taste mawkish & vulgar; the other indistinctive and gross." [86] Mark Twain has reason to correct "this queer statement." Already on the occasion of his stay in England in 1879 he had drawn up a list of differences between British and American English usage which contained "Gentleman & lady— Eng & Am definitions . . . female (woman)." [87] Having proclaimed Miss Martineau's statement to be true "only when one exactly reverses it," he now challenges his reader to "take upon himself a couple of difficult enterprises, if he will: to find an English book (let him begin with Dickens!) wherein 'female' is not used for 'woman,' and to find six American books wherein 'female' *is* used for 'woman.'" [88] Naturally Mark Twain did not want to make it too easy for those of his readers who were willing to take his challenge.

It appears that Mark Twain, despite his mention of the relation of the Indian legends to the Mississippi, still was not satisfied with the reasons he had already given for their extraction from School- craft's collection. He therefore continues, "The latter is used in 'Hiawatha'; but it is worth reading in the original form, if only that one may see how effective a genuine poem can be without the helps and graces of poetic measure and rhythm." The array of reasons, however, is not fully convincing; another return to the subject of Indian legends in chapter 60 indicates that Mark Twain found the matter to be a convenient means of filling out the final chapters of the manuscript. The inclusion of "A Legend of White-Bear Lake"— "a most idiotic Indian legend" [89]—is suggested by that locality, and though purportedly taken from a different "guide-book," it con- sists of pages 63 and 64 of the booklet used in chapter 49. [90] But its relation to the Mississippi, which is the author's justification for presenting it, is all but forgotten in a criticism that foreshadows "Fenimore Cooper's Literary Offenses."

Further deviations mar the effect of the concluding chapter. An observation on climatic differences between the South and the Northwest develops into an attack on newspaper clichés and stock items of the reporter's trade. "But I wander from my theme," the author concludes, and thus, in the following paragraphs returns to a description typical of his theme throughout the book, the devel- opment of a community to its present state, characteristically sup- plemented by statistics taken from the local newspaper. An impor- tant aspect of the idea of the standard work thus prevails in the very last stage of the composition. So does the debunking antiromantic view of civilization and man, to which his study had given rise.

Even Parkman had begun to question the thesis that civilization had been brought by the missionary,[91] but Mark Twain now specifies by calling the whisky jug the "van-leader of civilization."[92]

On December 2, 1882, Mark Twain had said that "the book is not done yet, for the powers of heaven and Earth and hell are leagued against it, and it may never be finished at all."[93] But not only was he able to write the final chapters and have them typed by December 28, he also managed to do the revisions and corrections based on Osgood's suggestions of October 29.[94]

These suggestions, which have been referred to in different contexts throughout this study, deserve another comment from the point of view of their possible relevance to the final shape of Mark Twain's standard work. They concern the cancellation or the revision of a total of 77 out of the 234 typescript pages Osgood read, and they refer to nine different items varying in length from 2 to 17 pages. There can be no doubt that these suggestions constitute another extraneous influence upon the book. In addition to that, they have been taken to furnish an instance of Mark Twain's ready submission to yet another authority representing the standards of Eastern respectability which the author was eager to embrace.

But there is an obvious difference between his reactions to the revisions proposed by Howells or enjoined by Mrs. Clemens and those proposed by the publisher of *Life on the Mississippi*. While Mark Twain never seems to have questioned the judgment of Howells and also seems to have followed that of his wife whenever feasible, his own tabulation given on the sheets received from his publisher shows that he considered Osgood's advice only in the case of thirty-eight of the seventy-seven pages involved. Although there is little point in discussing the adequacy of Osgood's judgment for each of the nine items, it is important to note that he is not actually setting himself up as a censor—as the continued reference to the deleted material as "suppressed" chapters and passages would seem to imply[95]—and that his suggestions for condension or rewriting are more frequent than those calling for a deletion. The tentative nature of all of Osgood's advice, moreover, is clearly expressed in his comment on "The Professor's Yarn" in chapter 36: "Consider whether 'The Professor's Yarn' is not suggestive of being 'lugged-in'. It is good, but rather long, and if retained could not the scene be changed to the Mississippi?"

There can be no doubt that in making such proposals Osgood is acting at the author's request—"I started Osgood to editing it," is what Mark Twain says in his letter of November 4, 1882, to William Dean Howells about the difficulties with his manuscript—and that Osgood was useful for trying out the manuscript on someone who Mark Twain thought represented the general reader. Although he complains to Howells that he finds that "large areas of it are condemned here and there and yonder" and that "the burden of these unfilled gaps" is harassing him, he seems not to have regarded Osgood's judgment as final, and certainly he saw it as less authoritative than that of Howells himself. For he also tells the latter that he ought to have finished the manuscript before showing it to anybody, "and then sent it across the ocean to you to be edited, as usual." [96] He therefore felt free to ignore what his publisher proposed. He retained "The Professor's Yarn" without condensing it or transferring it to the Mississippi. But he accepted Osgood's opinion that "The Professor's Yarn" had been "lugged in," and he thus rewrote the text of MSII 462–64 in an unsuccessful attempt to provide a more suitable introduction for it. More significant, and interesting in particular for an assessment of Osgood's role in shaping and revising the standard work, is Mark Twain's decision not to condense the "Dying Man's Confession." Osgood had thought that it was "too long for the climax" and, more important, that there were "some unpleasant details in it." Had such criticism involving the question of propriety and taste come from Howells or Mrs. Clemens, one can be certain that Mark Twain would have taken it more seriously. Not to follow Osgood's advice on this point, therefore, implies that his publisher never actually exerted the kind of "censorship" that other friends and relatives have been either credited with or blamed for.

Still, Osgood's reading of the manuscript was not insignificant. He seems to have read it as a friend and recent traveling companion, and also in his professional capacity as someone about to publish it as a subscription book. And Mark Twain, regardless of what he was to say about Osgood's qualifications as a publisher later,[97] seems to have valued his advice chiefly for the latter reason and therefore complied with some of the suggestions. In addition to some fairly short yarns and the tourist chapters (chapters 40A and 40B) Mark Twain struck out or condensed statistics and historical material or relegated some of it to the appendix. None of these changes, however, affected the basic concept of the standard work and the balance that the author had established between various kinds of material.

A final conclusion may be drawn from the matter under discussion. Osgood's as well as Mark Twain's careful tabulations of the number of pages involved in these suggested and actual changes and deletions indicate that the publisher had obviously begun to share the author's anxiety about the size of the manuscript and the date of its completion—a concern which will be seen to extend well into the phase of proofreading.

Mark Twain's "Speculations and Conclusions" of the final chapter, thus, do not form the perfect keystone in the structure of the book. The amount of work done during the last weeks of the composition and the now-obvious exasperation may well be the reason. The author extricated himself by striking "the home-trail," and, having thus completed the basic narrative pattern of the book, he left further "Speculations and Conclusions" about what he had discovered and rediscovered to be given in *Adventures of Huckleberry Finn* and *A Connecticut Yankee in King Arthur's Court*, both of which would have been different books if it were not for the writing of *Life on the Mississippi*.

6 On January 3, 1883, Osgood's firm asked for instructions concerning the award of "premiums offered for the largest bona fide lists of subscribers,"[98] but Mark Twain referred the letter to Charles L. Webster who, as the recently appointed subscription manager, was in charge of the general agencies[99]: "Charley, if there are any instructions to be given, you may give them—I will not interest myself in *any*thing connected with this wretched God-damned book SLC."[100] But apparently this was merely a momentary reaction to "the exhaustion of this ten days' revising & correcting."[101] A letter of January 6 to his publisher shows him taking a sincere interest in the production and marketing of the book:

> Yes, make two sets of the plates & dies, & print 50,000 copies of the book. Bliss usually issued with upwards of 40,000 orders, & only 20,000 books to supply them with. . . .
> We must give Webster all the thunder-&-lightning circulars & advertising enginery that is needful. We must sell 100,000 copies of the book in 12 months, & shan't want him complaining that we are the parties in fault if the sale falls short of it.[102]

There was also the chore of proofreading still to be done. Far from complaining about it, as he often did, his letter also states that in this respect he will cause no delay. But he explicitly adds: "I don't

The cancelled cut, originally appearing on page 441. This cut, which showed a head in profile (very suggestive of that of the author) being consumed in flames, was taken from the book as a result of the protests of Mrs. Clemens.

answer for Mrs. Clemens, who has not edited the book yet, & will of course not let a line of the proof go from here till she has read it & possibly damned it. But she says she will put aside *everything else*, & give her entire time to the proofs." [103]

It was Mrs. Clemens who was responsible for some of "the tribulations attendant upon [the book's] production" as recounted by Caroline Ticknor. [104] Her objections to an illustration showing the burning of Mark Twain in effigy (which appeared on page 441 of the page proofs and survives in an undetermined number of copies of the first edition) [105] resulted in the official cancellation of the cut. The relation of the cut to the text is somewhat ambiguous. Edward Wagenknecht stresses that "it occurs in connection with Mark Twain's discussion of New Orleans graveyards and burying customs generally in Chapters XLII and XLIII, and links up with [Mark Twain's] advocacy of cremation." [106] But Caroline Ticknor seems to be equally correct in interpreting Olivia Clemens's objection to the picture as being the result of its reference to the final sentences of chapter 43: "As for me, I hope to be cremated. I made that remark to my pastor once, who said, with what he seemed to think was an impressive manner: 'I wouldn't worry about that, if I had your chances.' " [107] Mrs. Clemens's further objections to an illustration for the story of Karl Ritter's revenge, as well as the author's own objections to two other illustrations, could not be considered. [108]

Another sign of the interest that Mark Twain himself took in the proofreading and in the final stage of the production of his subscription book is the attention he gave to the "Old Times on the Mississippi" series as reset from the *Atlantic Monthly*. In his letter of January 6 he told Osgood, *"No, I don't want to read proof of the old Atlantic matter*—but I want it read *almighty carefully* in Boston, & no improvements attempted," the final injunction bespeaking a confidence that did not by any means extend to all his book. But the proofsheets of these chapters were sent anyway, possibly to obtain his approval of the illustrations, which had been newly provided for this part of the work. And while several dozen alterations of the text, particularly those "necessitated either by the change of publication date or by the change from serial to book form," [109] are probably the result of Mark Twain's insistence on a meticulous proofreading in Boston rather than of his own exactitude, he does seem to have begun to look at the proofs of these chapters as well. At one point he specifically notes that chapter 4, the opening chapter of the *Atlantic* series, is still missing. [110] It must have reached him, however, because four of the forty-five more significant changes discussed by Arthur L. Scott occur in this chapter. The very nature of these and further revisions, as well as the letter to Osgood forbidding others to meddle with his text, would seem to indicate that most of them came from the author himself: "in the matter of profanity he was *sublime*," rather than *"perfect,"* [111] for instance, is a very Twainian improvement, and the same holds for the substitution in this sentence from the opening paragraph: "Before these events, the day was glorious with expectancy; after them [rather than: *after they had transpired*] the day was a dead and empty thing." Scott concludes that the revisions were made with "a minimum of effort" and that Mark Twain "followed his early practice of revising sporadically." [112] But the fact, also noted by Scott, that most of the more substantial revisions "occur in the first and last quarters" of the "Old Times on the Mississippi" series suggests that the author was interested in the relation of these chapters to the

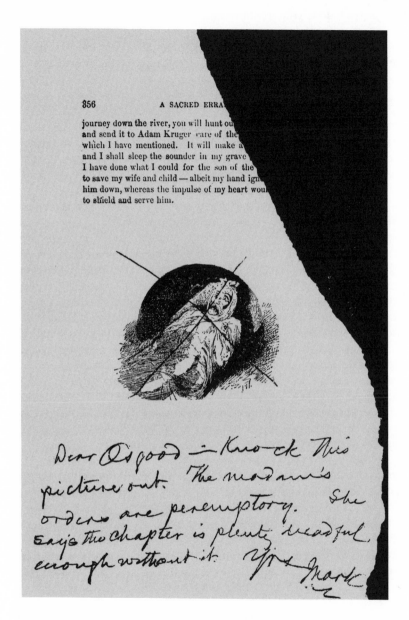

This is another picture which Mrs. Clemens regarded with a decidedly unsympathetic eye.

rest of the book. That he should have bothered at all to look at these chapters is more important than that he should have edited them somewhat sporadically and casually. After all, chapters 3 to 17 had already found the approval of William Dean Howells as well as that of the readers of the *Atlantic Monthly*.

This, however, was not true for the rest of the book, and on January 15, 1883, Mark Twain told Osgood, "you must glance through all the proof-slips (after Atlantic chapters) for about Baton Rouge and maybe in other places I have added footnotes and other stuff which you have not seen. I put in some Southern assassinations along there." [113] These additions survive chiefly in a lengthy footnote in chapter 40 where they were presented as "Extracts from the Public Journals." As a satirical substantiation of an assertion quoted in the text to the effect that "the Southern [was] the highest type of civilization this continent has seen," [114] this procedure closely parallels that used in one of Mark Twain's sources. In chapter 17 of his *American Notes* Charles Dickens had also juxtaposed statements concerning the mitigating influence of public opinion on the institution of slavery and assertions that the conduct of Southern society bears "the impress of civilisation and refinement" [115] on the one hand with two extended lists of items of contrary evidence quoted from the public journals of his day on the other. The last of these lists contains twelve individual reports of duels and assassinations, all of which could be substituted for the four reports to be found in Mark Twain's footnote.

Although Walter Blair is wrong in identifying these notes as stemming from the omitted chapter about Southern political slavery, [116] which in the manuscript followed chapter 47, [117] the omission of that chapter was certainly responsible for this late addition. Since Mark Twain was thus determined to have his say, one may conclude that his attack was the result of neither a momentary irritation nor lack of materials; he specifically tells Osgood that now "there will be 20 to 25,000 more words than necessary." But he also adds, "the scissors can be freely used," [118] and by doing so he provides another instance of his willingness to submit to the judgment of his publisher. But there can be little doubt that he expected Osgood to exercise such judgment primarily with regard to the actual size of the book.

This addition constituted the last stroke of work on the manuscript that can be accurately dated. The same day he wrote Cable, "I have just finished my book," and promised to return the volumes obtained from him for the composition.[119] But *Life on the Mississippi* also contains an epigraph, entitled "The 'Body of the Nation,' " that was apparently provided at this late stage [120] and that, though not part of the Morgan manuscript, probably did not find its way into the book without the author's approval. It is more likely, in fact, that Mark Twain himself chose the very passage from the "Editor's Table" in *Harper's New Monthly Magazine* of February 1863.[121] With its comparison of the basin of the Mississippi to other river basins of the world and with its emphasis on statistical data it has been taken to point to similar aspects in the work that it introduces, and it has led Edward Wagenknecht to ask: "Did any book ever begin less invitingly? And was there ever a less beguiling epigraph than 'The Body of the Nation'?" [122] But Mark Twain's true purposes in choosing the text become more obvious when it is examined in relation to the editorial it is taken from. Such examination reveals that the italics and capitals in the motto were not used in the original and that it was Mark Twain who thus sought to emphasize certain of its sentences and phrases. Only one of these sentences concerns primarily statistical matters (in comparing the size of the basin of the Mississippi to that of certain European countries) while the emphasis on the first and the last sentence points to the political importance of the Mississippi Valley as well as to its future development:

But *the basin of the Mississippi is the* BODY OF THE NATION. All the other parts are but members, important in themselves, yet more important in their relation to this. . . . Latitude, elevation, and rainfall all combine to render every part of the Mississippi Valley capable of supporting a dense population. *As a dwelling-place for civilized man it is by far the first upon our globe.*

In stressing these aspects Mark Twain apparently also tried to preserve the original context of the quotation. The "Editor's Table" of February 1863 in its entirety was devoted to Abraham Lincoln's Annual Message to Congress of December 1, 1862, and to its theme of national unity, for which the Mississippi Valley had begun to serve as a central symbol.[123] The passage quoted by Mark Twain is actually based on the following words spoken by Lincoln:

A glance at the map shows that, territorially speaking, it [the great interior region] is the great body of the republic. The other parts are but marginal borders to it. . . . In the production of provisions, grains, grasses, and all which proceed from them, this great interior region is naturally one of the most important in the world. Ascertain from the statistics the small proportion of the region which has, as yet, been brought into cultivation, and also the large and rapidly increasing amount of its products, and we shall be overwhelmed with the magnitude of the prospect presented.[124]

At a time when it had seemed possible "to frame a compromise that would avert a fight to the finish,"[125] Lincoln's words had given such currency to the prophecy that as much as two decades later the author of *Life on the Mississippi* could still expect his readers to interpret his epigraph as an avowal of the program of the Republican Party and its Reconstruction policy.

Mark Twain's very motto—and the true capstone of his work— thus emphasizes that the attack on Southern backwardness and maudlin romanticism had now definitely been made an integral part of his project and that his standard work, in addition to being a source of information about the Mississippi Valley and its history, was indeed intended to function like Cervantes's *Don Quixote* and to serve as an instrument of social as well as political change.

By April 12 the author had told Osgood that he liked the book,[126] presumably referring to the way it looked.

Life on the Mississippi was published on May 12, 1883, and sold "by subscription only." It was the first of Mark Twain's books to be reviewed in *Harper's Magazine*. The review stresses the very qualities that had distinguished the author's plan for the standard work. Rather than containing "the abounding strokes of whimsical humor that have tickled the fancy in other productions of this popular writer," the book is found to be a repository of an "amusing and interesting medley of fact and fiction—historical, topographical, autobiographical, and descriptive of aspects of life on and beside the Great River." In a variation of this praise the reviewer uses such phrases as "a graphic account teeming with solid information, occasionally alleviated by mirth-provoking oddities of thought and expression" and "animated sketches." In stating that *Life on the Mississippi* "describes the characteristic features of the river, and the art and mystery of its navigation, together with the numberless phases of character and incident that entered into and diversified the life of the river and of the people, cities, towns, and plantations that lined its shifting banks," and concluding, obviously with particular reference to chapters 4–20, that it is "an invaluable souvenir of a phase of American life and manners that has passed away never to be revived,"[1] the review implicitly characterizes the features of the idea of the standard work. The final sentence, applied to the work as a whole, also sets the keynote for what to this day has been said about the book's basic appeal for the reader—regardless of what other interests the scholars have taken in it.[2]

The review was a vindication for the author, not only of his plan for the standard work, but also of the actual procedure of composition, and testimony, at the same time, that he had been successful in realizing that plan. But I see no evidence that he really needed such a vindication. Besides the major phases of the composition and most of the resulting manuscript, Mark Twain's subsequent opinion about the work may be taken as ex post facto evidence that the author followed a specific plan throughout its making and that the necessary deviations did not greatly affect the original idea for the standard work. Despite the one isolated reference to a possible inferior quality of the incomplete manuscript[3] and his angry but momentary "I will not interest myself in *any*thing connected with this God-damned book,"[4] he never seems to have doubted the quality of his work. When the initial sales of *Life on the Mississippi* were lower than its author had expected,[5] he tried, in his usual manner, to lay the blame on his publisher. Though Osgood's protestations—"If it is a failure it is not due to lack of intelligent, conscientious & energetic effort on our part"[6]—practically suggested that Mark Twain try to find an explanation in the nature or the quality of the work itself, they did not once make him doubt the success of his composition. On the contrary, on December 21, 1883, he rejoins by saying that instead of the 30,000 copies actually sold the number should have been 80,000 and that "the publisher who sells less than 50,000 copies of a book for me has merely injured me, he has not benefitted me."[7] In 1888 Mark Twain has a leaflet listing the "Standard Publications of Charles L. Webster & Co.," his own firm, describe *Life on the Mississippi* as "a perfect encyclopædia of wit, humor, and fact."[8] Such a characterization confirms that in the author's opinion the essential aspects of the finished product corresponded to those of his plan for the work.

About 1890 and again in 1895, as has been mentioned, he explicitly reaffirmed his qualifications for writing the standard work by pointing to the singular combination of facts that had predestined him for the role of the historian of the river and its society. The Mississippi, he asserted, was his real field of work:

By a series of events—accidents—I was the only one who wrote about old times on the Mississipi. Wherever else I have been some better have been there before and will come after, but the Mississippi was a virgin field. No one could write that life but a pilot, because no one else but a pilot entered into the spirit of it. But the pilots were the last men in the world to write its history. As a class they did not naturally run to literature, and this was made more unlikely by another reason. Every pilot had to carry in his head thousands of details of that great river. Details, moreover, that were always changing, and in order to have nothing to confuse those details they entered into a compact never to read anything. Thus if they had thought of writing, they would have had no connected style, no power of describing anything; and moreover, they were so engrossed in the river that there was nothing in life unusual to them. Here then was my chance, and I used it.[9]

Mark Twain's interest in the subject of his standard work, and particularly in its historical aspect, furthermore, was not confined to the composition of *Life on the Mississippi* and *Adventures of Huckleberry Finn.* Even after the completion of the standard work and of the novel, a notebook entry, probably made early in 1885, testifies to its abiding appeal for the author: "Make a kind of Huck Finn narrative on a boat—let him ship as Cabin boy & another boy as cub pilot—& so put the great river & its bygone ways into history in form of a story." [10]

As late as May 1908, finally, *Life on the Mississippi* became the only book ever to have been singled out by Mark Twain for extensive stylistic revisions after publication. The nature of these revisions, complex and unfinished as they are, need not interest us here. But Guy A. Cardwell, who has examined the association copy preserved in the Barrett Collection at the Alderman Library of the University of Virginia, finds that "it is difficult to believe that he went to so much trouble without having a definite purpose in mind." [11] It is not at all impossible to assume, therefore, that his standard work might have been intended to become Volume One in the author's revised edition of the collected writings of Mark Twain.

Conclusion

The aesthetic evaluation of a literary composition as a rule does not reflect either the genesis or the use of sources as such. But the case may be made here that both can be essential to a final judgment. Critics have found the second part of *Life on the Mississippi* to be an "uneven, hasty and loosely put-together volume . . . not literature but a disorderly patchwork."[1] The account of the composition and the use of sources, however, uncovers significant patterns in the patchwork, which, regardless of their extraliterary origins and the reasons for their existence in the book, also function aesthetically as organizing principles for the materials presented. An even greater import of the genetic approach lies in the fact that it provides new insights into the author's aims and that it reveals negative evaluations to be frequently the result of untenable hypotheses concerning the author's intentions. The preceding account establishes that the second part of the book does not reflect Mark Twain's inability to continue the narrative in the spirit of the "Old Times on the Mississippi" series, but rather that he conceived and designed it as a complement and in such a way that both parts together should result in the standard work he had intended *Life on the Mississippi* to be from its inception. While previous incomplete accounts of the composition have apparently predisposed critics to arrive at hasty conclusions about the book's characteristics and quality, the revision of the record may lead to a re-examination of the validity of such findings.

This re-examination may not result in a significant gain in the aesthetic stature of *Life on the Mississippi*, but the account of the genesis of the book and the use of source materials in the course of its composition cannot fail to increase its value in another respect. Not only is it a repository of materials that reappear in later works, particularly in *Adventures of Huckleberry Finn* and *A Connecticut Yankee in King Arthur's Court*, but the account of the composition also demonstrates that the particular use that is made of these materials is the result not so much of the pressure of a contract as of a deliberate endeavor according to a carefully thought out plan, which therefore deserves attention in its own right. The ideas and attitudes developed to integrate and to order the materials further-more suggest that the book is also a conscious trying out of basic ideas of later works.

Finally, the genetic approach further exemplifies Mark Twain's working habits, particularly with regard to the use of source mate-rials. Walter Blair has already abundantly demonstrated that Bernard DeVoto missed an essential aspect of Mark Twain's methods of composition when he called the study of the author's sources "tire-some, repugnant, and quite meaningless."[2] The composition of *Life on the Mississippi* extends both the scope and the variety of sources, particularly in the direction of extraliterary materials of topical interest. While such evidence does not enhance the status of Mark Twain as an original artist with a primarily literary orienta-tion, it does establish a direct relation between his work and the culture of his day, a relation that continues to be a legitimate and important subject of Mark Twain scholarship.

To arrive at these conclusions, however, does not imply the claim that the originality of Mark Twain's mind and the complexity of his literary products can ever be reduced to an account of the writing of his works and a list of their source materials. There is much that must necessarily escape such a view. Listing Delaware among the states whose rivers drain into the Mississippi,[3] in the first chapter of his book, and calling whisky the van-leader of civilization, in the last chapter of it, are cases in point. They are like the significant "quarter twain" in the midst of an endless string of half twains that the ex-pilot discusses in chapter 13, and they remind us that his standard work, too, was written by a pilot turned humorist, whose "Perplexing Lessons" and "Continued Perplexities"—to pursue the telling metaphor of his very book—invite ever new "Sounding."

Notes

Preface

1. Sherwood Anderson, *Dark Laughter* (New York, 1925), p. 18. For a similar view see Barriss Mills, who as late as 1963 maintained: "[Mark Twain] spoiled it all by expanding the original sketches to include further reminiscences, new material based on revisiting the river in 1882, information and tables culled from newspapers, and various anecdotes to be found ready to hand. Inevitably this expanded version . . . dissipated and diluted whatever formal unity the earlier sketches had contained" ("*Old Times on the Mississippi* as an Initiation Story," *College English*, 25 [1964], 284).
2. See, however, Sherwood Anderson's letters of April 1918 and December 1919 to Van Wyck Brooks, which suggest that Anderson arrived at a similar view independently of Brooks's *The Ordeal of Mark Twain* (*Letters of Sherwood Anderson*, ed. Howard Mumford Jones and Walter Rideout [Boston, 1953], letters no. 29 and 45; and "Letters to Van Wyck Brooks," in *The Shock of Recognition*, ed. Edmund Wilson [New York, 1955], pp. 1256–90).
3. See Malcolm Cowley, "Introduction" to the Meridian Book edition of *The Ordeal of Mark Twain* (Cleveland, 1955), pp. 5–10.
4. See, for instance, Neal Frank Doubleday, who uses them to document Mark Twain's working habits. He explicitly states: "Mark Twain's letters of October

30 and November 4, 1882, are somewhat disconcerting accounts of the way in which the latter part of *Life on the Mississippi* was put together" (*Mark Twain's Picture of His America* [Boston, 1960], p. 154). See also Justin Kaplan in his "definitive" *Mr. Clemens and Mark Twain: A Biography* (New York, 1966), pp. 248–49.

5. The obvious discrepancy between the more readily available documents and a possible thematic unity of the work has occasionally led critics to neglect or to ignore completely Mark Twain's own statements and other documentation relating to the composition of the book. Stanley Brodwin, for instance, who argues in favor of a significant, triple-themed structure of the new chapters, practically confines himself to an intrinsic approach ("The Useful and the Useless River: *Life on the Mississippi* Revisited," *Studies in American Humor*, 2 [1976], 196–208), whereas James Cox, who sees a thematic unity in the confrontation between "the permanence of the river" and "the transient life of man," explicitly states: "The argument about the author's intention is always tenuous, especially when, as in this instance, we have no stated evidence as to what the intention was" ("Mark Twain: A Study in Nostalgia" [Ph.D. diss., Indiana University, 1955], p. 90).

6. Cox, "Mark Twain: A Study in Nostalgia," p. 73.

I. Introduction

1. See DeLancey Ferguson, *Mark Twain: Man and Legend* (Indianapolis, 1943), pp. 208–15; Walter Blair, *Mark Twain & Huck Finn* (Berkeley, 1960), pp. 285–99; Dewey Ganzel, "Twain, Travel Books, and *Life on the Mississippi*," *American Literature*, 34 (1962), 40–55; Dewey Ganzel, "Samuel Clemens and Captain Marryat," *Anglia*, 80 (1962), 405–16, esp. 406; Caroline Ticknor, "Mark Twain's 'Life on the Mississippi,' " *Glimpses of Authors* (Boston, 1922), pp. 132–51; Caroline Ticknor, " 'Mark Twain's' Missing Chapter," *The Bookman*, 39 (1914), 298–309.

2. *Mark Twain-Howells Letters: The Correspondence of Samuel L. Clemens and William D. Howells, 1872–1910*, ed. Henry Nash Smith and William M. Gibson, with the assistance of Frederick Anderson, 2 vols. (Cambridge, Mass., 1960), 1: 417.

3. Ferguson, *Mark Twain: Man and Legend*, p. 211.

4. *Mark Twain & Huck Finn*, p. 289.

5. "Twain, Travel Books, and *Life on the Mississippi*," p. 40.

6. *Mark Twain-Howells Letters*, 1: 418, n.6.

7. Making a typescript was, as Walter Blair remarks, "an unusual procedure at the time" (*Mark Twain & Huck Finn*, p. 288). Caroline Ticknor states that a typewritten copy was made "in order that his own clean manuscript might go to a friend and collector, who had made known to him a keen desire to possess it" (" 'Mark Twain's' Missing Chapter," p. 305). Here as in other details she seems to be wrong, for Mark Twain did not know Pierpont Morgan at that time. I suspect that the typescript was desirable not so much to preserve "his own clean manuscript," but rather to hide its blemishes, namely the use of source materials, often in the form of clippings, frequently without proper acknowledgment, from publisher and printers.

8. James R. Osgood & Company (W. Rowlands) to SLC, Boston, Sept. 16. 1882; Boston, Sept. 29. 1882; and Sept. 30. 1882, Mark Twain Papers, The Bancroft Library, University of California, Berkeley. (Subsequently abbreviated as MTP.)

9. These are preserved in the Theater Collection, Rogers Memorial Room, Harvard University. Page 233 of the typescript is bound in with the holograph manuscript of *Life on the Mississippi* in the Pierpont Morgan Library, New York City.

10. Autograph note, JRO to SLC, Oct 29. 1882, two columns in ink with SLC and JRO pencil notations. This is preserved together with two JRO autograph pages in pencil, which constitute a copy or a draft of the above, in the Theater Collection, Rogers Memorial Room, Harvard University.

11. The Pierpont Morgan Library holograph manuscript of *Life on the Mississippi*, bound in three volumes and cut after binding, consists of eight individually paginated portions. Reference to these portions is made by Roman numerals as follows: MSI = pp. 1–69 and one unnumbered page (LOM, pp. 1–31); MSII = pp. 1–774 (LOM, pp. 163–381, and LOM, HP, pp. 338–416); MSIII = pp. 1–115 (LOM, pp. 382–413, and LOM, HP, pp. 416–17); MSIV = pp. 1A–55 and pp. 58 1/2–64 (LOM, pp. 414–29 and pp. 441–43, and LOM, HP, p. 417); MSV = pp. 1–14 (LOM, pp. 429–34); MSVI = pp. 139–63 (LOM, pp. 434–41), MSVII = pp. 1–25 (LOM, pp. 443–50), and MSVIII = pp. 1–146 (LOM, pp. 450–96). Arabic numerals designate pages, and canceled pagination is indicated by square brackets. Except where noted, all references to the printed version of *Life on the Mississippi* are to the text of the so-called Definitive Edition (*The Writings of Mark Twain*, ed. Albert Bigelow Paine, 37 vols. [New York, 1922–25]), in which *Life on the Mississippi* is volume 12; the abbreviation LOM refers to this edition. (The pagination of this volume corresponds to that of *Life on the Mississippi* in the Author's National Edition [New York, 1898–1900; vol. 9] and to the Harper's Modern Classics edition [New York, 1950].) References to the printed text of deleted portions are to the Heritage Press edition of *Life on the Mississippi* ("With an introduction by Edward Wagenknecht and a number of previously suppressed passages, now printed for the first time, and edited with a note by Willis Wager" [New York, 1944]); the abbreviation LOM, HP refers to this edition. It should be noted that this is neither a critical nor a definitive edition; while "aside from the correction of . . . printing mistakes, the body of the . . . edition follows the regular, authorized text, which is essentially that of the first edition" (p. 388), the text of the "suppressed passages," given only if not "less than a sentence in length" and if not taken "verbatim from certain magazines cited in the following pages" (p. 385), preserves the final state of the manuscript. In one instance this results in an obvious inconsistency. In the "suppressed chapter" printed on pp. 396–98 "Uncle Mumford" and "Mr. H." of the printed version of *Life on the Mississippi* still appear under their real names Mr. Dunham and Mr. Harvey, and their identity is not clarified.

12. MSII 679[†].

13. MSII 749–74, LOM, HP, pp. 412–16.

14. In an undated letter marked "Friday" (probably December 29, 1882), Mark Twain informed Osgood that he had sent "all but '8th batch' " the previous night and that this eighth batch had been rescued by him, disinfected, and sent by express that morning (SLC to JRO [Hartford] Friday [December 29, 1882?], Pierpont Morgan Library [†]; a version appears in *Mark Twain's Letters to His Publishers, 1867–1894*, ed. Hamlin Hill [Berkeley, 1967], p. 160). By January 6,

1883, Mark Twain was eager to learn what Osgood had decided "to condemn in the last batches" (SLC to JRO, Hartford Jan 6/83, Newberry Library, Chicago [publ. in Benjamin Lease, "Mark Twain and the Publication of *Life on the Mississippi*: An Unpublished Letter," *American Literature*, 26 (1954), 248–50]); and by January 15, having probably received Osgood's objections to the chapter on "Southern Political Slavery" along with its galley proofs, he had made up his mind to delete it and instead insert additional indictments of the South in chapter 40 (SLC to JRO [Hartford] Jan 15 [1883], Yale Collection of American Literature, Morse Collection, Beinecke Library, Yale University; a version appears in *Mark Twain's Letters to His Publishers*, p. 162). The eighth batch remained in Osgood's hands together with the typescript and only after the author's death became part of the Morgan collection (see Ticknor, " 'Mark Twain's' Missing Chapter," pp. 298–305).

15. LOM, p. 314.

II.   Planning a Standard Work

1. SLC to Jane Clemens, January 20 [1866], MTP (†). See *Mark Twain-Howells Letters*, 1: 35, n. 1.
2. Quoted in Edgar Marquess Branch, "Introduction," *Early Tales & Sketches, Volume 1, 1851–1864*, ed. Edgar Marquess Branch and Robert H. Hirst (Berkeley, 1979), p. 35.
3. SLC to Olivia Langdon Clemens, Bennington, Vt., November 27, 1871 (*The Love Letters of Mark Twain*, ed. Dixon Wecter [New York, 1949], p. 166).
4. Quoted in Dixon Wecter, "Introduction," *Life on the Mississippi*, Harper's Modern Classics (New York, 1950), p. ix.
5. SLC to Elisha Bliss (*Mark Twain's Letters*, ed. Albert Bigelow Paine, 2 vols. [New York, 1917], 1: 187, 188).
6. Ibid., 1: 193.
7. See SLC to Orion Clemens, Buffalo [March or April] 4, 1871 (*Mark Twain's Letters*, 1: 185) and the introduction of the item in the *Galaxy* (reprinted in Samuel Langhorne Clemens, *Contributions to "The Galaxy," 1868–1871*, ed. Bruce R. McElderry, Jr. [Gainesville, Fla., 1961], p. 132).
8. *Mark Twain's Letters*, 1: 193.
9. Henry Nash Smith is correct in pointing out that in using this combination Mark Twain transcends the technique of the traditional travel narratives about the American West used in Washington Irving's *A Tour on the Prairies* (1835) and Francis Parkman's *The Oregon Trail* (1849) (*Mark Twain: The Development of a Writer* [Cambridge, Mass., 1962], pp. 52–53). The use of this technique in *Roughing It* and "Old Times on the Mississippi" at the same time contributes to the formation of a specifically American version of the traditonal theme of pilgrimage and the *queste*. This can be seen in the modern American novel just as much as in Mark Twain's *Adventures of Huckleberry Finn* and *A Connecticut Yankee in King Arthur's Court* (see, for instance, Paul Gerhard Buchloh, "Vom *Pilgrim's Progress* zum *Pilgrim's Regress*: Der Fortschrittsgedanke in der englischen

und amerikanischen Literatur," in *Die Idee des Fortschritts,* ed. Erich Burck [Munich, 1963], pp. 153–87).

10. SLC to OC, Elmira, July 15, 1870 (*Mark Twain's Letters,* 1: 175).

11. SLC to OC, Buffalo, 1870 (Ibid.).

12. SLC to OC, Elmira, July 15, 1870 (Ibid.).

13. SLC to OC, Buffalo, 1870 (Ibid.).

14. See *Traveling with the Innocents Abroad: Mark Twain's Original Reports from Europe and the Holy Land,* ed. Daniel Morley McKeithan (Norman, Okla., 1958), and Dewey Ganzel, *Mark Twain Abroad: The Cruise of the "Quaker City"* (Chicago, 1968).

15. Smith, *Mark Twain: The Development of a Writer,* p. 71. See also Robert Regan, " 'English Notes': A Book Mark Twain Abandoned," *Studies in American Humor,* 2 (1976), 157–70.

16. SLC to EB, May 15, 1871 (*Mark Twain's Letters,* 1: 187, 188).

17. SLC to Olivia Langdon Clemens, Hartford [August 10, 1871] (*The Love Letters of Mark Twain,* p. 159).

18. There are two notebooks (Notebook 2 and Notebook 3) kept during his piloting days, which provide a very detailed "technical documentation of Mark Twain's account of his piloting apprenticeship as given in *Life on the Mississippi*" ("Introduction," *Mark Twain's Notebooks & Journals, Volume I (1855–1873),* ed. Frederick Anderson, Michael B. Frank, and Kenneth M. Sanderson [Berkeley, 1975], p. 2). It is true that neither seems to have been available to him throughout the 1870s (see Edgar J. Burde, "Mark Twain: The Writer as Pilot," *PMLA,* 93 [1978], 890, n.9), but the rediscovery of the earlier one, on December 8, 1880 (see *Notebooks & Journals* I, p. 45), apparently did not induce Mark Twain to consult it in the course of the writing of the new chapters.

19. "Pudd'nhead Wilson's New Calendar," *Following the Equator,* 1, *The Writings of Mark Twain,* Definitive Edition (New York, 1923), 20: 220.

20. *The Writings of Mark Twain,* Author's National Edition, 7: ix.

21. Winnipeg, Canada, *Tribune,* July 27, 1895; quoted in Fred W. Lorch, "Mark Twain's 'Morals' Lecture During the American Phase of His World Tour in 1895–1896," *American Literature,* 26 (1954), 57–58.

22. *Mark Twain's Letters,* 2: 541–43; *The Portable Mark Twain,* ed. Bernard DeVoto (New York, 1946), pp. 773–75.

23. For a similar view of his experiences on the Mississippi see, as early as the writing of "Old Times on the Mississippi," SLC to William Dean Howells [Hartford] December 3, 1874 (*Mark Twain-Howells Letters,* 1: 47).

24. *Mark Twain in Eruption,* ed. Bernard DeVoto (New York, 1940), p. 216.

25. Henry Nash Smith has pointed out that the revival of the plan for a Mississippi book in 1871 and Mark Twain's idea to "spend 2 months on the river & take notes" occur "in the same letter in which he sets forth the formula for his lectures as a narrative plank with serious and humorous plugs inserted in it." Smith concludes that Mark Twain "conceived of a book as a longer discourse with an identical structure" (*Mark Twain: The Development of a Writer,* p. 71).

26. *Mark Twain-Howells Letters,* 1: 62.

27. Ibid., p. 55, n.5.

28. SLC to JR [n.p.] November 29 [1874?], Barrett Collection (†); copy in MTP.

29. *Mark Twain-Howells Letters,* 1: 58, 59.

30. WDH to SLC [Cambridge] April 27, 1875 (Ibid., p. 79).
31. SLC to JRO, Farmington Avenue, Hartford, Feb. 12 [1875], Theater Collection, Rogers Memorial Room, Harvard University (†); a version appears in *Mark Twain's Letters to His Publishers*, p. 85.
32. *Mark Twain-Howells Letters*, 1: 81.
33. SLC to WDH [Hartford, February ? 1875] (Ibid., p. 64).
34. SLC to WDH [Hartford, April 25 or 26, 1875] (Ibid., p. 78).
35. See, for instance, Blair, *Mark Twain & Huck Finn*, p. 50. The metaphor of the "dry tank" is, of course, Mark Twain's (see *Mark Twain in Eruption*, p. 197).
36. *Mark Twain-Howells Letters*, 1: 67.
37. SLC to [Elisha] Bliss [Hartford] Mch 1 [1875], MTP (†).
38. *Mark Twain-Howells Letters*, 1: 88.
39. *Mark Twain: A Biography*, 3 vols. (New York, 1912), 1: 533.
40. SLC to MMF, Hartford, April 14 [1877] (*Mark Twain to Mrs. Fairbanks*, ed. Dixon Wecter [San Marino, Calif., 1949], p. 204).
41. Quoted in Guy A. Cardwell, *Twins of Genius* (East Lansing, 1953), p. 81.
42. Ferguson, *Mark Twain: Man and Legend*, p. 214. Dixon Wecter writes: "We may regret that Clemens rejected [Osgood's] advice to shorten the yarn of Ritter in Chapter XXXI—though better counsel would have been its omission altogether" ("Introduction," *Life on the Mississippi*, p. xi).
43. A meticulous reconstruction of all phases of the trip, based on Mark Twain's two river notebooks, on his correspondence, and on contemporary newspaper reports, has been provided by Coleman O. Parsons in "Down the Mighty River with Mark Twain," *Mississippi Quarterly*, 22 (1969), 1–18, as well as by Guy A. Cardwell in "*Life on the Mississippi*: Vulgar Facts and Learned Errors," *Emerson Society Quarterly*, 19 (1973), 283–93, who also surveys the development of Mark Twain's plans for the project. For the precise dates of the tour see *Mark Twain's Notebooks & Journals, Volume II (1877–1883)*, ed. Frederick Anderson, Lin Salamo, and Bernard L. Stein (Berkeley, 1975), pp. 436–37.
44. See SLC to Edward H. House, Dec. 27/81, Barrett Collection, University of Virginia; copy in MTP.
45. SLC to JRO [Hartford] December 28, 1881 (*Mark Twain's Letters to His Publishers*, p. 147).
46. SLC to JCH, Hartford, April 2, 1882 (*Mark Twain's Letters*, 1: 418).
47. LOM, pp. 186, 405.
48. SLC to Olivia Langdon Clemens, Saturday Afternoon, 1/2 way to Memphis [April 22, 1882] (*The Love Letters of Mark Twain*, p. 208).
49. See Louis J. Budd, ed., "A Listing of and Selection from Newspaper and Magazine Interviews with Samuel L. Clemens, 1874–1910," *American Literary Realism, 1870–1910*, 10 (1977), 2, item 16.
50. Carl J. Weber suggests that Mark Twain had merely planned to return to the Mississippi and that it was Osgood who gave him the idea to turn his trip to literary uses. Osgood may have contributed to the genesis of the particular book that resulted, but he can hardly be called the spiritual father of the idea. (See *The Rise and Fall of James Ripley Osgood* [Waterville, Maine, 1959], pp. 191–93.)
51. *Notebooks & Journals II*, pp. 446–47.
52. Ibid., p. 455. On April 6, he actually wrote to the Office of the Secretary of War asking for such a map.
53. Ibid., p. 472.

54. Mark Twain's letter to his wife, written on May 17 from Quincy, Illinois, shortly before the end of the journey, states that he is "desperately homesick" and refers to the undertaking as "this hideous trip." But it certainly does not reflect the spirit in which the trip and the resulting book were undertaken. Other letters to Olivia Langdon Clemens written during the trip state that the author is having "a powerful good time" or "a most serene & enjoyable time," and comment very favorably on his experiences and impressions (see *The Love Letters of Mark Twain*, pp. 207–14). The letter of May 17 also mentions that Mark Twain "spent three delightful days in Hannibal" (*Mark Twain's Letters*, 1: 419), and on May 28, 1882, William Dean Howells wrote, "I have heard from Osgood what a glorious time you had" (*Mark Twain-Howells Letters*, 1: 403).

55. *Notebooks & Journals II*, pp. 472, 482; later used in chapter 2, "The River and Its Explorers."

56. *Notebooks & Journals II*, pp. 446, 456, 457, 458.

57. Notebooks 20 and 21, MTP; reproduced in *Notebooks & Journals II*, pp. 437–515, 521–74.

58. *Notebooks & Journals II*, pp. 454, 457.

59. An explanation for Mark Twain's hesitancy in reassuming the role of pilot that had given a kind of unity to the "Old Times on the Mississippi" series has recently been offered by Edgar J. Burde. Burde sees the second part of *Life on the Mississippi* dominated by the stance of Captain William Brown, to whose memory "all occurrences are of the same size" and who "cannot distinguish an interesting circumstance from an uninteresting one" (LOM, p. 112; Burde, "Mark Twain: The Writer as Pilot," pp. 878–92).

60. "An 'Innocent' Interviewed: Mark Twain Pays a Visit to St. Louis," reprinted in Budd, "Newspaper and Magazine Interviews with Samuel L. Clemens," p. 38.

61. Contract between SLC and James R. Osgood & Company for the publication of *Life on the Mississippi*, April 10, 1882, reproduced in Frederick Anderson and Hamlin Hill, "How Samuel Clemens Became Mark Twain's Publisher: A Study of the James R. Osgood Contracts," *Proof*, 2 (1972), 139–42.

62. See *Mark Twain's Letters*, 1: 401–3, 417–18.

63. A clipping of the review is preserved as an enclosure in a letter of September 12, 1882, from Joel Chandler Harris to Mark Twain, MTP.

64. *Notebooks & Journals II*, pp. 482, 455.

65. Blair, *Mark Twain & Huck Finn*, p. 289.

66. Ferguson, *Mark Twain : Man and Legend*, p. 214.

67. Bernard DeVoto, *Mark Twain at Work* (Cambridge, Mass., 1942), p. viii.

68. See, especially, Blair, *Mark Twain & Huck Finn*; Howard G. Baetzhold, "The Course of Composition of *A Connecticut Yankee*: A Reinterpretation," *American Literature*, 33 (1961), 195–214; John S. Tuckey, *Mark Twain and Little Satan* (West Lafayette, Ind., 1963); Bryant Morey French, *Mark Twain and "The Gilded Age"* (Dallas, 1965).

III.   Devising a Narrative Structure

1. SLC to E. B. Peck, February 11, 1882 (published in *Twainian*, 16 [1957], 4).

2. Notebook entries apparently made for a book about the Mississippi occur

already in Notebook 18 (February–September 1879) and Notebook 19 (July 1880–January 1882). Relevant entries in Notebook 20 occur as early as February 1882.
3. *Notebooks & Journals II*, p. 454.
4. Ibid., p. 482.
5. *Mark Twain & Huck Finn*, p. 289; see above, p. 2.
6. See *Notebooks & Journals II*, pp. 338–39.
7. The discovery of these sheets also refutes Dewey Ganzel's questioning of Blair's redating of the working notes for *Huckleberry Finn* ("Twain, Travel Books, and *Life on the Mississippi*," esp. pp. 49–55; cf. Walter Blair, "When Was *Huckleberry Finn* Written?" *American Literature*, 30 [1958], 1–25). Since the use of violet ink in MSVI 139–62 occurred in 1879 and no other use of this ink has been discovered after 1880, the working notes written in the same ink must have been made before the latter date and not, as Ganzel contends, on the basis of Mark Twain's reading of travel books in connection with the composition of *Life on the Mississippi*, in 1882. Although Ganzel's argument rests on the possibility of the use of violet ink after 1880, his supporting evidence seems convincing in itself. However, the correlation that he establishes between the travel books, the additional chapters of *Life on the Mississippi*, and events in Mark Twain's life after the trip on the one hand, and the working notes in Group A for *Huckleberry Finn* on the other, in itself does not constitute prima facie evidence. It is quite obvious that Mark Twain read some of the travel memoirs already before he wrote chapters 17–18 of the novel in 1879–80, perhaps even specifically for its composition. Walter Blair states that "Clemens may have read [Alexander Mackay, *Western World* (London, 1850)] before the [1882] trip, for it recounts the lynching of some gamblers in Natchez" (*Mark Twain & Huck Finn*, p. 411, n. 29). In Notebook 20 he wrote: "Natchez . . . (Hanging the gamblers)" (*Notebooks & Journals II*, p. 457). Although most of the travel memoirs found in Mark Twain's library at the time of his death do not contain the dates of their acquisition and can be assumed to have come into his possession in July 1882 (see below, chapter 4, section 2), he had owned a copy of the first volume of Harriet Martineau's *Retrospect of Western Travel* since 1875 and was given the second volume of the work (in a different binding) by his brother-in-law, Theodore Crane, as a Christmas present in 1877. (The volumes are listed as No. 319 in the Anderson Auction Catalogue of 1911, p. 49. The first volume has Mark Twain's autograph [S. L. Clemens] and the date 1875, the second volume contains the autograph notation "T. W. Crane to SLClemens Xmas 77".) The correlation Ganzel sees between the travel books and Group A of the working notes for *Huckleberry Finn* is therefore the result of a reading prior to 1882 of Harriet Martineau's *Retrospect of Western Travel*, probably also of Alexander Mackay's *Western World*, and certainly of other undetermined travel memoirs to which Mark Twain returned in 1882 for the composition of *Life on the Mississippi*. The even handwriting of the working notes for which the author used violet ink, furthermore, indicates that they are not notes that were taken while the author was actually reading. A correlation of Group A with "events in Twain's life after his trip" ("Twain, Travel Books, and *Life on the Mississippi*," pp. 49–50) as seen in a notation about the punishment of a deaf child on page 11 of the notes certainly does not exist. His daughter Jean need not yet have had scarlet fever (which she actually had that summer) to make the author think of this disease as explanation for a

five-year-old girl's suddenly becoming deaf. Since the same incident is given in an entry in Notebook 20—"Some rhymes about the little child whose mother boxed its ears for inattention & presently when it did not notice the heavy slamming of a door, perceived that it was deaf" (*Notebooks & Journals II*, p. 510)—it has apparently been assumed to constitute one of the many entries made during the trip. But it is evident from a preceding one that it was made after September 20 and not, therefore, in New Orleans. The inaccurate form of the entry and its corrections on page 11 of the working notes, furthermore, indicate that its writing antedates that of the notebook entry and that the working notes for the novel helped to complement the working notes for the standard work. Not only the completed chapters of *Huckleberry Finn*, but also the working notes presumably kept with the manuscript thus became a "source" for *Life on the Mississippi*.

8. See, for instance, Franklin R. Rogers, "Introduction," *Mark Twain's Satires & Burlesques*, ed. Franklin R. Rogers (Berkeley, 1967), pp. 1–16.

9. Studies devoted to the question of narrative technique include the following: Walter Blair, *Mark Twain & Huck Finn*; Bernard DeVoto, *Mark Twain at Work*; Kenneth S. Lynn, *Mark Twain and Southwestern Humor* (Boston, 1959); Franklin R. Rogers, *Mark Twain's Burlesque Patterns As Seen in the Novels and Narratives 1855–1885* (Dallas, 1960); Henry Nash Smith, *Mark Twain: The Development of a Writer*; Albert E. Stone, Jr., *The Innocent Eye: Childhood in Mark Twain's Imagination* (New Haven, 1961); Leo Marx, "The Pilot and the Passenger: Landscape Conventions and the Style of *Huckleberry Finn*," *American Literature*, 28 (1956), 129–46; and Horst H. Kruse, "Annie and Huck: A Note on *The Adventures of Huckleberry Finn*," *American Literature*, 39 (1967), 207–14.

10. See Horst Kruse, "Die literaturkritischen Urteile in Mark Twains *Life on the Mississippi*: Ihre Kriterien und ihre Funktion," parts 1 and 2, *Die Neueren Sprachen*, Heft 7, 1966: 297–309, and Heft 8, 1966: 355–63.

11. *Notebooks & Journals II*, p. 256.

12. LOM, p. 263. His notebook of the period identifies the date as November 19, 1878, and the widow as a "Frau Kratz" who lived at 45 Nymphen[burger]strasse (*Notebooks & Journals II*, p. 282).

13. *Harper's New Monthly Magazine*, 14, 80 (January 1857), 232–41. Regarding the availability of the journal, see below, chapter 4, n. 194.

14. "My Own Funeral," p. 236. For Mark Twain's description of this expedient see LOM, pp. 263–64.

15. This presupposes the dating of the first stage of the manuscript as given above. He has Ritter say, "It is believed that in all these eighteen years that have elapsed since the institution of the corpse-watch, no shrouded occupant of the Bavarian deadhouses has ever rung its bell" (LOM, p. 278). On the basis of the notebook entry of January 4, 1879, however, an earlier date seems unlikely.

16. See Frank Baldanza, *Mark Twain: An Introduction and Interpretation* (New York, 1961), p. 96; Douglas G. Browne and Alan Brock, *Fingerprints: Fifty Years of Scientific Crime Detection* (London, 1953), pp. 33–34; Anne P. Wigger, "A Study of *Pudd'nhead Wilson and Those Extraordinary Twins*" (MS, MTP, p. 37). The earliest discussion of fingerprints, according to the latter, occurs in Henry Faulds, "On the Skin-furrows of the Hand" (*Nature: A Weekly Illustrated Journal of Science*, 22 [October 28, 1880], 605). The method described by Faulds suggests that it was actually this article which induced Mark Twain to use the fingerprint

142

material in *Life on the Mississippi*. This early interest in the matter seems to have occasioned his reading of Francis Galton's book *Finger Prints* immediately upon its publication in 1892, which then led to a rediscovery of this method of identification for the composition of *Pudd'nhead Wilson* (see Anne P. Wigger, "The Source of the Fingerprint Material in Mark Twain's *Pudd'nhead Wilson and Those Extraordinary Twins*," *American Literature*, 28 [1957], 517–20). The idea to use thumb-prints for an illustration in the first edition of *Life on the Mississippi* (p. 346) apparently came to Mark Twain as an afterthought. An added page, MSII 345 1/2, contains a pencil notation in the author's hand, "Fac-similes of some Thumb-prints to be slung in here" (†). It may well have been suggested by an article on "Thomas Bewick" in the September number of the *Century Magazine* for 1882, which also contained William Dean Howells's essay on Mark Twain. The article shows an illustration of "Bewick's Thumb-Mark" (Austin Dobson, "Thomas Bewick," 24 [n.s. 2], 5 [September 1882], 665).

17. LOM, pp. 268, 270–71.
18. LOM, p. 266; MSII [11] 339. This dating of events is essential to the logic of the story and therefore must have existed in the early versions.
19. LOM, p. 273; MSII [33] 361.
20. See SLC to George Washington Cable, Hartford, July 17, 1881 (Cardwell, *Twins of Genius*, p. 81).
21. LOM, p. 265; MSII [9] 337.
22. *Mark Twain: Man and Legend*, p. 214.
23. *Notebooks & Journals II*, p. 462. The relation of this entry to both an experience of the author in Munich in 1878 and *Life on the Mississippi* is also demonstrated in a marginal comment in his copy of Lady Emmeline Stuart Wortley's *Travels in the United States, Etc., During 1849 and 1850* (New York, 1851) which, along with similar works, he procured and read in the course of the composition of his book (see below, chapter 4, section 2): "Claiming a corpse, for the jewels & money.— the Todt-Gallerie Munich" (p. 127; Yale Collection of American Literature, Morse Collection, Beinecke Library, Yale University [†]).
24. MSII [68] 397.
25. MSII 209.
26. MSII 117. Mr. Dad Dunham was to become "Uncle Mumford" in the printed version. This change does not appear in the manuscript.
27. LOM, p. 5.
28. See below, chapter 4, section 5.
29. MSII [55] 384.
30. LOM, p. 284.
31. *Notebooks & Journals II*, p. 458. Datable early April 1882.
32. See, in particular, Notebooks 13, 14, 15, and 16 as well as the editorial comments on Mark Twain's procedure, *Notebooks & Journals II*, pp. 9, 44, 114, 155.
33. *Notebooks & Journals II*, pp. 465, 466, 524, 536–37.
34. *Mark Twain's Letters*, 1: 417–18.
35. *Mark Twain-Howells Letters*, 1: 401.
36. *Notebooks & Journals II*, p. 527.
37. See SLC to OLC, Saturday Afternoon, 1/2 way to Memphis [April 22, 1882] (*The Love Letters of Mark Twain*, p. 208).
38. See *Mark Twain: A Biography*, 2: 739, 740; Arlin Turner, "Notes on Mark Twain

in New Orleans," *McNeese Review*, 6 (1954), 10–22; *The Love Letters of Mark Twain*, pp. 211–12; and Blair, *Mark Twain & Huck Finn*, p. 287.

39. See *Notebooks & Journals II*, pp. 536, 526–27.

40. *Notebooks & Journals II*, p. 467. Angle brackets indicate cancellations made by the author.

41. Ibid., p. 540.

42. LOM, pp. 207, 201.

43. LOM, pp. 201, 207.

44. *Mark Twain: A Biography*, 2: 736, 737.

45. MSII 69 (†).

46. LOM, pp. 186, 190, 210.

47. Blair, *Mark Twain & Huck Finn*, p. 292.

48. The process of transference can be followed in Notebook 20. The entry "The bear that Bill Hood & I released from his chain 'for fun' & he took possession of the boat" (*Notebooks & Journals II*, p. 455) becomes "Dad Dunham & the pet bear" (*Notebooks & Journals II*, p. 474). The idea to "Get up a rambling yarn about a fellow who went into battle with a Testament in front & 6 decks of cards behind" (*Notebooks & Journals II*, p. 492) is recorded in ink, the name "Dunham" is later added in pencil. The episode followed chapter 34 of the book and was deleted from the final version (see LOM, HP, p. 396).

49. Osgood's list of suggested omissions and revisions dated October 29, 1882, contains the following: "Condense the 'Dying Man's Confession'. Some unpleasant details in it, and story too long for the climax." Mark Twain's pencil notation reads "Retained" (Theater Collection, Rogers Memorial Room, Houghton Library, Harvard University [†]).

50. LOM, pp. 187–88; *Notebooks & Journals II*, pp. 521, 522.

51. LOM, p. 496.

52. MSII 89A–E; MSII 93A–D; cf. LOM, pp. 192–95. See below, chapter 4, section 4.

53. Mark Twain's own documentation indicates Charles Augustus Murray (*Travels in North America, 1834–36*, 2 vols. [New York, 1839]) as a source for the first addition, Captain Marryat (*A Diary in America, With Remarks on Its Institutions* [New York, 1839] and *Second Series of a Diary in America* [Philadelphia, 1840]) for the footnote; the second addition may well have been suggested by his reading in these and other travel accounts.

54. SLC to WDH, Hartford, January 28, 1882 (*Mark Twain-Howells Letters*, 1: 386–89).

55. Lem Gray was later emended to "Robert Styles" and then "Rob Styles" on MSII 117 and MSII 118, obviously because Lem Gray died on August 23, 1882, from wounds received in a boiler explosion aboard the *Gold Dust*. The new name, clearly fictitious, implies an adequate characterization of the captain who is assuming various roles.

56. LOM, pp. 201, 207.

57. See *Notebooks & Journals II*, pp. 441, 442–43, 444.

58. *Notebooks & Journals II*, p. 486.

59. Cf. DeVoto, *Mark Twain at Work*, pp. 66, 68.

60. MSII 122–23; LOM, HP, p. 389.

61. See *Notebooks & Journals II*, pp. 382, 462, 476.

IV.   A Summer's Work

1. SLC to Frank Fuller, Hartford, July 5th, 1882, MTP (†).
2. SLC to Jane Clemens [Hartford, July 1882], MTP (†).
3. JRO to SLC [Boston] July 6, 1882, MTP.
4. MSII 144.
5. *Notebooks & Journals II*, p. 482.
6. The Anderson Auction Catalogue of his library lists as item 376, Francis Parkman, *The Conspiracy of Pontiac*, 2 vols.; *The Oregon Trail; Frontenac and New France under Louis XIV*, 4 vols., Boston, 1880. The autograph "SLClemens" is in two of the volumes and the item is described as containing "numerous marked paragraphs and marginal notes" (Anderson Auction Catalogue, 1911, p. 56, MTP). In 1885 he acquired, probably as a birthday present, Parkman's *Montcalm and Wolfe*, 2 vols. (Boston, 1885). These copies, which are now in the Mark Twain Memorial Library in Hartford, bear the autograph "Saml L. Clemens, Hartford, Conn. Nov. 30th 1885." Late in the 1890s, when recalling the Oliver Wendell Holmes Breakfast of December 1879, he remembered a blunder "with a man I worshipped—Francis Parkman" (NB 42, TS, p. 50, MTP; quoted in *Mark Twain-Howells Letters*, 1: 284).
7. See *Notebooks & Journals II*, pp. 359, 404, 405, 411, 472, 482.
8. See *Mark Twain's Notebooks & Journals, Volume III (1883–1891)*, ed. Robert Pack Browning, Michael B. Frank, and Lin Salamo (Berkeley, 1979), p. 98.
9. Chapter 1 (LOM, p. 8) contains an incomplete cross reference to chapter 44 (LOM, p. 361).
10. LOM, p. 6.
11. JRO to SLC [Boston] Sep. 22, 1882, MTP.
12. Pages [1]–22 became MSII 495–518.
13. *Mark Twain & Huck Finn*, pp. 289, 291.
14. Of the items not taken from the Grangerford parlor but used in "The House Beautiful" in *Life on the Mississippi* the following are mentioned in Cook's book: the "new and deadly invention" of the coal furnace (p. 111), the bric-a-brac and souvenirs of family travels, a shell, quartz specimens, and Indian arrowheads (pp. 101, 123).
15. LOM, p. 316.
16. See "Introduction," *Life on the Mississippi*, p. xii.
17. *Notebooks & Journals II*, p. 548.
18. The case can still be made, however, in view of similar remarks about a Grand Tower packet plying between St. Louis and St. Genevieve (LOM, pp. 196–97). These remarks are also based on actual observation and refer to the *Fannie Tatum* (see *Notebooks & Journals II*, p. 548).
19. Item 123, AAA Gallery, sale no. 4228, January 29/30, 1936. I have not been able to determine the present location of the document. The above quotation is taken from the auction catalogue (†).
20. See *Notebooks & Journals II*, pp. 484–86, 498.
21. LOM, pp. 2, 261, 327, 342, and LOM, HP, p. 414.
22. LOM, pp. 224, 368–70, 497–506.
23. See *Notebooks & Journals II*, p. 458.
24. WR to SLC [Boston] July 22, 1882, MTP.
25. The first of these was to have followed chapter 29, the other two, chapter 40. They

comprise MSII 261–87 and MSII 559–612 and are printed in the Heritage Press edition, pp. 391–95, 402–7, 407–11.

26. "Twain, Travel Books, and *Life on the Mississippi*," pp. 41–42.

27. *Mark Twain & Huck Finn*, pp. 289–90.

28. Ralph Keeler and A. R. Waud (illustrator), "New Orleans," "On the Mississippi," "St. Louis," in *Every Saturday: An Illustrated Weekly Journal*, 2d ser. 3, nos. 79–102 (July 1–December 9, 1871).

29. James R. Osgood & Co. (W. Rowlands) to SLC, Boston. Sept. 16. 1882, MTP.

30. See JRO to SLC, Boston, July 31, 1882, MTP.

31. Cf. Walter Francis Frear, *Mark Twain and Hawaii* (Chicago, 1947), pp. 9, 23, 55–57, and Ferguson, *Mark Twain: Man and Legend*, pp. 107–8.

32. See chapter 3, n. 7.

33. "Twain, Travel Books, and *Life on the Mississippi*," pp. 46–48.

34. Cf. LOM, HP, p. 402.

35. "Twain, Travel Books, and *Life on the Mississippi*," p. 42.

36. LOM, HP, p. 402.

37. LOM, p. 249.

38. As far as Hesse-Wartegg's *Mississippi-Fahrten* is concerned, however, it seems as if Osgood himself may have joined the search for materials and brought the book home from his European travels that summer.

39. Robert Underwood Johnson to SLC, New York, August 9, August 16, August 29, 1882, MTP. See below, section 3.

40. LOM, HP, p. 411.

41. LOM, HP, p. 407; MSII [29] 588.

42. It was Osgood who, in his list of suggestions of October 29, 1882, proposed that Mark Twain "condense or re-write" the two chapters.

43. See also Brodwin, "The Useful and the Useless River," who feels that these passages give the book "a more dynamic sociological and literary scope" (p. 208, n. 14).

44. *Mark Twain & Huck Finn*, p. 290.

45. See William Dean Howells, *My Mark Twain* (New York, 1910), p. 49.

46. LOM, p. 334.

47. MSII 713 (†).

48. See below, section 6.

49. MSIII 32 (†).

50. Departing from his usual procedure, Mark Twain did not have either his wife Olivia or other "editors" review the manuscript before it was sent to Osgood. Mrs. Clemens did her obligatory reading of the book only after the galley proofs had arrived in Hartford. See below, chapter 5, section 6.

51. "Mark Twain: Audience and Artistry," *American Quarterly*, 15 (1963), 25–40.

52. RUJ to SLC, New York, August 9, 1882, MTP.

53. "Mark Twain," *Century Magazine*, 24 (n. s. 2), 5 (September 1882), 783.

54. *Mark Twain-Howells Letters*, 1: 405.

55. *Mark Twain: A Biography*, 2: 732; see also *Mark Twain-Howells Letters*, 1: 404, n. 3.

56. See, for instance, Paul J. Carter, Jr.,"The Influence of William Dean Howells upon Mark Twain's Social Satire," *University of Colorado Studies, Series in Language and Literature*, no. 4 (1953), pp. 93–100.

57. Commercial considerations of this kind are also stressed by Willis Wager: "The chapter on current political and civic conditions in the South [47 A] would have

particularly offended Southern subscribers . . . " (LOM, HP, p. 387). The interest Mark Twain took in the sales of his books is evident in his correspondence with Osgood after the publication of *Life on the Mississippi* (see below, chapter 6). See also Samuel Charles Webster, *Mark Twain: Business Man* (Boston, 1946), and Hamlin Hill, "Mark Twain: Audience and Artistry." Guy A. Cardwell, on the other hand, sees no evidence that Osgood and Clemens actually ever discussed the problem of selling the book in the South ("Mark Twain, James R. Osgood, and Those 'Suppressed' Passages," *New England Quarterly*, 46 [1973], 163–88).

58. LOM, pp. 192–93, 193 n.
59. LOM, HP, p. 411.
60. See Ganzel, "Twain, Travel Books, and *Life on the Mississippi*, " p. 42, and Blair, *Mark Twain & Huck Finn*, pp. 289–90.
61. MSII 251A–H; LOM, pp. 243–47. MSII 251E–H are pp. 89–92 of Captain Frederick Marryat, *Second Series of a Diary in America*.
62. MSII 247A–B; LOM, p. 241.
63. MSII 247–247A; LOM, p. 240.
64. LOM, p. 240. By implication Mark Twain further praised this writer when in an added footnote in chapter 33 (MSII 412 verso; LOM, p. 289) he quoted from Edward Atkinson's "Significant Aspects of the Atlanta Cotton Exposition" in *Century Magazine*, 23 (n. s. 1), 4 (February 1882), 563–74.
65. MSII 256A–B; LOM, p. 250.
66. *Mark Twain & Huck Finn*, p. 289.
67. *Notebooks & Journals II*, pp. 456, 457, 567–68, 563–67.
68. MSII 465–MSII [28] 490. According to Walter Blair, the evidence of paper and ink suggests that the chapter is one of many unused portions of *A Tramp Abroad* (*Mark Twain & Huck Finn*, p. 289, n. 7).
69. MSII 464 (†).
70. LOM, p. 304.
71. *North American Review*, 135, 310 (September 1882), 266–82.
72. *Notebooks & Journals II*, p. 502. Though the entry could have been occasioned by the fate of "poor Moore," the reference to a relation between earth-burial and plague clearly reflects Cobb's mention of Cooper's statement that the "malignity of the cholera, which scourged London in the year 1854, was enhanced by the excavations made for sewers in the soil where in 1665 those dying from the plague were buried," and another mention of an instance of the outbreak of the plague caused by excavations in ground where, three hundred years previously, the victims of pestilence had been buried ("Earth Burial and Cremation," p. 271). The article also states that it is possible to cremate a body "at a cost of less than a dollar for fuel" (p. 279). Further proof for the source of the notebook entry is provided by another entry immediately following that quoted above: "Parallel Fijian slavery with political assessment slavery" (*Notebooks & Journals II*, p. 502), which reflects his reading of Dorman B. Eaton's article "Political Assessments" in the same number of the *North American Review* (pp. 197–219).
73. LOM, pp. 347–48.
74. "I'm for cremation. It would shock people to burn an abandoned sinner whom they believed was going straight to eternal cremation" (*Notebooks & Journals II*, p. 300).
75. "Earth Burial and Cremation," p. 272.

76. SLC to AET, New Orleans, June 1, 1857, MTP (†); printed in Minnie M. Brashear, *Mark Train: Son of Missouri* (Chapel Hill, 1934), p. 178.
77. LOM, pp. 77–80, 344, 345, 347, 353.
78. LOM, pp. 346–47.
79. LOM, p. 347; "Earth Burial and Cremation," p. 280.
80. LOM, p. 347; MSII 640.
81. MSII 640–42; see LOM, HP, p. 412.
82. Willis Wager, "A Note on These Suppressed Passages," LOM, HP, p. 387.
83. LOM, p. 345.
84. MSII 634–35, MSII 636 (†).
85. MSII 636 (†). Angle brackets indicate cancellations in the manuscript.
86. "Earth Burial and Cremation," pp. 267, 268.
87. LOM, p. 345.
88. MSII 633 (†).
89. "Earth Burial and Cremation," p. 269.
90. *Century Magazine,* 24 (n. s. 2), 1 (May 1882), 1–16.
91. Ibid., p. 6.
92. "Earth Burial and Cremation," p. 266.
93. Ibid., p. 277. Italics mine.
94. See below, section 6, for an account of the development of Mark Twain's attack on Sir Walter Scott.
95. LOM, p. 348. It is very likely that materials used in chapter 43 stem, like the Ritter story, the Professor's Yarn and the account of Lem Hackett's drowning, from unused portions of *A Tramp Abroad* or are based on notes originally made for it. Mark Twain had obviously intended to include a chapter devoted to "funeral yarns." Notes for it occur in Notebook 17 (*Notebooks & Journals II,* pp. 256, 267, 277) and in Notebook 18 (*Notebooks & Journals II,* pp. 343, 345). But it is well known that the subject had long interested him. Notebook 14 contains, among other items listed for future literary use, the notation "About Undertakers" (*Notebooks & Journals II,* p. 50).
96. *The Education of Henry Adams* (New York, 1931), p. 234.
97. "Murder by Burial," *Century Magazine,* 24 (n. s. 2), 6 (October 1882), 943.
98. It is quite possible that he did read the column, for it appeared in the same number of the *Century Magazine* which also contained the last installment of William Dean Howells's *A Modern Instance,* commented upon in his letter of October 3, 1882 (*Mark Twain-Howells Letters,* 1: 417). For another possible influence of this number of the *Century Magazine* on *Life on the Mississippi* see chapter 3, n. 16.
99. Autograph note, JRO to SLC, Oct 29. 1882, Theater Collection, Rogers Memorial Room, Harvard University.
100. Ibid., autograph note by Mark Twain on Osgood's letter to him (†).
101. The influence of Howells's *Century* article on Mark Twain's critical attitude in *Life on the Mississippi* was probably reinforced by two reviews of his recent works by another of his favorite writers. On September 12, 1882, Joel Chandler Harris sent his review of *The Stolen White Elephant,* which stresses the serious purpose behind the book. In an accompanying letter he explains, "Did Osgood send you the notice of 'The Prince and the Pauper'? That notice expressed my ideas more fully, and I think, by George! that Mr. Howells had it framed in

front of him when he wrote the Century sketch" (JCH to SLC, Atlanta, Ga., 12 September, 1882, MTP).

102. Howells first made this comparison in his review of *A Connecticut Yankee* in the *Atlantic Monthly* in 1890. See also *My Mark Twain*, pp. 146–47.

103. LOM, pp. 377–78.

104. *A Connecticut Yankee in King Arthur's Court*, p. 397.

105. See Smith, *Mark Twain: The Development of a Writer*, p. 167.

106. LOM, pp. 333, 375.

107. LOM, p. 376.

108. *Notebooks & Journals II*, pp. 546, 484.

109. See New Orleans *Times-Democrat*, August 26, 1882, p. 35.

110. *Notebooks & Journals II*, pp. 489–90.

111. Ibid., p. 553.

112. Working notes for the novel and fourteen pages of "Middle Age phrases for a historical story" indicate that he drew on Scott's works for phrases, descriptions, and incidents. These notes, which were probably made about 1879, are preserved as DV 114 and DV 115, MTP.

113. See SLC to William Dean Howells, Elmira, August 22, 1874 (*Mark Twain–Howells Letters*, 1: 21). About a year earlier, during his stay in Edinburgh, Mark Twain had purchased the twelve-volume Abbotsford Edition of *The Waverley Novels*. See Alan Gribben, *Mark Twain's Library: A Reconstruction*, 2 vols. (Boston, 1980), 2: 618, as well as pp. 612–18, for an annotated list of books by Scott that Mark Twain read or owned.

114. SLC to BM, New York City, May 4, 1903, and May 8, 1903 (*Mark Twain's Letters*, 2: 737–38).

115. The copy which bears the autograph "Clara L. Clemens, Sept. '82 Elmira" is now in the Mark Twain Library at West Redding, Connecticut.

116. LOM, pp. 317, 318.

117. *North American Review*, 135, 308 (July 1882), 95–96, 98.

118. See Blair, *Mark Twain & Huck Finn*, pp. 205–7, 227–30.

119. Paine, *Mark Twain: A Biography*, 1: 521.

120. See *Mark Twain in Hartford*, ed. Henry Darbee (Hartford, Conn., 1958), pp. [20–21].

121. SLC to KG, Hartford, February 24, 1882, MTP (†). See also SLC to Charles Warren Stoddard, Hartford, October 26, 1881 (*Mark Twain's Letters*, 1: 404).

122. LOM, p. 408.

123. *North American Review*, 135, 310 (September 1882), 243–52.

124. "Architecture in America," pp. 245, 243, 248–49, 245–46.

125. LOM, p. 350. The addition occurs on the verso of MSII 656. The author's personal notebook contains an entry, "House with all the modern inconveniences," which seems to have been made after September 20, but before he left Elmira (*Notebooks & Journals II*, p. 505).

126. *Notebooks & Journals II*, p. 485: "In the south is little or no architecture, but New England is full of it. The town hall in Belmont is finer & more beautiful & more pure & elegant art than anything in south, perhaps."

127. LOM, p. 462.

128. "Mark Twain's Images of Hannibal," *Texas Studies in English*, 37 (1958), 14.

129. "Architecture in America," pp. 250–51.

130. MSII 277–78; LOM, HP, p. 394.

131. LOM, pp. 322, 317.
132. In thanking Howells for a complimentary copy he wrote on March 18, 1872: "We bought it & read it some time ago, but we prize this copy most on account of the autograph" (*Mark Twain-Howells Letters*, 1: 10).
133. The list is to be found in Notebook 19 and was apparently made in July 1880 (see *Notebooks & Journals II*, pp. 361–66). Notebooks 19 and 20 (July 1880 to February 1883) contain a number of references to the proposed anthology, and it was only immediately before his Mississippi journey that he reminded himself, "Put away the Library of Humor books" (*Notebooks & Journals II*, p. 464).
134. *Their Wedding Journey* (Boston, 1871), p. 283.
135. LOM, p. 386.
136. *Their Wedding Journey*, p. 284.
137. Published in Fred W. Lorch, "Mark Twain in Iowa," *Iowa Journal of History and Politics*, 27 (1929), 411, 412.
138. *Contributions to "The Galaxy,"* pp. 59–60.
139. *Notebooks & Journals II*, p. 553.
140. MSII 720, 722.
141. The addition occurs on the verso of MSII 717. Baker's assistance in procuring materials for *Life on the Mississippi* is discussed in section 7 below.
142. SLC to William Dean Howells, Elmira, August 22, 1887 (*Mark Twain-Howells Letters*, 2: 595).
143. *Mark Twain: A Biography*, 3: 1537.
144. See n. 142.
145. This edition is listed in the Anderson Auction Catalogue of 1911, item no. 65, MTP. A comment on Carlyle's *History of Frederick the Great* occurs in Notebook 20. A reference to the fourth volume, p. 252—"Nothing left of you [i.e. Belleisle] but this sad faculty of sowing chaff in the fashionable manner!"—occurs shortly thereafter (*Notebooks & Journals II*, p. 503). These entries were made between the second half of August and September 20, 1882.
146. See Olin H. Moore, "Mark Twain and Don Quixote," *PMLA*, 37 (1922), 324–46.
147. LOM, p. 377.
148. *Notebooks & Journals II*, p. 359.
149. *Domestic Manners of the Americans*, chapter 23; quoted in *Mark Twain & Huck Finn*, p. 411, n. 23.
150. *La Salle and the Discovery of the Great West* (Boston, 1879), p. 83. Another description during the same phase of composition also echoes Parkman's sentence. In chapter 44 Mark Twain contrasts "the venerable Cathedral" and "the pretty square in front of it": "the one dim with religious light, the other brilliant with the worldly sort . . . " (LOM, p. 356). For a similar contrast see the concluding chapter 34 of Parkman's *The Jesuits in North America*; see below, chapter 5, n. 92.
151. LOM, pp. 374–75.
152. *A Tramp Abroad*, 1, *The Writings of Mark Twain*, Definitive Edition (New York, 1923), 9: 242.
153. "The French Revolution and *Huckleberry Finn*," *Modern Philology*, 4 (1957), 21–35, and *Mark Twain & Huck Finn*, pp. 176–81.
154. See Blair, *Mark Twain & Huck Finn*, pp. 179–80.
155. "The Coming Revolution in England," *North American Review*, 135, 311 (October 1882), 304.

156. LOM, p. 376; MSII 733H.
157. LOM, p. 376; MSII 733 I, MSII 733 J.
158. *Mark Twain & Huck Finn*, p. 292.
159. "The Course of Composition of *A Connecticut Yankee*: A Reinterpretation," p. 202.
160. After the completion of *A Tramp Abroad* Mark Twain had written to William Dean Howells on January 8, 1880: "Next time I make a contract before writing the book, may I suffer the righteous penalty & be burned, like the injudicious believer" (*Mark Twain-Howells Letters*, 1: 287).
161. Evidences of this ability are to be found throughout his writings. Mark Twain's success in assimilating materials has probably prevented a recognition of the full extent of the author's "borrowings." As the use of notes collected for his attack on Whitelaw Reid already indicates, evidences of the use of random materials in *Life on the Mississippi* are not confined to the chapters devoted to the attack on the South. In one of the two deleted chapters in which Mark Twain portrays the America of the past seen by the foreign tourist he further documents the prevalence of "rum-tippling" by inserting a footnote based on his reading of the *Autobiography of Lyman Beecher, D.D.* (MSII 581A; LOM, HP, p. 406. The reference is to *Autobiography, Correspondence, Etc., of Lyman Beecher*, ed. Charles Beecher, 2 vols. [New York, 1864], 1: 245). The context shows that the footnote was planned at the time of the composition, but was inserted only after the chapter had been incorporated in the manuscript. The reading of Lyman Beecher's autobiography therefore preceded the composition of these two chapters, and it is highly probable that Beecher's famous stand against dueling is reflected in Mark Twain's own attack on the custom in the second of the deleted chapters. Both authors (Mark Twain now for the first time) use the same argument, the suffering of the widow and the orphans of the duelist, and Mark Twain echoes Beecher's statement that "with the exception of a small section of the Union, the whole land is defiled with blood. From the lakes of the North to the plains of Georgia is heard the voice of lamentation and woe—the cries of the widow and fatherless" (p. 155), by remarking that "this imbecile custom, this ridiculous custom, this cruel and brutal custom, (since the heartbroken widow and orphans do the real suffering necessary to heal the hurt honor of the victor; whereas him they have never offended, and do not deserve such bitterness and misery at his hands,) has wholly departed from the North . . . " (MSII [45] 604; LOM, HP, p. 410). If, as is quite possible, the reading of Lyman Beecher's autobiography preceded the composition of chapter 27 of *Huckleberry Finn*, there may be another reason for the presence of a copy of Henry Clay's speeches (in direct verbal juxtaposition to "Dr. Gunn's Family Medicine, which told you all about what to do if a body was sick or dead") in Mark Twain's description of the Grangerford parlor. Not only was it "standard equipment in that period for a house in Kentucky, whose adored spokesman Clay was" (Blair, *Mark Twain & Huck Finn*, p. 229), its author is also mentioned in a footnote to the account of Beecher's sermon against dueling: "That sermon has never ceased to be a power in the politics of this country. More than anything else, it made the name of brave old Andrew Jackson distasteful to the moral and religious feeling of the people. It hung like a millstone on the neck of Henry Clay" (p. 154).
162. "The French Revolution and *Huckleberry Finn*," pp. 28, 35.

163. See "Interviews with Samuel L. Clemens," pp. 2–3, items 15 and 18, p. 39, as well as *Notebooks & Journals II*, p. 512, n. 265.

164. JHC to SLC, St. Louis, August 23, 1882, MTP.

165. MSIII 61–71 were inserted between MSIII 60 and MSIII [61] 78.

166. MSIII [66] 83, LOM, p. 406. The comparison made between present and past ("We made Natchez [three hundred miles] in twenty-two hours and a half— much the swiftest passage I have ever made over that piece of water") is still more obvious in some notations from his reading directly reflected here. On the margin of a chapter entitled "Mississippi Voyage" in volume 2 of his copy of Harriet Martineau's *Retrospect of Western Travel* (New York, 1838) he wrote, "Think of this weary slow travel!—Two days out, to Natchez—we went there in 22 1/2 hours" (pp. 9, 15 [†]).

167. The last paragraph, for instance, reads, "Up to the present time, a term of thirty-five years, we ascertain, by reference to the diary, he has made four hundred and sixty round trips to New Orleans, which gives a distance of one million one hundred and four thousand miles, or an average of eighty-six miles a day" (LOM, p. 400).

168. See Ivan Benson, *Mark Twain's Western Years* (Stanford, 1938), p. 82.

169. The matter from the *Missouri Republican* of September 6, 1860, provided by John H. Carter and inserted in chapter 50 of *Life on the Mississippi* has been discussed in another context relating to Mark Twain. Allan Bates has discovered that Sam Clemens followed his famous Sergeant Fathom letter of May 17, 1859, with another burlesque of contemporary river reports which he published in the *Missouri Republican* on August 30, 1860. He points out that this item with its renewed if less obvious attack on the venerable Captain Sellers may have occasioned the very article on the latter's career which appeared in the same paper exactly one week later on September 6, 1860. Bates remarks, "Current newspapers reveal nothing timely about this laudatory article; it may well have been intended to soothe tempers which had been ruffled by the *Republican's* publication a few days earlier of Sam Clemens's burlesque" ("Sam Clemens, Pilot-Humorist of a Tramp Steamboat," *American Literature*, 39 [1967], 108–9). If this is so, then this is perhaps the very reason why Mark Twain remembered the article and thought of it when he began to gather and to order materials for incorporation in his standard work. The young Sam Clemens, recollecting the reaction to his Sergeant Fathom letter of fifteen months earlier and perhaps expecting the kind of response which the New Orleans *Daily Delta* actually showed by calling it "by far the best thing we have read since the days of the Sergeant Fathom letter, in a pilot's report, emanating from Sam. Clemens, of the Arago" (New Orleans *Daily Delta*, September 2, 1860; reprinted by Bates, p. 105), must have scanned the pages of the *Republican* for some time to come and thus have encountered the impressive record of Sellers's life as a Mississippi pilot. Considering the nature of that article and the fact that Sellers's diary must indeed have been available to the person who wrote it—possibly a newspaper friend who rallied to his defense—it is understandable that it should later have been mistaken for an obituary notice.

170. SLC to JRO [Elmira] July 19/82, Yale Collection of American Literature, Morse Collection, Beinecke Library, Yale University (†); a version appears in *Mark Twain's Letters to His Publishers*, p. 157.

171. See also Ernest E. Leisy, "Mark Twain and Isaiah Sellers," *American Literature*,

13 (1943), 398–405, and Guy A. Cardwell's summary of more recent findings in "Samuel Clemens' Magical Pseudonym," *New England Quarterly*, 48 (1975), 175–93. I am drawing on facts presented in both articles, but I interpret them differently.

172. An account of the meeting with Stevenson, which was said to have been "quite affecting," is to be found in the New Orleans *Times-Democrat* of May 3, 1882 (see Parsons, "Down the Mighty River with Mark Twain," p. 8). Stevenson is also likely to have been one of the "old-time pilots" who accompanied Mark Twain on his tours aboard the tugboat *W. M. Wood* between May 2 and May 4, although by then he actually was a commission merchant and wholesale cotton dealer (see *Notebooks & Journals I*, p. 58). The fact that he should have preserved and been able to provide the material in question may be explained by the supposition that in 1859 he was among those who were shown Mark Twain's "performance" and who "eagerly rushed it into print" (LOM, p. 402).

173. *Notebooks & Journals II*, pp. 555, 469 (angle brackets indicate cancellations made by the author).

174. SLC to James R. Osgood [Elmira] July 19/82, Yale Collection of American Literature, Morse Collection, Beinecke Library, Yale University (†); a version appears in *Mark Twain's Letters to His Publishers*, p. 157.

175. MSIII 72 verso.

176. LOM, p. 401.

177. See Cardwell, "Samuel Clemens' Magical Pseudonym," p. 180.

178. Leisy, "Mark Twain and Isaiah Sellers," p. 399.

179. Paul Fatout, "Mark Twain's Nom de Plume," *American Literature*, 34 (1962), 5.

180. "Samuel Clemens' Magical Pseudonym," p. 188.

181. The clipping from the *Daily Crescent*, which in turn was used by Albert Bigelow Paine as copy for his reprint of the burlesque article in Appendix B of his biography, does not identify the source, and Paine, following Mark Twain's assertion (in *Life on the Mississippi*) as to the newspaper and his own reasoning about the date, erroneously gives it as "*True Delta* (New Orleans), May 8 or 9 [1859]" (*Mark Twain: A Biography*, 3: 1675).

182. LOM, p. 402.

183. See, for instance, Leisy, "Mark Twain and Isaiah Sellers," p. 402, and Cardwell, "Samuel Clemens' Magical Pseudonym," p. 186.

184. I am grateful to Everett Emerson for an exact transcription on the basis of the holograph in the Pierpont Morgan Library.

185. These are printed in Benson, *Mark Twain's Western Years*, pp. 81–82.

186. In *Life on the Mississippi* "four" is given as a number and the faulty definitive article before Big Black Island is deleted.

187. "Samuel Clemens' Magical Pseudonym," p. 185.

188. *Mark Twain's Western Years*, p. 81.

189. This direct association of the writing of his own burlesque piece with the *True Delta* perhaps explains why in *Life on the Mississippi* the author mistakenly names that paper as the place of its publication.

190. *Mark Twain: A Biography*, 3: 1593, n. 1.

191. PMB to SLC, New Orleans, Sept 26th 1882, MTP.

192. *Notebooks & Journals II*, p. 458.

193. Ibid., pp. 469, 555.

194. These are taken from J. S. C. Abbot, "Heroic Deeds of Heroic Men—IV—Siege

and Capture of Port Hudson," *Harper's New Monthly Magazine*, 30, 178 (March 1865), 425–39, and "X—Charles Ellet and His Naval Steam Rams," *Harper's New Monthly Magazine*, 32, 189 (February 1866), 295–312, and are incorporated as MSII 483, MSII 486, MSII 545 1/2 D and the original and subsequently deleted Appendix A. Mark Twain explicitly instructed his typist to copy Appendix A (page 302 of "Charles Ellet and His Naval Steam Rams") as well as Appendix B and C, presumably to disguise his borrowings (see above, chapter 1, n. 7). The puzzling fact that he should have been able to borrow extensively from this particular magazine during the Elmira period of composition is explained by an entry in Notebook 13 made between July 15 and July 31, 1877: "2nd hand bookstore—get full Harper Monthly for Sue, & some miscellaneous books" (*Notebooks & Journals II*, p. 38). Sue, here, refers to Mark Twain's sister-in-law, Mrs. Theodore Crane, of Quarry Farm, Elmira.

195. *Notebooks & Journals II*, pp. 563–67.
196. *Mark Twain's Letters*, 1: 423.
197. SLC to John Garth, Hartford, July 3, 1882 (Ibid.).
198. SLC to Jane Clemens [Hartford, July 1882], MTP.
199. SLC to Frank Fuller, Hartford, July 5th. 1882, MTP (†).
200. James R. Osgood to SLC [Boston] July 6, 1882, MTP.
201. Invoice, de Graff to SLC, September 5, 1882, MTP.
202. OLC to SEM, Elmira, Aug. 13th 1882, Moffett Collection, MTP.
203. SLC to JRO, Elmira, Sept. 18, 1882, copy in MTP (†); a version appears in *Mark Twain's Letters to His Publishers*, pp. 157, 158.
204. SLC to Joseph H. Twichell, Elmira, September 19, 1882, copy in MTP (†).
205. SLC to Jane Clemens, Hartford Conn. Oct. 9th. 1882 (typewritten), Moffett Collection, MTP (†).
206. JRO to SLC [Boston] September 22, 1882, MTP.
207. JRO to SLC [Boston] October 14, 1882, MTP.
208. SLC to WDH, "HARTFORD CONN. OCT. 3D, 1882" (*Mark Twain-Howells Letters*, 1: 417).
209. See SLC to WDH, Hartford, November 4, 1882 (Ibid., pp. 418–20).
210. *Mark Twain at Work*, p. 58.

V. "Trying to Build the Last Quarter of the Book"

1. SLC to GWC, New York [September 29, 1882] (Cardwell, *Twins of Genius*, p. 84).
2. SLC to GWC, Hartford, October 16, 1882 (Ibid., p. 86).
3. GWC to SLC, New Orleans, November 7, 1882 (Ibid., p. 87).
4. SLC to GWC, Hartford, November 11, 1882 (Ibid., p. 88).
5. "Insert the 4 pages 772 AB&c—reduce them in fac simile & crowd them onto a single page of my book, to be read by a magnifier."
6. See SLC to HMC, Hartford, Dec. 2/82, MTP.
7. SLC to GWC, Hartford, January 15, 1883 (Cardwell, *Twins of Genius*, p. 89).
8. SLC to WDH, HARTFORD, CONN. OCT. 3D, 1882 (*Mark Twain-Howells Letters*, 1: 417 [orthography of the original retained]).
9. Ibid., p. 414.
10. WDH to SLC, Boston, March 22, 1882 (Ibid., p. 395).
11. SLC to WDH, Hartford, March 27, 1882 (Ibid., p. 398).

12. *Mark Twain: Man and Legend*, p. 211. See also Paine, *Mark Twain's Letters*, 1: 423.
13. James R. Osgood to SLC, Boston, Apl. 1. 1882, MTP. See also *Mark Twain-Howells Letters*, 1: 398–99, n. 3.
14. *Notebooks & Journals II*, p. 464.
15. SLC to JCH, Elmira, September 5, 1882, copy in MTP.
16. See n. 21.
17. Howells's letter of September 1 must have been followed by an unrecorded reply from Mark Twain, presumably written about the middle of September, telling him that he will "kill Clark" and also informing him that he suffers from malaria. This explains why Howells, writing from Switzerland on October 17, suggested that Mark Twain join him in Florence for the winter, from where he "could go home with some of the old Etruscan malaria in your bones, instead of the wretched pinch-beck Hartford article that you are suffering from now. . . . If you come, you need not kill Clarke; you could bring his material with you." Meanwhile Mark Twain had followed up his reply by announcing that he had returned to Hartford, but that he had not been able to see Clark. Since he did not have Howells's current address, he sent the letter to London, but is plainly afraid that it might "wind up in the pe[r]dition of some European dead[-]letter office." It did not reach Howells in Switzerland until after October 17. The beginning of Mark Twain's letter of November 4 is in reply to Howells's suggestion that Mark Twain spend the winter in Europe, but he then proceeds to record the developments concerning the composition of his book: "at last I have said with sufficient positiveness that I will finish the book at no particular date; that I will not hurry it; that I will not hurry myself; that I will take things easy and comfortably, write when I choose to write, leave it alone when I so prefer" (*Mark Twain-Howells Letters*, 1: 418). These statements clearly reflect decisions which had been reached already by October 14. The concluding report of Cable's visit in Hartford and a "midnight dinner in Boston the other night, where we gathered around the board of the Summerset Club," finally, would clearly refute all statements made in the preceding letter if it was actually written on October 30.
18. This portion of the manuscript consists of six individually paginated parts (MSIII–MSVIII) of different lengths and also shows several inserts and rearrangements.
19. SLC to William Dean Howells, Hartford, November 4, 1882 (*Mark Twain-Howells Letters*, 1: 418).
20. The sources used in these two chapters are discussed in sections 3, 4, and 5.
21. SLC to EHH, "HARTFORD, CONN. DEC. 2D. 1882" [typewritten], Barrett Collection (†); photostat copy in MTP.
22. SLC to WDH, Hartford, November 4, 1882 (*Mark Twain-Howells Letters*, 1: 418).
23. SLC to OC, Hartford, Nov. 18, 1882 [typewritten], MTP (†).
24. LOM, pp. 383, 384.
25. "Sugar is made & plowed & planted in this way: (Go on with a confused & absurd statement, & wind up with wishing I had taken notes. Editing Agricultural paper style)" (*Notebooks & Journals II*, p. 481. See also p. 479). The reference is to "How I Edited an Agricultural Paper," written about 1870 and included in *Sketches New and Old, The Writings of Mark Twain*, Definitive Edition (New York, 1922), 7: 280–87.
26. LOM, p. 384.

27. See *Notebooks & Journals II*, p. 556.

28. Ibid., pp. 555–56.

29. LOM, pp. 385–86.

30. In the manuscript Mark Twain used capital letters where indicated. Here and in other places these were occasionally lost because the typescript was made on a typewriter with upper case types only.

31. See above, pp. 55–56.

32. MSIII 15 (†).

33. LOM, p. 142.

34. LOM, p. 386.

35. LOM, p. 386.

36. "In the course of the tugboat gossip, it came out that . . ." (p. 391); "But I did not learn that . . ." (p. 391); "The tugboat gossip informed me . . ." (p. 395); "I was told . . ." (p. 396); "We had some talk about Captain Isaiah Sellers . . ." (p. 398).

37. LOM, p. 404.

38. The entries elaborated in chapter 49 occur in Notebook 20, *Notebooks & Journals II*, pp. 446, 447, 472, 475, and 476, and in Notebook 21, *Notebooks & Journals II*, pp. 531–32 and 533–34.

39. Ibid., p. 474.

40. LOM, pp. 395–96.

41. LOM, p. 386.

42. *Notebooks & Journals II*, p. 310.

43. As Willis Wager has already pointed out, the Morgan manuscript shows an intermediate stage in the presentation of this episode; "the spirit was supposed to be that of [Mark Twain's] brother Henry. . . . Then Mark Twain changed the identity of the supposed spirit to a more distant relative of his. And, in the printed book, it appears as that of the uncle of a friend of Twain's" ("A Note on These Suppressed Passages," LOM, HP, p. 387).

44. *Notebooks & Journals II*, p. 306.

45. The Anderson Auction Catalogue of 1911 lists as item no. 246, D[aniel] D[unglas] Home, *Incidents in My Life* (New York, 1863).

46. See Dixon Wecter, *Sam Clemens of Hannibal* (Boston, 1952), p. 90, and Brashear, *Mark Twain: Son of Missouri*, pp. 131, 133.

47. Wecter, *Sam Clemens of Hannibal*, p. 90.

48. Hannibal *Tri-Weekly Messenger*, December 23, 1852; quoted in Wecter, *Sam Clemens of Hannibal*, p. 90.

49. MSIII 27, 28 (†).

50. LOM, pp. 382, 408–9.

51. Autograph notation by Mark Twain in Martineau, *Retrospect of Western Travel*, 2: 9, 15, MTP (†).

52. LOM, p. 413.

53. LOM, p. 397.

54. *Notebooks & Journals II*, p. 508.

55. The two supporting letters—the first addressed to the Reverend Joseph H. Twichell, the second to the philanthropist and temperance advocate Page—have survived in the Morgan manuscript, while the copy of the original letter was returned to Twichell.

56. After the chapter had been set up in print Osgood apparently returned the copy of the first letter to Twichell and also sent a proof of the chapter. The latter

156

replied: "I return herewith the proof submitted me. I do not find anything in it to correct in particular, since I gave Mr. Clemens leave to tell the story. I'm a little dubious as to the propriety of its being told, but that is none of your affair, and anyway there's no help now for it, I suppose" (quoted in Ticknor, *Glimpses of Authors*, p. 138).

57. MSIV 1A–2A (†).

58. LOM, pp. 427, 442, 450–51, 451.

59. *"The American Claimant" and Other Stories and Sketches, The Writings of Mark Twain*, Definitive Edition (New York, 1923), 15: 326. The story was first published in the *Century Magazine*, 23 (n. s. 1), 1 (November 1881), 35–46.

60. Baldanza, *Mark Twain: An Introduction and Interpretation*, p. 49.

61. *Nook Farm: Mark Twain's Hartford Circle* (Cambridge, Mass., 1950), p. 209.

62. LOM, pp. 461, 466.

63. *Notebooks & Journals II*, p. 469.

64. LOM, p. 462.

65. At one point in the course of the composition of *A Connecticut Yankee* Mark Twain himself specifically used the term "a *contrast* [of civilizations]" (SLC to Mary Mason Fairbanks, November 16, 1886, *Mark Twain to Mrs. Fairbanks*, p. 257).

66. See below, section 5.

67. John Disturnell, comp., *Sailing on the Great Lakes and Rivers of America* (Philadelphia, 1874).

68. *La Salle and the Discovery of the Great West*, pp. 270–71, 270.

69. *Notebooks & Journals II*, p. 479. Angle brackets indicate cancellations made by the author.

70. LOM, p. 473.

71. LOM, p. 474.

72. *Notebooks & Journals II*, p. 480.

73. *Mark Twain as a Literary Artist* (Norman, Okla., 1950), p. 278.

74. *La Salle and the Discovery of the Great West*, p. 267, n. 1.

75. LOM, p. 492.

76. LOM, p. 470.

77. LOM, p. 480. I have not been able to verify DeLancey Ferguson's identification of the booklet as having been "put out by a railroad company" (*Mark Twain: Man and Legend*, p. 211).

78. LOM, pp. 477, 480.

79. By the author of "Three Weeks in Cuba" [Benson J. Lossing], *Harper's New Monthly Magazine*, 7, 38 (July 1853), 177–90.

80. *La Salle and the Discovery of the Great West*, p. 271, n. 1.

81. LOM, p. 482.

82. LOM, p. 483. The reference is to Henry Rowe Schoolcraft, *Algic Researches, Comprising Inquiries Respecting the Mental Characteristics of the North American Indians; First Series; Indian Tales and Legends*, 2 vols. (New York, 1839).

83. The latter, taken from the first volume of *Algic Researches*, pp. 84–86, is used in chapter 59; the former, from *Algic Researches*, pp. 96–121, forms Appendix D of *Life on the Mississippi*.

84. Cf. Ticknor, " 'Mark Twain's' Missing Chapter," pp. 299–300, and *Glimpses of Authors*, pp. 141–44.

85. LOM, p. 526.

86. LOM, HP, p. 403; MSII 9A.

87. *Notebooks & Journals II*, p. 349.

88. LOM, HP, p. 403, n.; MSII 9B. See also Mark Twain's autograph notation "American neglect of word 'woman' " in his copy of *Society in America* in the Mark Twain Library, Hartford, and a nine-page manuscript attacking archaic definitions of the terms "lady" and "gentleman" in recently published dictionaries (DV 311, MTP, dated 1878–79 by A. B. Paine).

89. LOM, pp. 483–84, 493.

90. The two pages are inserted as clippings on MSVIII 140 and 141. The clipping identifies the story as stemming "from the facile pen of T. M. Newson, author of Indian Legends."

91. See *The Jesuits in North America*, chapter 34. Mark Twain's own copy of the book contains a number of pencil markings and underlinings for this chapter (MTP).

92. LOM, p. 490.

93. SLC to Edward H. House, "HARTFORD, CONN. DEC. 2D. 1882", Barrett Collection (†); photostat copy in MTP.

94. When advising Osgood on December 29 that he had sent the "eighth batch," Mark Twain also asked his publisher to telephone Fairchild "& say I am going to write & thank him for his invitation as soon as I get over the exhaustion of this ten days' revising & correcting" (SLC to JRO [Hartford] Friday [December 29, 1882], Pierpont Morgan Library (†); a version appears in *Mark Twain's Letters to His Publishers*, p. 160).

95. For a discussion of the question of "suppression" see Cardwell, "Mark Twain, James R. Osgood, and Those 'Suppressed' Passages," pp. 176–78.

96. *Mark Twain-Howells Letters*, 1: 418.

97. See, for instance, SLC to James R. Osgood, Hartford Dec 21. [1883] (*Mark Twain's Letters to His Publishers*, pp. 164–65, and n. 3).

98. James R. Osgood & Co. to SLC, Boston, January 3, 1883 (*Mark Twain: Business Man*, ed. Samuel Charles Webster [Boston, 1946], p. 207).

99. See Paine, *Mark Twain: A Biography*, 2: 741.

100. *Mark Twain: Business Man*, p. 207.

101. See above, n. 94.

102. SLC to James R. Osgood & Co., Hartford Jan 6/83 (published in Lease, "Mark Twain and the Publication of *Life on the Mississippi*," pp. 248–50).

103. Ibid.

104. " 'Mark Twain's' Missing Chapter," p. 301. See also Ticknor, *Glimpses of Authors*, pp. 132–51.

105. See Merle Johnson, *A Bibliography of the Works of Mark Twain*, rev. ed. (New York, 1935), p. 42.

106. "Introduction," LOM, HP, p. xiv.

107. LOM, p. 353.

108. LOM, 1st ed., pp. 356, 301, 363. See Ticknor, " 'Mark Twain's' Missing Chapter," p. 302, and *Glimpses of Authors*, pp. 137–38.

109. Arthur L. Scott, "Mark Twain Revises *Old Times on the Mississippi*, 1875–1883," *Journal of English and Germanic Philology*, 54 (1955), 635.

110. See the excerpt from an undated letter written after Mark Twain had begun to read the proofs, published in Ticknor, " 'Mark Twain's' Missing Chapter," pp. 304–5.

111. LOM, p. 41; Scott, "Mark Twain Revises *Old Times on the Mississippi*," p. 635.

112. LOM, p. 32; Scott, "Mark Twain Revises *Old Times on the Mississippi*," pp. 636, 638.
113. SLC to JRO [Hartford] January 15 [1883], Yale Collection of American Literature, Morse Collection, Beinecke Library, Yale University (†); a version appears in *Mark Twain's Letters to His Publishers*, p. 162.
114. LOM, pp. 336, 334.
115. *American Notes for General Circulation*, *The Works of Charles Dickens*, National Edition (London, 1907), 12: 276.
116. Cf. *Mark Twain & Huck Finn*, p. 294.
117. LOM, HP, pp. 412–16.
118. SLC to JRO [Hartford] January 15 [1883] (*Mark Twain's Letters to His Publishers*, p. 162).
119. See above, note 7.
120. As the epigraph did not become part of the Morgan manuscript, it is unlikely that it was chosen earlier, in response, for instance, to Osgood's letter of September 22, 1882, asking for "your preface, or such introductory or explanatory matter as you choose to prefix" (JRO to SLC [Boston] Sep. 22, 1882, MTP). Osgood certainly had in mind some prefatory matter written by Mark Twain himself.
121. *Harper's New Monthly Magazine*, 26, 153 (February 1863), 413–18.
122. "Introduction," LOM, HP, p. ix.
123. See Henry Nash Smith, *Virgin Land: The American West as Symbol and Myth* (New York, 1957), pp. 185–89.
124. *The Collected Works of Abraham Lincoln*, ed. Roy P. Basler, 8 vols. (New Brunswick, 1953), 5:528–29.
125. Smith, *Virgin Land*, p. 187.
126. See JRO to SLC, Boston, Apr. 12, 1883, MTP.

VI. Publication

1. "Editor's Literary Record," *Harper's New Monthly Magazine*, 67, 401 (October 1883), 799.
2. Quoting from the "Invitation to Learning" radio program J. Donald Adams wrote in 1957: "The broadcast began with the undebatable statement that 'Life on the Mississippi' is 'one of the greatest eyewitness accounts' in our literature, 'a vivid, first-hand report on a vanished way of life.' It should rank, certainly, on any sensible list of the ten best American books. Together with 'Huckleberry Finn,' it remains one of the high-water marks of Twain's achievement" ("Speaking of Books," *New York Times Book Review*, April 7, 1957, p. 2). A recent thumbnail sketch of "The Mississippi River in History" by Thomas D. Clark (*Mississippi Quarterly: A Journal of Southern Culture*, 16 [1963], 181–90) shows that even the historian still presents the same materials and still places the same emphases that we find in *Life on the Mississippi*, an eloquent testimony of the success of Mark Twain's ambition to produce the standard work.
3. See SLC to William Dean Howells, Hartford, November 4, 1882 (*Mark Twain-Howells Letters*, 1: 418).
4. Autograph note to Charles L. Webster; see above, chapter 5, section 6.

5. See James D. Hart, *The Popular Book: A History of American Literary Taste* (Berkeley, 1950), p. 149.
6. JRO to SLC, Boston, December 8, 1883, MTP.
7. SLC to JRO, Hartford Dec 21. [1883], Theater Collection, Rogers Memorial Room, Houghton Library, Harvard University (†); a version appears in *Mark Twain's Letters to His Publishers*, p. 165. The number of the copies sold by subscription, however, is not a true measure of the popularity of a specific book. "The big sale," Mark Twain told Osgood on April 17, 1883, "is always before issue—after issue, the agents immediately load up the bookstores & canvassing ceases. . . . *The orders that come in after the issue* of a subscription book don't amount *to a damn*—just write that up amongst your moral maxims; for it is truer than nearly anything in the Bible" (Theater Collection, Rogers Memorial Room, Houghton Library, Harvard University [†]; a version appears in *Mark Twain's Letters to His Publishers*, pp. 162–63). But it was its sale during the decade following publication that made *Life on the Mississippi* one of the bestsellers of 1883. See Hart, *The Popular Book*, p. 309.
8. *Standard Publications of Charles L. Webster & Co.* [1888], p. 4, Documents and Clippings File (Items Relating to General Grant), MTP.
9. Winnipeg, Canada, *Tribune*, July 27, 1895; quoted in Fred W. Lorch, "Mark Twain's 'Morals' Lecture," pp. 57–58.
10. *Notebooks & Journals III*, p. 91.
11. "Mark Twain: A Self-Emasculated Hero," *Emerson Society Quarterly*, 23 (1977), 181.

VII. Conclusion

1. Leo Marx, "The Pilot and the Passenger: Landscape Conventions and the Style of *Huckleberry Finn*," *American Literature*, 28 (1956), 136, 139.
2. "Mark Twain and the Limits of Criticism," *Forays and Rebuttals* (Boston, 1936), p. 377; quoted in Walter Blair, "The French Revolution and *Huckleberry Finn*," p. 21.
3. This disconcerting statement would have continued to go unnoticed if it were not for James M. Cox, who persuades me that evidence such as this of Mark Twain's humor in *Life on the Mississippi* stands in need of further investigation.

Appendix

T A B L E   A
Chronological Survey of the Phases of Composition

1.	Chapters 4–17 ("Old Times on the Mississippi")	Hartford, 1874–1875
2.	Chapter 3 (Chapter 16 of the manuscript of *Adventures of Huckleberry Finn*)	Elmira, 1876
3.	Chapters 31 (first version), 34A, 36, 54 (probably all original *A Tramp Abroad* material; order of composition unknown)	1878–1879
4.	Chapter 31 (second version)	1881
5.	Chapter 31 (third version)	Hartford, March to May 1882
6.	Chapters 18–21, 32, 31 (fourth version)	Hartford, May to
7.	Chapters 22–25 (first half)	June 20, 1882
8.	Chapters 25 (second half), 38	Elmira, July 1882
9.	Chapters 40A–40B	Elmira, beginning
10.	Chapter 29A	of August 1882
11.	Chapters 26–44, 50; chapters 45–47 perhaps begun; incorporation of chapters 31, 32, 34A, 36, 38; chapters 1–2; incorporation of chapter 3	Elmira, middle of August to end of September 1882
12.	Chapters 45–47 completed	Hartford, beginning of October 1882
13.	Chapter 47A	Hartford, beginning of November 1882
14.	Chapters 48–49, 51–60 (order of composition unknown); incorporation of chapter 50 (after the writing of part of chapter 51); incorporation of chapter 54	Hartford, November to ca. December 19, 1882
15.	Revisions and corrections, elimination of chapters 29A, 34A, 40A, 40B; epigraph (?)	Hartford, ca. December 19 to ca. December 29, 1882
16.	Proofreading, elimination of chapter 47A; addition of material in footnote to chapter 40 (LOM, pp. 334–36); epigraph (?)	Hartford, beginning of January to January 15, 1883

TABLE B
Phases of Composition
(Numbers in parentheses refer to the phases of composition given in Table A)

Chapter		Chapter	
Epigraph	(15, 16)	34	(11)
1	(11)	34A	(3)
2		35	
3	(2)	36	(3)
4		37	
5		38	(8)
6		39	
7		40	
8		40A	(9)
9		40B	
10	(1)	41	
11		42	
12		43	(11)
13		44	
14		45	
15		46	(12)
16		47	
17		47A	(13)
18		48	(14)
19	(6)	49	
20		50	(11)
21		51	(14)
22		52	
23	(7)	53	
24		54	(3)
25	(8)	55	
26		56	
27	(11)	57	(14)
28		58	
29A	(10)	59	
30		60	
31	(3) (4) (5) (6)		
32	(6)		
33			

Table C
Source Materials for the Composition of
Life on the Mississippi Discussed in this Study

1. Abbot, John Stephens Cabot. "Heroic Deeds of Heroic Men—IV—Siege and Capture of Port Hudson." *Harper's New Monthly Magazine,* 30,178 (March 1865), 425–39.

2. ———. "Heroic Deeds of Heroic Men—X—Charles Ellet and His Naval Steam Rams." *Harper's New Monthly Magazine,* 32, 189 (February 1866), 295–312.

3. Atkinson, Edward. "Significant Aspects of the Atlanta Cotton Exposition." *Century Magazine,* 23 (n. s. 1), 4 (February 1882), 563–74.

4. ———. "Views of Mr. Atkinson on the Levee Question." New Orleans *Times-Democrat,* April 28, 1882.

5. Beecher, Lyman. *Autobiography, Correspondence, Etc., of Lyman Beecher, D.D.* Edited by Charles Beecher. 2 vols. New York, 1864.

6. Beers, W. George. "The Canadian Mecca." *Century Magazine,* 24 (n. s. 2), 1 (May 1882), 1–16.

7. Bird, Robert Montgomery. *Nick of the Woods, or: The Jibbenainosay: A Tale of Kentucky.* Philadelphia, 1837.

8. Carlyle, Thomas. *History of the French Revolution.* London, n.d. [ca. 1865].

9. Cervantes, Miguel. *Don Quixote.*

10. Cobb, Augustus G. "Earth Burial and Cremation." *North American Review,* 135, 310 (September 1882), 266–82.

11. Cobbett, William. *A Year's Residence in the United States of America . . . in Three Parts.* London, 1816–17.

12. Coke, Edward Thomas. *A Subaltern's Furlough: Descriptive of Scenes in Various Parts of the United States, Upper and Lower Canada, New Brunswick, and Nova Scotia, During the Summer and Autumn of 1832.* 2 vols. New York, 1833.

13. Combe, George. *Notes on the United States of North America During a Phrenological Visit in 1838–9–40.* 3 vols. Edinburgh, 1841.

14. Cook, Clarence Chatham. "Architecture in America." *North American Review,* 135, 310 (September 1882), 243–52.

15. ———. *The House Beautiful: Essays on Beds and Tables, Stools and Candlesticks.* New York, 1877.

16. Crawford, Francis Marion. "False Taste in Art." *North American Review,* 135, 308 (July 1882), 89–98.

17. [Dallas, Jacob A.] "Up the Mississippi." *Emerson's Magazine and Putnam's Monthly,* 5, 40 (October 1857), 433–56.

18. Dickens, Charles. *American Notes for General Circulation.*

19. Disturnell, John, comp. *Sailing on the Great Lakes and Rivers of America. . . .* Philadelphia, 1874.

20. Dobson, Austin. "Thomas Bewick." *Century Magazine,* 24 (n. s. 2), 5 (September 1882), 643–66.

21. Eaton, Dorman B. "Political Assessments." *North American Review,* 135, 310 (September 1882), 197–219.

22. "Editor's Table." *Harper's New Monthly Magazine,* 26, 153 (February 1863), 413–18.

166

23. Faulds, Henry. "On the Skin-furrows of the Hand." *Nature: A Weekly Illustrated Journal of Science,* 22 (October 28, 1880), 605.

24. Fearon, Henry Bradshaw. *Sketches of America: A Narrative of a Journey of Five Thousand Miles Through the Eastern and Western States of America.* 3d ed. London, 1819.

25. Freeman, Edward Augustus. *A Visit to the United States.*

26. Hall, Basil. *Travels in North America, in the Years 1827 and 1828.* 3 vols. Edinburgh, 1829.

27. Hamilton, Thomas. *Man and Manners in America.* 2d ed. 2 vols. Philadelphia, 1833.

28. von Hesse-Wartegg, Ernst. *Mississippi-Fahrten: Reisebilder aus dem amerikanischen Süden (1879–1880).* Leipzig, 1881.

29. Howells, William Dean. *Their Wedding Journey.* Boston, 1871.

30. Hulme, Thomas. *A Year's Residence in the United States of America.* Part 3 of Cobbett, *A Year's Residence. . . .* London, 1816–17.

31. Hyndman, H. M. "The Coming Revolution in England." *North American Review,* 135, 311 (October 1882), 299–322.

32. Keeler, Ralph, and A. R. Waud. "New Orleans," "On the Mississippi," "St. Louis." *Every Saturday: An Illustrated Weekly Journal,* 2d ser. 3, nos. 79–102 (July 1–December 9, 1871).

33. [Lossing, Benson J.] "Sketches on the Upper Mississippi." *Harper's New Monthly Magazine,* 7, 38 (July 1853), 177–90.

34. Mackay, Alexander. *The Western World; or, Travels in the United States in 1846–47. . . .* 3 vols. London, 1849.

35. Marryat, Captain Frederick. *A Diary in America, With Remarks on Its Institutions.* New York, 1839.

36. ———. *Second Series of a Diary in America.* Philadelphia, 1840.

37. Martineau, Harriet. *Retrospect of Western Travel.* 2 vols. New York, 1838.

38. Murray, Charles Augustus. *Travels in North America During the Years 1834, 1835 & 1836. . . .* 2 vols. London, 1839.

39. Parkman, Francis. *The Jesuits in North America.* 15th ed. Boston, 1880.

40. ———. *La Salle and the Discovery of the Great West.* Boston, 1879.

41. Schoolcraft, Henry Rowe. *Algic Researches, Comprising Inquiries Respecting the Mental Characteristics of the North American Indians. First Series. Indian Tales and Legends.* 2 vols. New York, 1839.

42. Sturge, Joseph. *A Visit to the United States in 1841.* Boston, 1842.

43. *The Times-Democrat.* New Orleans. August 26, 1882. Decuple Sheet. Trade Edition of the Mississippi Valley: History—Description—Production—Commerce. Review of the Principal Cities with Business Notices and Advertisements.

44. de Tocqueville, Alexis. *Democracy in America.* 2 vols. Cambridge, Mass., 1862.

45. "Topics of the Time: Murder by Burial." *Century Magazine,* 24 (n. s. 2), 6 (October 1882), 942–43.

46. Trollope, Frances. *Domestic Manners of the Americans.* 2 vols. London, 1832.

47. Wortley, Lady Emmeline Stuart. *Travels in the United States, Etc., During 1849 and 1850.* New York, 1851.

Various Additional Sources

48. Cincinnati *Commercial*
49. *Commodore Rollingpin's Almanac*
50. *Harper's New Monthly Magazine*, March 1858 (for an illustration)
51. Louisville, Kentucky, *Evening Post*
52. [Mark Twain's "Sergeant Fathom Letter"], New Orleans *Daily Crescent*, May 17, 1859
53. *New Orleans Directory of 1882*
54. New Orleans *Times-Democrat*
55. A New York newspaper
56. St. Louis *Globe-Democrat*
57. St. Paul *Pioneer Press*
58. "Special River Correspondence: A Veteran Navigator . . . ," St. Louis *Missouri Republican*, September 6, 1860
59. "A Tourists' Guide which the St. Louis and St. Paul Packet Company are going to issue this summer . . . " (LOM, p. 480); incorporating (59a) T. M. Newson, "A Legend of White-Bear Lake"

60. Letter of Isaiah Sellers of May 4, 1859
61. Letter of Jack Hunt to Charles Williams, St. Louis, June 9, 1872 ("the Convict's Letter")
62. Letter of S. G. Buckingham to J. H. Twichell, Springfield, July 7, 1873
63. Letter of S. Lewis B. Speare to Page, Charlestown, July 11, 1873

Mark Twain Manuscripts

64. *Huckleberry Finn* manuscript
65. *A Tramp Abroad* material; material used in chapter 31 based on (65a) Anon., "My Own Funeral," *Harper's New Monthly Magazine*, 14, 80 (January 1857), 232–41

Table D
Survey of Source Materials Used in Individual Chapters of *Life on the Mississippi* (Numbers in parentheses refer to the list of source materials in Table C)

Chapter

Epigraph	(22)							
1	(40)	(54)	(35)	(36)				
2	(40)	(54)	(35)	(36)				
3	(64)							
16	(49)							
22	(38)	(35)	(36)					
25	(18)	(50)	(32)					
26	(64)							
27	(26)	(46)	(38)	(35)	(36)	(34)	(40)	
28	(48)	(4)						
29	(28)	(36)	(46)					
29A	(46)	(26)	(25)	(27)				
30	(54)							
31	(65; 65a)	(23)	(20)					
33	(3)	(54)						
34A	(65?)							
35	(1)	(2)	(54)					
36	(65)							
37	(55)							
38	(64)	(18)	(15)	(27)				
39	(54)	(46)	(4)					
40	(26)	(46)	(18)	(16)	(14)			
40A+B	(30)	(11)	(24)	(26)	(46)	(12)	(27)	(38)	(37)
	(44)	(35)	(36)	(13)	(42)	(18)	(34)	(47)	(21)
	(5)							
41	(43)	(14)	(16)	(10)				
42	(10)	(6)	(45)					
43	(14)	(10)						
44	(14)	(35)	(36)	(40)				
45	(54)							
46	(9)	(31)	(46)	(8)	(39)	(40)		
47A	(54)	(51)	(53)					
48	(29)	(17)						
50	(58)	(52)	(60)					
52	(61)	(62)	(63)					
53	(8?)	(18?)						
54	(65)							
55	(7)							
58	(54?)							
59	(59)	(33)	(40)	(19)	(41)			
60	(59a)	(40)	(19)	(33)	(57)			

Appendices

A	(54)	B	(4)	D	(41)
[A]	(2)	C	(46)		

Selected Bibliography

Unpublished Material

The Mark Twain Papers, The Bancroft Library, University of California, Berkeley.
The Pierpont Morgan Library, New York City.
Theater Collection, Rogers Memorial Room, Houghton Library, Harvard College, Cambridge, Massachusetts.
Berg Collection, New York Public Library, New York City.
Yale Collection of American Literature, Morse Collection, Beinecke Library, Yale University, New Haven, Connecticut.
Mark Twain Library and Memorial, Hartford, Connecticut.
Manuscript Division, Tulane University Library, New Orleans.
Mark Twain Memorial Library, Redding, Connecticut.
Mark Twain Museum, Hannibal, Missouri.
Mark Twain Memorial, Florida, Missouri.

Writings of Mark Twain

The Autobiography of Mark Twain. Edited by Charles Neider. New York: Washington Square Press, 1961.
Contributions to "The Galaxy," 1868–1871. Edited by Bruce R. McElderry. Gainesville, Fla.: Scholars' Facsimiles & Reprints, 1961.

"A Curious Experience." *Century Magazine,* 23 (n. s. 1), 1 (November 1881), 35–46.
Life on the Mississippi. Boston: James R. Osgood, 1883.
Life on the Mississippi. New York: Heritage Press, 1944.
Life on the Mississippi. New York: Harper & Brothers, 1950.
The Love Letters of Mark Twain. Edited by Dixon Wecter. New York: Harper & Brothers, 1949.
Mark Twain: Business Man. Edited by Samuel Charles Webster. Boston: Little, Brown, 1946.
Mark Twain in Eruption. Edited by Bernard DeVoto. New York: Harper & Brothers, 1940.
Mark Twain-Howells Letters: The Correspondence of Samuel L. Clemens and William D. Howells, 1872–1910. Edited by Henry Nash Smith and William M. Gibson with the assistance of Frederick Anderson. 2 vols. Cambridge, Mass.: Harvard University Press, 1960.
Mark Twain to Mrs. Fairbanks. Edited by Dixon Wecter. San Marino: Huntington Library, 1949.
Mark Twain to Uncle Remus 1881–1885. Edited by Thomas H. English. Atlanta: The Library, Emory University, 1953.
Mark Twain's Letters. Edited by Albert Bigelow Paine. 2 vols. New York: Harper & Brothers, 1917.
Mark Twain's Letters to His Publishers, 1867–1894. Edited by Hamlin Hill. Berkeley: University of California Press, 1967.
Mark Twain's Notebook. Edited by Albert Bigelow Paine. New York: Harper & Brothers, 1935.
Mark Twain's Notebooks & Journals, Volume I (1855–1873). Edited by Frederick Anderson, Michael B. Frank, and Kenneth M. Sanderson. Berkeley: University of California Press, 1975.
Mark Twain's Notebooks & Journals, Volume II (1877–1883). Edited by Frederick Anderson, Lin Salamo, and Bernard L. Stein. Berkeley: University of California Press, 1975.
Mark Twain's Notebooks & Journals, Volume III (1883–1891). Edited by Robert Pack Browning, Michael B. Frank, and Lin Salamo. Berkeley: University of California Press, 1979.
[Mark Twain's "Sergeant Fathom Letter"]. New Orleans *Daily Crescent,* May 17, 1859, p. 7. (Reprinted as Appendix B in A. B. Paine, *Mark Twain: A Biography,* 3: 1593–96).
Mark Twain's Travels with Mr. Brown. Edited by Franklin Walker and G. Ezra Dane. New York: Alfred A. Knopf, 1940.
Old Times on the Mississippi. Toronto: Belfast Brothers, 1876.
The Portable Mark Twain. Edited by Bernard DeVoto. New York: The Viking Press, 1946.
Traveling with the Innocents Abroad: Mark Twain's Original Reports from Europe and the Holy Land. Edited by Daniel Morley McKeithan. Norman: University of Oklahoma Press, 1958.
The Writings of Mark Twain. Author's National Edition. 25 vols. New York: Harper & Brothers, 1898–1900.
The Writings of Mark Twain. Definitive Edition. 37 vols. New York: Gabriel Wells, 1922–25.

Books and Articles

Abbot, John Stephens Cabot. "Heroic Deeds of Heroic Men—IV—Siege and Capture of Port Hudson." *Harper's New Monthly Magazine*, 30, 178 (March 1865), 425–39.

———. "Heroic Deeds of Heroic Men—X—Charles Ellet and His Naval Steam Rams." *Harper's New Monthly Magazine*, 32, 189 (February 1866), 295–312.

Adams, Henry. *The Education of Henry Adams*. New York: The Modern Library, 1931.

Adams, J. Donald. "Speaking of Books." *New York Times Book Review*, 62 (April 7, 1957), 2.

Anderson, Frederick, and Hamlin Hill. "How Samuel Clemens Became Mark Twain's Publisher: A Study of the James R. Osgood Contracts." *Proof*, 2 (1972), 117–43.

Anderson, Sherwood. *Dark Laughter*. New York: Boni & Liveright, 1925.

———. *Letters of Sherwood Anderson*. Edited by Howard Mumford Jones and Walter Rideout. Boston: Little, Brown, 1953.

Andrews, Kenneth R. *Nook Farm: Mark Twain's Hartford Circle*. Cambridge, Mass.: Harvard University Press, 1950.

Atkinson, Edward. "Significant Aspects of the Atlanta Cotton Exposition." *Century Magazine*, 23 (n. s. 1), 4 (February 1882), 563–74.

———. "Views of Mr. Edward Atkinson on the Levee Question." New Orleans *Times-Democrat*, April 28, 1882.

Baender, Paul, and Frederick Anderson. "Twain in Progress: Two Projects." *American Quarterly*, 16 (1964), 621–23.

Baetzhold, Howard G. "The Course of Composition of *A Connecticut Yankee*: A Reinterpretation." *American Literature*, 33 (1961), 195–214.

Baldanza, Frank. *Mark Twain: An Introduction and Interpretation*. New York: Barnes & Noble, 1961.

Bates, Allan. "Sam Clemens, Pilot-Humorist of a Tramp Steamboat." *American Literature*, 39 (1967), 102–9.

Beecher, Lyman. *Autobiography, Correspondence, Etc., of Lyman Beecher, D.D.* Edited by Charles Beecher. 2 vols. New York: Harper & Brothers, 1864.

Beers, W. George. "The Canadian Mecca." *Century Magazine*, 24 (n. s. 2), 1 (May 1882), 1–16.

Bellamy, Gladys Carmen. *Mark Twain as a Literary Artist*. Norman: University of Oklahoma Press, 1950.

Benson, Ivan. *Mark Twain's Western Years*. Stanford: Stanford University Press, 1938.

Bird, Robert Montgomery. *Nick of the Woods, or: The Jibbenainosay: A Tale of Kentucky*. Edited by Mark Van Doren. New York: Vanguard Press, 1928.

Blair, Walter. "The French Revolution and *Huckleberry Finn*." *Modern Philology*, 55 (1957), 21–35.

———. *Mark Twain & Huck Finn*. Berkeley: University of California Press, 1960.

———. "When Was *Huckleberry Finn* Written?" *American Literature*, 30 (1958), 1–25.

Branch, Edgar Marquess. "Introduction." *Early Tales & Sketches, Volume 1, 1851–1864*. Edited by Edgar Marquess Branch and Robert H. Hirst. *The Works of Mark Twain*, vol. 15. Berkeley: University of California Press, 1979.

Brashear, Minnie M. *Mark Twain: Son of Missouri*. Chapel Hill: University of North Carolina Press, 1934.

Brodwin, Stanley. "The Useful and the Useless River: *Life on the Mississippi* Revisited." *Studies in American Humor*, 2 (1976), 196–208.

Brooks, Van Wyck. *The Ordeal of Mark Twain*. Edited with an introduction by Malcolm Cowley. Cleveland: The World Publishing Company, 1955.

Browne, Douglas G., and Alan Brock. *Fingerprints: Fifty Years of Scientific Crime Detection*. London: George G. Harrap, 1953.

Brownell, George H. "A Question as to the Origin of the Name 'Mark Twain.' " *Twainian*, 1 (1942), 5.

Buchloh, Paul G. "Vom *Pilgrim's Progress* zum *Pilgrim's Regress*: Der Fortschrittsgedanke in der englischen und amerikanischen Literatur." In *Die Idee des Fortschritts*, edited by Erich Burck, pp. 153–87. Munich: Beck, 1963.

Budd, Louis J. *Mark Twain: Social Philosopher*. Bloomington: Indiana University Press, 1962.

———, ed. "A Listing of and Selection from Newspaper and Magazine Interviews with Samuel L. Clemens, 1874–1910." *American Literary Realism*, 10 (1977), 1–100.

Burde, Edgar J. "Mark Twain: The Writer as Pilot." *PMLA*, 93 (1978), 878–92.

Cardwell, Guy Adams. "The Bowdlerizing of Mark Twain." *Emerson Society Quarterly*, 21 (1975), 179–93.

———. "*Life on the Mississippi*: Vulgar Facts and Learned Errors." *Emerson Society Quarterly*, 19 (1973), 283–93.

———. "Mark Twain, James R. Osgood, and Those 'Suppressed' Passages." *New England Quarterly*, 46 (1973), 163–88.

———. "Samuel Clemens' Magical Pseudonym." *New England Quarterly*, 48 (1975), 175–93.

———. "A Self-Emasculated Hero." *Emerson Society Quarterly*, 23 (1977), 173–87.

———. *Twins of Genius*. East Lansing: Michigan State College Press, 1953.

Carlyle, Thomas. *History of Friedrich II. of Prussia Called Frederick the Great*. London: Chapman & Hall, n.d. [ca.1865].

———. *History of the French Revolution*. London: Chapman & Hall, n.d. [ca.1865].

Carter, Paul J., Jr. "The Influence of William Dean Howells upon Mark Twain's Social Satire." *University of Colorado Studies, Series in Language and Literature*, no. 4 (1953), pp. 93–100.

Clark, Harry Hayden. "Mark Twain." In *Eight American Authors: A Review of Research and Criticism*, edited by Floyd Stoval, pp. 319–63. New York: Norton, 1963.

Clark, Thomas D. "The Mississippi River in History." *Mississippi Quarterly: A Journal of Southern Culture*, 16 (1963), 181–90.

Cobb, Augustus G. "Earth Burial and Cremation." *North American Review*, 135, 310 (September 1882), 266–82.

Cook, Clarence Chatham. "Architecture in America." *North American Review*, 135, 310 (September 1882), 243–52.

———. "Beds and Tables, Stools and Candlesticks. . . . " *Scribner's Monthly*, 10, 2 (June 1875)–15, 1 (May 1877). [11 installments.]

———. *The House Beautiful: Essays on Beds and Tables, Stools and Candlesticks*. New York: Scribner's Sons, 1877.

Cox, James M. "Mark Twain: A Study in Nostalgia." Ph.D. dissertation, Indiana University, 1955.

Crawford, Francis Marion. "False Taste in Art." *North American Review,* 135, 308 (July 1882), 89–98.

[Dallas, Jacob A.] "Up the Mississippi." *Emerson's Magazine and Putnam's Monthly,* 5, 40 (October 1857), 433–56.

Darbee, Henry, ed. *Mark Twain in Hartford.* Hartford: The Mark Twain Library and Memorial Commission, 1958.

DeVoto, Bernard. *Forays and Rebuttals.* Boston: Little, Brown, 1936.

———. *Mark Twain at Work.* Cambridge, Mass.: Harvard University Press, 1942.

———. *Mark Twain's America.* Boston: Little, Brown, 1932.

Dickens, Charles. *American Notes for General Circulation. The Works of Charles Dickens.* National Edition. 40 vols. London: Chapman & Hall, 1906–8. Vol. 12, pp. 1–298.

Disturnell, John, comp. *Sailing on the Great Lakes and Rivers of America: Embracing a Description of Lakes Erie, Huron, Michigan & Superior, and Rivers St. Mary, St. Clair, Detroit, Niagara & St. Lawrence; Also, the Copper, Iron and Silver Region of Lake Superior, Commerce of the Lakes, &c. Together with Notices of the Rivers Mississippi, Missouri and Red River of the North; Cities, Villages and Objects of Interest. Forming Altogether a Complete Guide to the Upper Lakes, Upper Mississippi, Upper Missouri, &c. Also, Railroad and Steamboat Routes.* With Map and Embellishments. Philadelphia: J. Disturnell, 1874.

Dobson, Austin. "Thomas Bewick." *Century Magazine,* 24 (n. s. 2), 5 (September 1882), 643–66.

Doubleday, Neal Frank, ed. *Mark Twain's Picture of His America.* Boston: D.C. Heath, 1960.

Eastman, Mary H. *Dahcotah, or, Life and Legends of the Sioux Around Fort Snelling.* New York: Harper & Brothers, 1849.

Eaton, Dorman B. "Political Assessments." *North American Review,* 135, 310 (September 1882), 197–219.

"Editor's Literary Record." Anon. rev. of *Life on the Mississippi. Harper's New Monthly Magazine,* 67, 401 (October 1883), 799.

"Editor's Table." *Harper's New Monthly Magazine,* 26, 153 (February 1863), 413–18.

Fatout, Paul. "Mark Twain's Nom de Plume." *American Literature,* 34 (1962), 1–7.

Faulds, Henry. "On the Skin-furrows of the Hand." *Nature: A Weekly Illustrated Journal of Science,* 22 (October 28, 1880), 605.

Fearon, Henry Bradshaw. *Sketches of America: A Narrative of a Journey of Five Thousand Miles Through the Eastern and Western States of America.* 3d ed. London: Longman, Hurst, Rees, Orme and Brown, 1819.

Ferguson, DeLancey. *Mark Twain: Man and Legend.* Indianapolis: Bobbs-Merrill, 1943.

Forster, Edward Morgan. *Aspects of the Novel.* London: Arnold, 1927.

Frear, Walter Francis. *Mark Twain and Hawaii.* Chicago: The Lakeside Press, 1947.

French, Bryant Morey. *Mark Twain and "The Gilded Age."* Dallas: Southern Methodist University Press, 1965.

Ganzel, Dewey. *Mark Twain Abroad: The Cruise of the "Quaker City."* Chicago: University of Chicago Press, 1968.

———. "Samuel Clemens and Captain Marryat." *Anglia,* 80 (1962), 405–16.

———. "Twain, Travel Books, and *Life on the Mississippi.*" *American Literature,* 34 (1962), 40–55.

Gribben, Alan. *Mark Twain's Library: A Reconstruction*. 2 vols. Boston: G. K. Hall, 1980.

Guggisberg, Hans Rudolf. *Das europäische Mittelalter im amerikanischen Geschichtsdenken des 19. und des frühen 20. Jahrhunderts*. Basel: Helbing und Lichtenhahn, 1964.

Hart, James D. *The Popular Book: A History of American Literary Taste*. Berkeley: University of California Press, 1950.

von Hesse-Wartegg, Ernst. *Mississippi-Fahrten: Reisebilder aus dem amerikanischen Süden (1879–1880)*. Leipzig: C. Reissner, 1881.

Hill, Hamlin. *Mark Twain and Elisha Bliss*. Columbia: University of Missouri Press, 1964.

———. "Mark Twain: Audience and Artistry." *American Quarterly*, 15 (1963), 25–40.

Home, Daniel Dunglas. *Incidents in My Life*. New York: Carleton, 1863.

Howells, William Dean. "Mark Twain." *Century Magazine*, 24 (n. s. 2), 5 (September 1882), 780–83.

———. *My Mark Twain*. New York: Harper & Brothers, 1910.

———. *Their Wedding Journey*. Boston: James R. Osgood, 1871.

Hyndman, H. M. "The Coming Revolution in England." *North American Review*, 135, 311 (October 1882), 299–322.

Johnson, Merle. *A Bibliography of the Works of Mark Twain*. Rev. ed. New York: Harper & Brothers, 1935.

Kaplan, Justin. *Mr. Clemens and Mark Twain: A Biography*. New York: Simon and Schuster, 1966.

Keeler, Ralph, and A. R. Waud. "New Orleans," "On the Mississippi," "St. Louis." *Every Saturday: An Illustrated Weekly Journal*, 2d ser., 3, nos. 79–102 (July 1–December 9, 1872).

Kruse, Horst H. "Annie and Huck: A Note on *The Adventures of Huckleberry Finn*." *American Literature*, 39 (1967), 207–14.

———. "Die literaturkritischen Urteile in Mark Twains *Life on the Mississippi*: Ihre Kriterien und ihre Funktion." Teil 1 + 2. *Die Neueren Sprachen*, 65 (N.F. 15) (1966), 297–309; 355–63.

Lease, Benjamin. "Mark Twain and the Publication of *Life on the Mississippi*: An Unpublished Letter." *American Literature*, 26 (1954), 248–50.

Leisy, Ernest E. "Mark Twain and Isaiah Sellers." *American Literature*, 13 (1942), 398–405.

Lincoln, Abraham. *The Collected Works of Abraham Lincoln*. Edited by Roy P. Basler. 8 vols. New Brunswick: Rutgers University Press, 1953.

Long, Eugene Hudson. *Mark Twain Handbook*. New York: Hendricks House, 1957.

Lorch, Fred W. "Mark Twain in Iowa." *Iowa Journal of History and Politics*, 27 (1929), 408–56.

———. "Mark Twain's 'Morals' Lecture During the American Phase of His World Tour in 1895–1896." *American Literature*, 26 (1954), 52–66.

[Lossing, Benson J.] "Sketches on the Upper Mississippi." *Harper's New Monthly Magazine*, 7, 38 (July 1853), 177–90.

Lynn, Kenneth S. *Mark Twain and Southwestern Humor*. Boston: Little, Brown, 1959.

Mackay, Alexander. *The Western World; or, Travels in the United States in 1846–47. . . .* 3 vols. London: R. Bentley, 1849.

Marryat, Captain Frederick. *A Diary in America, With Remarks on Its Institutions*. New York: William H. Colyer, 1839.

————. *Second Series of a Diary in America*. Philadelphia, 1840.

Martineau, Harriet. *Retrospect of Western Travel*. 2 vols. New York: Harper & Brothers, 1838.

Marx, Leo. "The Pilot and the Passenger: Landscape Conventions and the Style of *Huckleberry Finn*." *American Literature*, 28 (1956), 129–46.

Mills, Barriss. "*Old Times on the Mississippi* as an Initiation Story." *College English*, 25 (1964), 283–89.

Moore, Olin H. "Mark Twain and *Don Quixote*." *PMLA*, 37 (1922), 324–46.

Murray, Charles Augustus. *Travels in North America During the Years 1834, 1835 & 1836, Including a Summer Residence with the Pawnee Tribe of Indians, in the Remote Prairies of the Missouri, and a Visit to Cuba and the Azore Islands*. 2 vols. London: R. Bentley, 1839.

"My Own Funeral." Anon. *Harper's New Monthly Magazine*, 14, 80 (January 1857), 232–41.

Paine, Albert Bigelow. *Mark Twain: A Biography*. 3 vols. New York: Harper & Brothers, 1912.

Parkman, Francis. *The Conspiracy of Pontiac*. 2 vols. Boston: Little, Brown, 1880.

————. *Count Frontenac and New France Under Louis XIV*. Boston: Little, Brown, 1880.

————. *The Jesuits in North America in the Seventeenth Century*. 15th ed. Boston: Little, Brown, 1879.

————. *La Salle and the Discovery of the Great West*. Boston: Little, Brown, 1879.

————. *The Oregon Trail*. Boston: Little, Brown, 1880.

Parsons, Coleman O. "Down the Mighty River with Mark Twain." *Mississippi Quarterly*, 22 (1969), 1–18.

Regan, Robert. " 'English Notes': A Book Mark Twain Abandoned." *Studies in American Humor*, 2 (1976), 157–70.

Rogers, Franklin R. "Introduction." *Mark Twain's Satires & Burlesques*. Berkeley: University of California Press, 1967.

————. *Mark Twain's Burlesque Patterns As Seen in the Novels and Narratives 1855–1885*. Dallas: Southern Methodist University Press, 1960.

Salomon, Roger B. *Twain and the Image of History*. New Haven: Yale University Press, 1961.

Schmidt, Paul. "River vs. Town: Mark Twain's *Old Times on the Mississippi*." *Nineteenth-Century Fiction*, 15 (1960), 95–111.

Schoolcraft, Henry Rowe. *Algic Researches, Comprising Inquiries Respecting the Mental Characteristics of the North American Indians. First Series. Indian Tales and Legends*. 2 vols. New York: Harper & Brothers, 1839.

Scott, Arthur L. "Mark Twain Revises *Old Times on the Mississippi*, 1875–1883." *Journal of English and Germanic Philology*, 54 (1955), 634–38.

Smith, Henry Nash. "Introduction." *Adventures of Huckleberry Finn*. Edited by Henry Nash Smith. Cambridge, Mass.: Riverside Press, 1958.

————. "Mark Twain as an Interpreter of the Far West: The Structure of *Roughing It*." In *The Frontier in Perspective*, edited by Walker D. Wyman and Clifton B. Kroeber, pp. 205–28. Madison: University of Wisconsin Press, 1957.

————. *Mark Twain: The Development of a Writer*. Cambridge, Mass.: Harvard University Press, 1962.

————. "Mark Twain's Images of Hannibal." *Texas Studies in English*, 37 (1958), 3–23.

————. *Virgin Land: The American West as Symbol and Myth*. New York: Vintage Books, 1957.

"Special River Correspondence: A Veteran Navigator. . . . " St. Louis *Missouri Republican*, September 6, 1860.

Stone, Albert E., Jr. *The Innocent Eye: Childhood in Mark Twain's Imagination*. New Haven: Yale University Press, 1961.

Ticknor, Caroline. *Glimpses of Authors*. Boston: Houghton, Mifflin, 1922.

———. " 'Mark Twain's' Missing Chapter." *The Bookman*, 39 (1914), 298–309.

The Times-Democrat. New Orleans. August 26, 1882. Decuple Sheet. Trade Edition of the Mississippi Valley: History—Description—Production—Commerce. Review of the Principal Cities with Business Notices and Advertisements.

Todd, William B. "Problems in Editing Mark Twain." In *Bibliography and Textual Criticism: English and American Literature, 1700 to the Present*, edited by O M Brack, Jr., and Warner Barnes, pp. 202–8. Chicago: University of Chicago Press, 1969.

"Topics of the Time: Murder by Burial." *Century Magazine*, 24 (n. s. 2), 6 (October 1882), 942–43.

Trollope, Frances. *Domestic Manners of the Americans*. Edited by Donald Smalley. New York: Alfred A. Knopf, 1949.

Tuckey, John S. *Mark Twain and Little Satan: The Writing of "The Mysterious Stranger."* West Lafayette: Purdue University Studies, 1963.

Turner, Arlin. *Mark Twain and George W. Cable: The Record of a Literary Friendship*. East Lansing: Michigan State University Press, 1960.

———. "Notes on Mark Twain in New Orleans." *The McNeese Review*, 6 (1954), 10–22.

Wagenknecht, Edward. "Introduction." *Life on the Mississippi*. New York: Heritage Press, 1944.

———. *Mark Twain: The Man and His Work*. Rev. ed. Norman: University of Oklahoma Press, 1961.

Wager, Willis J. "A Critical Edition of the Morgan Manuscript of Mark Twain's *Life on the Mississippi*." Ph.D. dissertation, New York University, 1942.

———. "A Note on These Suppressed Passages." *Life on the Mississippi*. New York: Heritage Press, 1944.

Weber, Carl J. *The Rise and Fall of James Ripley Osgood: A Biography*. Waterville, Maine: Colby College Press, 1959.

Wecter, Dixon. "Introduction." *Life on the Mississippi*. New York: Harper & Brothers, 1950.

———. *Sam Clemens of Hannibal*. Boston: Houghton, Mifflin, 1952.

Wigger, Anne P. "The Source of the Fingerprint Material in Mark Twain's *Pudd'nhead Wilson and Those Extraordinary Twins*." *American Literature*, 28 (1957), 517–20.

———. "A Study of *Pudd'nhead Wilson and Those Extraordinary Twins*." MS, MTP.

Wilson, Edmund, ed. *The Shock of Recognition*. New York: The Modern Library, 1955.

Wortley, Lady Emmeline Stuart. *Travels in the United States, Etc., During 1849 and 1850*. New York: Harper & Brothers, 1851.

Index

Illustrations on pages 119 and 121 are from Caroline
Ticknor, " 'Mark Twain's' Missing Chapter," *The
Bookman* 39 (1914): 300, 303. Other illustrations are
from the first edition of *Life on the Mississippi* (1883).

Library of Congress Cataloging in Publication Data

Kruse, Horst Hermann.
  Mark Twain and "Life on the Mississippi".
  Rev. and enl. translation of: Mark Twains Life
on the Mississippi.
  Bibliography: p.
  Includes index.
  1. Twain, Mark, 1835–1910. Life on the Mississip-
pi. 2. Twain, Mark, 1835–1910—Biography.
3. Mississippi River in literature. 4. Authors,
American—19th century—Biography.   I. Title.
PS1314.K713   1981   977   81-7570
ISBN 0–87023–330–0   AACR2